THE WOMEN OF KARBALA

Ritual Performance and Symbolic Discourses
in Modern Shi'i Islam

EDITED BY KAMRAN SCOT AGHAIE

University of Texas Press Austin

The publication of this book was assisted by a University Cooperative Society
Subvention Grant awarded by The University of Texas at Austin.

Library of Congress Cataloging-in-Publication Data

The women of Karbala : ritual performance and symbolic discourses in modern Shi'i
Islam / edited by Kamran Scot Aghaie.— 1st ed.
        p.   cm.
Includes bibliographical references and index.
ISBN 0-292-70936-6 (cloth : alk. paper) — ISBN 0-292-70959-5 (pbk. : alk. paper)
1. Shī'ah—Rituals. 2. Religious life—Shī'ah. 3. Muslim women—Religious life.
4. Karbalā', Battle of, Karbalā', Iraq, 680. I. Aghaie, Kamran Scot.
BP194.4.W66   2005
297.8'2'082—dc22

                                                                2005007772

This book is dedicated to my wife Jackie.

Contents

A Note on Transliteration

Transliteration is always a difficult problem in the field of Islamic or Middle Eastern Studies. However, this book posed particular difficulties, because the chapters include about half a dozen languages. This is further complicated by the fact that many terms in the book move from one language to another with minor changes. We tried using several systems, including a strict Arabic system; however, each approach posed serious difficulties and led to confusion. In the end we adopted a flexible system.

Whenever possible the original transliteration system of the author is used. However, there is one very important exception to this general rule: Terms that appear repeatedly throughout the different chapters, such as *Hosayn, Ali Ebn-e Abi Taleb, Ta'ziyeh, Majles, Fatemeh,* or *Moharram,* are transliterated according to modern Persian. While this is admittedly problematic, especially in the chapters on Arab or South Asian communities, it proved to be the least problematic of all the systems that we considered for use. More than half the chapters deal with Iran or use significant Persian terms. Also, many of the terms used in South Asia, even those originating from Arabic, entered the language through Iran and Persian. This is particularly true in the case of terms related to Shi'ism. Even in the cases of chapters dealing with Arab communities, which were at times the most problematic, the Persian transliteration often (although certainly not always) is not far from the colloquial Arabic pronunciation.

Acknowledgments

First of all, I would like to thank the authors for their patience. This book took longer to complete than I had originally anticipated, which must have tested their patience. I would also like to express my gratitude to the reviewers of this manuscript for taking the time to give me their insightful comments and feedback. The manuscript was significantly improved by their input.

I must thank Jackie most of all, for putting up with me when I was in the crazy final stages of completing this book. My thanks also go out to my mother and my sister Laila. Over the years, they have encouraged me to pursue my career goals and have also helped out at different times by reviewing and editing my work. I am also indebted to Nosrat Hemmatiyan and Kamal Hosayni for their friendship, hospitality, and help when I was in Tehran conducting research. Hushang Dabbagh and his family, longtime close friends of my father's, were similarly supportive and welcoming when I was researching in Isfahan and Shahreza. I view them as my family in Iran.

I would also like to extend my gratitude to Dr. Asghar Karimi in Tehran for his generous advice and consultation. I am amazed by the breadth and depth of his knowledge of Iranian popular culture. He is a wonderful colleague, and I have benefited greatly from his knowledge and experience. I would also like to give a special thanks to Faegheh Shirazi for being such a wonderful colleague and friend. She bravely served as the "guinea pig," showing the way so that the rest of us junior faculty could follow. I must also thank Abraham Marcus, Ian Manners, Harold Liebowitz, and Richard Lariviere, who helped me complete this project by providing a supportive and nurturing environment here at the University of Texas at Austin. Moh Ghanoonparvar was also very supportive and helpful in giving advice about practical matters related to publishing.

I would like to thank everyone who helped me in completing and preparing my manuscript for publication. Diane Watts did a wonderful job digitizing and cleaning up the photographs for this manuscript. Elisabeth Sheiffer did an excellent job in helping me format and edit the final manuscript for submission to the press. I am also indebted to Mehrnoosh Massah for her assistance with my research in Iran. Thanks also go to Annes McCann-Baker for her advice on the ins and outs of academic publishing.

Many grants and fellowships made this book possible. I would like to thank the Vice President of Research at the University of Texas at Austin for providing financial support in the form of the Faculty Research Grant, the URI Summer Research Assignment, and the University Cooperative Subvention Grant. Richard Lariviere, the dean of the College of Liberal Arts, was also generous in appointing me as the Dean's Fellow for spring 2003, which allowed me to complete this book. I would also like to express gratitude to the Religious Studies Program at UT Austin for granting me the Religious Studies Forum-Research Award.

Gendered Aspects of the Emergence and Historical Development of Shi'i Symbols and Rituals

KAMRAN SCOT AGHAIE

This book deals with the minority group called Shi'is, which today make up approximately fifteen percent of Muslims. While Iran has the single largest concentration of Shi'is, our analysis will include Shi'i communities in Iran, Iraq, Lebanon, India, Pakistan, and the United States. Before discussing the arguments put forth in this book, we should review the emergence and historical development of Shi'i symbols and rituals.

Karbala and the Emergence of Shi'ism

The roots of the Sunni-Shi'i schism lie in the crisis of succession that occurred upon the death of the Prophet Mohammad in 632 CE. However, this sectarian division took several centuries to fully develop. Upon the death of the Prophet Mohammad, the main challenge facing the young Muslim community was who should succeed the Prophet and in what capacity. It was also unclear who had the right to select a successor. The caliphate is the system of government that evolved out of this crisis. According to this system, the empire was ruled by a caliph, who commanded both temporal and religious authority but did not possess any of the supernatural or metaphysical qualities of the Prophet, such as infallibility, supernatural knowledge and ability, or the ability to receive revelation. While some Muslims supported the ruling caliphs, others believed that the Prophet's son-in-law and cousin, Ali Ebn-e Abi Taleb, should have succeeded the Prophet upon his death. Later, they believed that Ali's descendants should be his successors, beginning with his two sons, Hasan (d. 669) and Hosayn (d. 680).

These Muslims believed that the Prophet named Ali as his successor on more than one occasion before his death. For example, they believed that the Prophet gave a speech shortly before his death at a place called Ghadir Khom; according to one account, "he took Ali by the hand and said to the people: 'Do you not acknowledge that I have greater claim on each of the believers than they have on themselves?' And they replied: 'Yes!' And he took Ali's hand and said: 'Of whomsoever I am Lord [Mawla], then Ali is also his Lord. O God! Be thou the supporter of whoever supports Ali and the enemy of whoever opposes him.'"[1] Over the centuries support for Ali slowly evolved into a belief called the "imamate." The "imamate" differed from the caliphate in that the imam had to be a descendant of the Prophet and was usually considered to have supernatural qualities and abilities, such as infallibility and supernatural religious knowledge. The imam also had to be appointed by either the Prophet or the previous imam in an unbroken chain of succession leading back to the Prophet. According to this view, the Prophet endorsed the imamate before his death in 632.[2] Sunnis and Shiʿis have passionately disagreed about both the authenticity and the correct interpretation of these accounts. This crisis of succession after the Prophet's death, followed by a series of political events that unfolded during the first few centuries of Islamic history, led to this religious division.

The term "Shiʿi" derives from the phrase "Shiʿat Ali," or "partisans of Ali." The term "Sunni" derives from the phrase "Ahl al-Sunnah wa al-Jamaʿah," which means "those who follow the [prophetic] Traditions and the [official/orthodox] Consensus." As these terms imply, the term "Shiʿi" derives from their support of the Prophet Mohammad's progeny as his successors, beginning with Ali. Sunni orthodoxy, which developed largely in response to Shiʿi ideological and political challenges, rejected this notion in favor of the caliphs, who in fact did succeed the Prophet and who actually ruled during these early centuries. While the disputes and schisms may have begun with the crisis of succession, they evolved in accordance with later political and theological trends. For example, regional, ethnic, or tribal loyalties frequently sparked political rebellions. Sectarian rhetoric often accompanied such rebellions. Proto-Shiʿi sentiments were often the most effective way to challenge the legitimacy of the ruling caliphs. The Shiʿi imams, who were descendants of the Prophet and who had varying degrees of popular support among the masses, were rivals of the Sunni caliphs, who actually ruled the empire. For much of their early history, Sunnis have been associated with the state and the ruling elites, while Shiʿis were more often associated with political opposition to the Sunni rulers and elites. While there were several Shiʿi states, particularly in the tenth century, their long-term political influence was at its greatest when it took the form of opposition movements that challenged the legitimacy of the ruling caliphs.

After the death of the Prophet Mohammad, political divisions began to manifest themselves right away. The authority of the first caliph, Abu Bakr, was challenged by Arab tribes that tried to secede from the empire. During the reign of the third caliph, Osman, discontent with his policies led to protest, which eventually turned violent, and he was killed by an angry mob in 656. However, the conflicts that had the greatest impact on the Sunni-Shi'i split were a series of challenges to Ali's authority between 656 and 661, as well as the Battle of Karbala, which took place in 680. For example, in 656 the Prophet's widow, Ayesheh, led a rebellion against Ali, which was later called the Battle of the Camel. This was followed in 657 by a rebellion, called the Battle of Seffin, by the leading Muslim general, Mo'aviyeh, with whom Ali was forced to negotiate. Mo'aviyeh established the Umayyad caliphate in 661 after Ali was assassinated by a radical political opposition group called the Khavarej.

One of the most consistent and significant trends throughout the early centuries of Islamic history was that Shi'i imams, who were descendants of the Prophet and who had varying degrees of popular support among the masses, were rivals of the Sunni caliphs, who actually ruled the empire. This rivalry was particularly intense during the Umayyad period and came to a head with the Battle of Karbala in 680, during the reign of the second Umayyad caliph, Yazid (d. 683). In this battle the Prophet's grandson, Hosayn, along with seventy-two of his family and supporters, were massacred by Yazid's troops. Many different accounts of this important battle have been written by such prominent historians as the classical Arab scholar al-Tabari (d. 923). However, we are not concerned here with the historical accuracy of the narratives that purport to recount the details of this battle. For our purposes it is only necessary to keep in mind what Shi'is have historically considered to be the "correct" representations of this event.

Like many other famous historical events, the Battle of Karbala has been told and retold over the centuries without a single authoritative version emerging to completely supplant all others. The most commonly accepted narratives of the Battle of Karbala begin with an account of the discontent of Muslims (especially in southern Iraq) under the rule of Yazid (r. 680–683). Yazid is portrayed as politically oppressive and morally corrupt. The Prophet Mohammad's grandson Hosayn (in Medina) received several letters from the caliph's subjects in southern Iraq asking him to travel to Iraq in order to lead them in an uprising against Yazid. After sending scouts

Figure I.1. A "coffeehouse" painting depicting the return of Hosayn's horse from the battlefield, without its master (in a *hay'at* in Tajrish, in northern Tehran, 1997). © Kamran Scot Aghaie

to assess the situation in southern Iraq, Hosayn and a number of his close relatives left the Hejaz and began the trip to Iraq.

The caravan was surrounded by an overwhelming force sent by Yazid, and a standoff ensued in which Hosayn refused to give an oath of allegiance (*bay'at*) to Yazid. At the end of ten days of waiting, negotiating, and occasionally fighting, a final battle took place; Hosayn, all his adult male relatives and supporters, and some of the women and children were brutally killed. The survivors, consisting of women and children, along with Hosayn's son Ali (Zayn al-Abedin) (d. 712–713), who was too ill to take part in the fighting, were then taken captive and transported, along with the heads of the martyrs, which had been placed on spears, to Yazid's court in Damascus. Along the way they were exhibited in chains in the public markets of the cities through which they passed, and a series of unpleasant incidents occurred, as a result of which Hosayn's relatives, especially his sister Zaynab and his son, Zayn al-Abedin, publicly condemned Yazid for his cruelty toward the descendants of the Prophet Mohammad. The important roles of these women in the symbolism of Karbala are the focus of this book.

Mourning for Hosayn, Zaynab, and the martyrs of Karbala began almost immediately, as Hosayn's surviving relatives and supporters lamented the tragedy. As part of the long-term trend toward the development of popular mourning rituals based on commemoration of Karbala, popular elegies of the martyrs were composed during the remainder of the Umayyad period (680–750) and the first two centuries of Abbasid rule (roughly 750–930). Karbala symbolism was important in many rebellions throughout this period, including the political overthrow of the Umayyads by the Abbasids in 749–750. The political uses of Karbala symbols and simple mourning practices date almost as far back as the Battle of Karbala itself. However, the earliest reliable account of the performance of public mourning rituals which in any way resemble what we now call Moharram processions (especially with a political connotation) concerns an event that took place in 963, during the reign of Moʿezz al-Dowleh, the Buyid ruler of southern Iran and Iraq.

The Buyid rulers, who were Shiʿis themselves, promoted Shiʿi rituals, along with a celebration of the Ghadir Khom incident, in order to promote their religious legitimacy and to strengthen the sense of Shiʿi identity in and around Baghdad. It should be noted, however, that during this period popular sentiment for the family of the Prophet was not restricted exclusively to the Shiʿis. The famous fourteenth-century Arab historian Ebn al-Kathir states that "on the tenth of *Moharram* of this year [AH 352], Muʿizz ad-Dawla Ibn Buwayh, may God disgrace him, ordered that the markets be closed, and that the women should wear coarse woolen hair cloth, and that they should go into the markets with their faces uncovered/unveiled and their hair disheveled, beating their faces and wailing over Hussein Ibn Abi Talib." He continues somewhat apologetically, "The people of the *Sunna* could not prevent this spectacle because of the *Shiʿa's* large numbers and their increasing power (*zuhur*), and because the sultan was on their side.[3] One of the interesting aspects of this account is that it demonstrates that women have been involved in these rituals from the very beginning and that their role was significant enough that it was singled out for comment. Rituals like this in which believers mourned and commemorated the tragedy of Karbala continued to be practiced throughout the middle ages.

A major development in Shiʿi rituals occurred with the establishment of the Safavid state in 1501 in a territory largely encompassing the modern state of Iran. The Safavids were originally a Sufi order, but the founder of the dynasty, Shah Ismaʿil, decreed that the official state religion would be orthodox Twelver Shiʿism. Shiʿi symbols and rituals were very important to the self-definition of the Safavid dynasty. They made fairly liberal use of Shiʿi symbols and rituals (such as the Moharram procession) to promote their legitimacy vis-à-vis their Sunni rivals to the east (the Uzbeks and the Mughals) and their more dangerous rival to the west (the Ottomans). Shiʿi rituals took on new meanings and new forms during the Safavid era. The fact that the rulers themselves were Shiʿis meant that these rituals could be used to bolster their legitimacy. It also meant that public rituals could be performed without any regard for Sunni attitudes toward these rituals. Shiʿis could publicly express their sense of community identity and their negative sentiments toward Sunnis. Earlier rituals had been performed within a society in which the Sunnis made up the majority, but the Safavid period created a new environment that was relatively more isolated from Sunnis. Because of the large numbers of Shiʿis living under Safavid rule, rituals became more elaborate and the demand for talented authors of elegies dramatically increased.[4]

One of the most important rituals that became popular during the Safavid period was the *rowzeh khani,* a ritual sermon recounting and mourning the tragedy of Karbala. This ritual was inspired in part by Hosayn Vaʾez Kashefi's 1502 composition, *Rowzat al-shohada (The Garden of Martyrs).*[5] This seminal work became one of the main sources for a series of "Karbala narratives" and is one of the most often quoted sources in later narratives and histories retelling the story of the battle and its aftermath. Excerpts from Kashefi's work also served as the basis for scripts that were used in the *rowzeh khani* sermons, which eventually became one of the primary rituals of Shiʿis around the world and which bears the same name as Kashefi's book.[6] *Rowzeh khani* consists of a sermon based on a text like *Rowzat al-shohada,* with a great deal of improvisation on the part of a specially trained speaker. The speaker strives to move the audience to tears through his recitation of the tragic details of the Battle of Karbala.[7] Mourning for the martyrs of Karbala has been viewed by Shiʿis as a means of achieving salvation, a belief illustrated by the often-repeated quotation, "Anyone who cries for Husayn or causes someone to cry for Husayn shall go directly to paradise."[8]

From Iran and Iraq, Shiʿism spread into parts of South Asia as well. According to popular belief in South Asia, Shiʿi rituals were first introduced into South Asia at the end of the fourteenth century by the conqueror Timur (Tamerlane), who is believed to have converted to Shiʿism prior to his invasion into the Indian subcontinent from Afghanistan.[9] As Cole has argued, Shiʿism spread along with the migration of Iranian elites (i.e., scholars, poets, artisans, merchants) from the Iranian plateau and Iraq into South Asia. One important side effect of this influx of Iranians into the region was the establishment of Persian-influenced elite culture. In some cases this elite culture was also Shi'i, which led to the spread of Shi'ism in parts of South Asia. In the sixteenth and seventeenth centuries, Shi'i states were established in southern India. For example, the Nizam Shahi dynasty (r. 1508–1553) ruled in Ahmadnagar, the Qutb Shahi dynasty (1512–1687) ruled in Hyderabad, and the Adil Shahi dynasty ruled in the Deccan kingdom of Bijapur. These dynasties were able, to varying degrees, to encourage Shi'i practices until Mughal dominance or even conquest discouraged such practices.[10]

While this period was characterized by Shi'i rule in certain provinces, one should be careful not to overstate the importance of these political trends. In many ways, the more subtle spread of Persian, Shi'i, elite culture was a more influential factor in the spread of Shi'ism in South Asia. This is particularly important to keep in mind in northern Indian areas like Kashmir and Awadh, where large Shi'i minorities lived, mostly under Sunni rule. This elite culture survived well into the modern period, and was quite influential in certain areas, where Shi'i elites (including some women) promoted Shi'i beliefs and ritual practices, depending on the degree of tolerance of the Sunni rulers. For example, elegies were recited both in private and in public, public processions were sometimes organized, the Karbala narrative was told in the form of sermons in domestic rituals in the homes of Shi'i elites, and replicas of the tomb of Hosayn (ta'ziyehs) were built for use in these various rituals, and they remain a central feature of South Asian Moharram rituals today.[11]

Similar trends can be seen in the Arab Shi'i provinces that were located outside of Safavid control. In Iraq and Lebanon, major Shi'i communities flourished while living under Sunni rule, which fluctuated between tolerance and persecution. In fact, during the eighteenth century, when political decentralization, economic chaos, and Afghan invasions were weakening the religious establishment in the Iranian plateau, the Shi'i shrine cities in southern Iraq, in particular Najaf and Karbala, flourished relatively independent of state influence. The important influence of the Iraqi Shi'is continued in some ways into the nineteenth century as well. During the period of decline of Iran's religious establishment, many of the greatest Shi'i scholars were either from Iraq or chose to study and work there. In this environment, Shi'i beliefs, practices, and rituals continued to develop and evolve, as they had in previous centuries.

While state sponsorship was not a necessary component in the preservation and evolution of Shi'i beliefs and ritual practices, it was nevertheless important. In nineteenth-century Iran, after the Qajars brought greater security, prosperity, and religious patronage, a newer and more elaborate

Figure I.2. *Ta'ziyeh* performance with an audience consisting mostly of women (Tehran, 1997). © Kamran Scot Aghaie

ritual emerged, called either *shabih khani* or *ta'ziyeh khani*. The *ta'ziyeh* (i.e., different from the South Asian *ta'ziyeh*) was an elaborate ritual drama or theatrical performance of the Karbala story based on the narratives used in the *rowzeh khani*. The *ta'ziyeh* involved a large cast of professional and amateur actors, a director, a staging area, elaborate costumes, and props. This ritual reached its greatest level of popularity during the late Qajar period, after which it underwent a slow decline until it became much less common in the large cities in the 1930s and 1940s. However, *ta'ziyehs* have persisted in Iran on a smaller scale to the present day, especially in traditional neighborhoods in cities and in rural areas.[12]

While Moharram rituals were more prevalent in areas where Shi'is were concentrated, such as Lebanon, Iran, southern Iraq, Hyderabad, and Awadh, some Sunnis (especially those oriented more toward popular culture and Sufism) also commemorated Karbala in similar observances. In some areas, such as South Asia, Sunnis have often been enthusiastic participants in Shi'i rituals. In the modern era, the rituals of Sunnis and Shi'is have become more distinct from each other. However, throughout much of Islamic history the differences between them based on ideological constructs were often less prevalent. This was particularly true of popular practice, which could often be at variance with the views of the elite ulama. In the twentieth century, Sunni involvement in commemorations of Karbala has declined, whereas Shi'i involvement has continued to evolve and change as it did in previous centuries.[13]

Gender Dynamics and Scholarship on the Karbala Paradigm

The story of Karbala is centered on the battle and martyrdom of Hosayn and his followers at Karbala. This is the axis around which the story revolves. For Shi'is, the event is the axis around which all of history revolves.[14] However, historians have typically emphasized the battle, which in turn has led to an overemphasis on the male martyrs and a virtual exclusion of any focus on the role of women.

Here, we extend our analysis of the historical narratives to include the events leading up to the battle, those surrounding the battle, and those following the battle—all of which involve women. The authors in this volume will demonstrate the importance of the gender-coded symbols derived from these aspects of the original narratives, despite the fact that modern historians have often considered them to be marginal to the symbolism of Karbala. This approach to studying the Karbala narratives allows for a more comprehensive portrayal of the events under study, while at the same time providing a basic theoretical construct within which gender concepts can be analyzed.

While traditionally the exclusion of women from historical analysis throughout the field of history and Middle Eastern/Islamic studies has been so common as to be more or less the norm, there are several specific reasons why women's involvement in the rituals and symbols of Karbala have been at times overlooked or at least underemphasized by many historians. First, as stated above, the most central component of the event itself, being a battle involving Hosayn and his male followers on the battlefield has often been assumed to be not only a male event, but also the source of nearly all of the symbols of Karbala. This assumption is reinforced by the fact that in the primary sources used to reconstruct the rebellion itself, the role of men on the battlefield is an important part of the narrative. However, it is inappropriate for a historian to focus exclusively upon symbols derived from the battle itself without understanding the broader conceptions of the movement of Hosayn. This point has often been stressed by Muslim writers representing a more or less normative perspective. According to this argument, the "event" of Karbala should not be defined as simply the battle itself, but rather it is best understood as including the events leading up to the battle, surrounding the battle (i.e., on the sidelines), and following the battle. This basic battle narrative then must be placed within a universalist narrative which begins with Adam and ends with the return of the *mahdi* at the end of the temporal world, all of which has historically been included by most Shiʿi scholars within the "Karbala narrative."

When the modern historian examines the events before, around, and after the battle itself, he or she sees that both men and women participated in these "peripheral" events, and that many of the important symbols of Karbala are drawn from these events. For example, it would be inappropriate to treat the public statements and actions of Hosayn's sister Zaynab, immediately following the battle as separate from the movement itself.[15] For example, Morteza Motahhari (the prominent modern Shiʿi theologian) has portrayed Zaynab as spokesperson for the cause after the massacre as the second half of Hosayn's movement (i.e., not merely a marginal role).[16] Zaynab's public criticism of Yazid and his followers has been stressed in most of the narratives.[17]

Furthermore, Fatemeh's role as mother and educator of Hosayn, as well as her role as one of the purified fourteen who suffered for the cause of Islam, cannot be separated from the Karbala event, even though she was not present at the battle itself (although in many narratives she is brought into the narrative symbolically or metaphysically).[18] There have been countless books with such titles as *The Fourteen Purified Ones*, which present the biographies of the twelve imams, the Prophet Mohammad, and Fatemeh. In these books, all fourteen are portrayed as suffering for the same cause regardless of whether they were present at Karbala or not.[19] The importance of Fatemeh is also demonstrated by the large number of poems and Moharram chants devoted to her memory.[20] And as demonstrated earlier, Fatemeh is given a great deal more coverage than most of the male characters in some narratives, like Vaʾiz Kashefi's *Rowzat al-shohada*.

Similarly, Hosayn's followers, both men and women, were not only prominent players in the events themselves, but have also been important sources of symbolism for Shiʿism and have very often served as role models. For example, many of the poems chanted during Moharram rituals are based on such figures as Moslem Ebn-e Aqil, Zaynab's two sons, Zaynab, Fatemeh, the other eleven imams, the Prophet, Qasem, and Abbas.[21] Furthermore, Hosayn has always been a role model to be emulated in various ways by both men and women. What has not been sufficiently developed in the research is the ways in which certain qualities Hosayn represents have been gender-coded as "male," "female," or "gender-neutral." An approach that takes these factors into account also shows how women, not

Figure I.3. A large billboard located at the entrance to Behesht-e Zaynab, the martyrs' cemetery in Isfahan. A young mourning girl is shown next to tulips and a goblet, both symbolizing martyrdom—all under the watchful eyes of Khomeini himself (Isfahan, 2001). © Kamran Scot Aghaie

just men, have at times been talked about as role models for both women and men.

And, although Muslim historians and religious scholars have written more about male actors in the event, women have not been excluded entirely. Rather, men have primarily written about men and to a male audience, with women being ever-present yet subsidiary characters. This trend can be observed throughout the twentieth century and beyond. For example, when using the symbolism of Karbala in writing about a contemporary social issue such as the legitimacy of the Iranian monarchy, male political or religious leaders were often addressing primarily other male activists and leaders using the symbolism most closely associated with men at Karbala. This dynamic has been complicated by the practical realities of these movements, which involved a great deal of active involvement of women as protesters, and in some cases as fighters and martyrs. For example, Khomeini often referred to the active involvement of women in the struggle against the shah: "This movement [the revolution] was a national movement . . . women, men and children all rose up." [22] And after the revolution, women served in certain capacities in the domestic security forces, charged with the task of policing women's social behavior.

Furthermore, when women were mentioned in these texts, as was frequently the case, they were usually placed outside the discussion in the sense that men were the speakers and they were speaking about women rather than to them. Thus it is possible for women to have been so often mentioned without necessarily being explicitly addressed as an audience. This is an important point in regard to more recent sources dealing with women or explicitly gender-related issues: topics and issues that had previously been underemphasized were brought to the foreground or even focused upon exclusively.

An example of the underdevelopment of gender analysis in relation to the Karbala paradigm is the research on *ta'ziyeh*, which has often been of interest to scholars primarily as a theatrical form.[23] *Ta'ziyeh*, which entails a theatrical reenactment of the Karbala narrative, has historically included male performers and a mixed audience of men and women. However, many researchers have focused upon the performers at the expense of the event as a whole, which has led to an overemphasis on males. While *ta'ziyeh* has typically not featured female actors, it does have female characters, such as Zaynab or the martyr Roqayyeh Khatun, which can be analyzed as such.[24]

This problem has been further complicated by two recent trends in Iran, the first of which has been the televising of *ta'ziyeh* since the Islamic Revolution in 1978–1979 (which led to increased government control over such activities).

Another good example is provided by a trend that has begun recently in Iran. The *ta'ziyeh* tradition has been displaced in certain ways by a new movie genre that has represented the historical event in a radically different format.[25] While the movie genre is not actually a ritual it serves a similar role as the *ta'ziyeh* in the sense that it has been one of the primary vehicles for public viewing of the narrative of Karbala. The televising of *ta'ziyeh* has led to the excision of women characters from the play because the government sponsors the view that men should not dress up as women.[26] This has also led to innovative ways of including (or excluding) female characters without using actual actors: hearing a female voice off stage, speaking to these women without getting a response, or merely cutting out certain parts altogether. Thus women as characters have become less visible on stage.

The second trend is significant because the new movie genre has reached a broader audience, allowing women to view the performance without having to leave the privacy of their homes, thus redefining the public sphere and their participation within it. Another important development has been the inclusion of women actresses in key roles in these movies. So while female

Figure I.4. In the background, a poster depicting Fatemeh, holding red tulips symbolizing the male martyrs of her family; in the foreground, a young girl plants tulips over the graves of the martyrs. Bagh-e Behesht-e Ali (Qom, 2001). © Kamran Scot Aghaie

characters have been disappearing from view in *ta'ziyeh*, female characters and actresses have been appearing in new and more visible forms in the movie genre.

Another reason why scholarly interest has traditionally underemphasized or ignored gender is that Western historians have privileged the political over the social and cultural, focusing on Hosayn as a symbol of martyrdom and rebellion, with the female characters and gender-coded symbols being ignored or at least underdeveloped. While this study is not entirely an exception to this general rule, it is hoped that it does not focus on such political issues at the expense of other important issues such as those related to the various uses of gender-coded symbols as a form of social discourse.

The "Karbala narrative" is centered on the battle of Karbala, in which Hosayn and most of his followers were martyred. However, this battle is only the central axis around which the story revolves. The Karbala narrative, in turn, is the axis around which all of history revolves for Shiʿis. Modern historians studying this set of symbols have often placed primary emphasis on the battle itself. This has led to an overemphasis being placed upon the male martyrs at the expense of female characters in the narrative. Similarly, research on Moharram rituals has often focused almost exclusively upon the central procession and the physical self-flagellation of male participants in these rituals. The net result has been the exclusion, almost entirely, of the participation of women in these rituals.[27]

The Present Study

The main arguments presented in this study are as follows:

- Shiʿi women have generally been very actively involved in religious rituals, both in women-only rituals and in gender-mixed public rituals. While women's roles are similar in some ways to those of men, they are also distinct. Space and activities are often gender specific, but the two genders often interact, mirror, or contrast each other. Close examination of the gender dynamics present in such rituals can illuminate broader gender dynamics in these societies.
- Shiʿi symbols have been gender coded in significant ways. These symbols have been used to define the ideals of women's behavior. Further, some symbols are gender specific while others are gender neutral. These sets of symbols have been used to reinforce distinctions between the genders, while at the same time stressing the centrality of women to the symbolic repertory of Shiʿism.
- While Shiʿi symbols and rituals have been used at times to restrict women's activities and social roles, they have also served as a means for empowering women and have helped to promote a sense of gender-specific identities for women.
- While there are various universalistic components to Shiʿi beliefs and

practices, the religious experiences of Shi'i women have generally been extremely diverse and varied. Practices may vary on the basis of personal preferences, religious interpretations, popular cultural practices, ideals or norms of gender interaction/segregation, regional customs, education levels, or socioeconomic background.

In Chapter 1, Negar Mottahedeh analyzes the gender dynamics of *ta'ziyeh* ritual dramas as they developed during the Qajar period. She discusses the significance of female characters in this theatrical tradition, along with the practice according to which male actors usually played female characters. She argues that women in some instances organized ritual dramas that were attended and performed exclusively by women.

Chapter 2, by Kamran Scot Aghaie, focuses on the gender dynamics of Shi'i symbols and rituals in Qajar Iran. Shi'i symbols and rituals served a variety of social, psychological, and spiritual functions for Iranian women. While rituals served to reinforce gender segregation, they also provided opportunities for women to play significant roles in both public and private religious events. Women were enthusiastic patrons and participants in both gender-mixed rituals and women-only rituals. These rituals helped women to promote their social status and to develop and maintain social networks. The rituals also gave women a means for spiritual growth and emotional release: a means to ask for divine intercession in their spiritual life, as well as in their practical personal and family crises. The symbols involved in these rituals were gender coded in that they portrayed ideals of male and female behavior. While these symbols served to restrict female behavior in certain ways, they also helped to provide a sense of female identity and to reinforce the centrality of women to Shi'i beliefs.

In Chapter 3, Ingvild Flaskerud analyzes women's religious rituals in modern Shiraz, especially ritual space, objects, and visual imagery. She focuses on how Shi'i women participate in rituals in order to achieve salvation and divine intercession in this world and the next. After explaining the origins and dynamics of a distinctively Shi'i aesthetic tradition, she discusses the iconography of images, space and objects in women's rituals in Shiraz.

In Chapter 4, Faegheh Shirazi studies the diverse representations of female characters in elegies, chants, and slogans in popular Iranian rituals. She argues that women are represented as participating in social and political struggles, such as jihad, although not always in the same ways as men. These popular representations were used to promote a sense of religious and nationalist support for the Islamic regime in Iran, as well as Iran's

Figure I.5. A young girl having fun playing with her father's ritual chains (Tehran, 1997). © Kamran Scot Aghaie

efforts to win the war against Iraq. Role models such as Fatemeh, Zaynab, Roqayyeh, and Sakineh were used to promote ideals of motherhood and domestic responsibility, which were in turn linked to the nation's political success and survival. Shirazi argues that these representations of female characters demonstrate the central role women and female religious characters have played both in Shiʻi history and in contemporary Iranian politics.

In Chapter 5, Peter J. Chelkowski studies visual representations of female characters in Shiʻi religious dramas, in particular Zaynab and Shahbanu, the Persian wife of Hosayn. He discusses how the female characters portrayed in visual representations serve as models of chastity, purity, and self-sacrifice. He then explores the diverse ways in which the Islamic regime in Iran has used these images to represent ideals of social and political behavior for women. He describes and analyzes samples of this iconography in many different forms, including performances, as well as posters, stamps, and murals. Throughout this chapter, Chelkowski demonstrates the continuities and discontinuities between the *ta'ziyeh* iconography and recent political iconography.

In the next chapter, Shemeem Burney Abbas analyzes how gendered themes are expressed through the narrative voice of Sakineh in women's mourning rituals in Pakistan. Her ethnographic account of the rituals, along with a linguistic analysis of the contents of the ritual chants and sermons, shows that in Pakistan, much of the oral history of the Karbala tragedy is reenacted in Sakineh's voice.

In Chapter 7, Syed Akbar Hyder examines the diverse ways in which Zaynab is represented in modern Urdu poems and pious elegies, in particular the elegies of the prominent South Asian Zaker Rashid Torabi. He then discusses several other poets, including Iftikhar Arif, Vahid Akhtar, and the female poet Parvin Shakir. He explores the central role of Zaynab as the "conqueror of Damascus" in the symbolic narratives of Karbala. Hyder's literary analysis explores the symbolic rhetoric and stylistic devices used in representing Zaynab within the South Asian tradition. He concludes by showing how Shi'i symbols and ideals have been articulated within the discourses on gender in South Asia.

In Chapter 8, Rehana Ghadially studies one of the diverse manifestations of Shi'ism, the Isma'ili, in the Bohra community of India. In analyzing mixed-gender public rituals, she finds that both men and women are heavily involved. However, the more public the ritual, the less involved women tend to be. Conversely, the more private the ritual, the more active the women participants are. She also demonstrates how space and activities are gendered, as well as the central role of women in the process of reinforcing universalistic Shi'i ideals and maintaining communal identities through ritual practices. She argues that women-only rituals provide women with stronger sense of their centrality to the Shi'i faith. She also explores the tensions between patriarchal social norms and the emancipatory aspects of women's involvement in these rituals.

In Chapter 9, Mary Elaine Hegland compares the two major Shi'i immigrant communities in the United States of America, Iranians and South Asians. Her comparative analysis demonstrates that the religious practices of these two communities are quite distinct. She argues that South Asian women are far more active in Shi'i rituals than their Iranian counterparts, attributing this to the different socioeconomic backgrounds and demographics of these two communities, along with their distinct religious and political experiences. She also finds that their beliefs and practices have changed over time and across regions. As these women migrated to the United States, their attitudes toward rituals underwent varying degrees of change as they adapted to their new environments and priorities. Her research demonstrates how Muslim women's religious experiences can significantly differ despite their shared religion.

In their study of women's rituals in Iraq, Elizabeth Warnock Fernea and Basima Q. Bezirgan call into question the long observed assumption of a rigid dichotomization of public versus private space in Muslim societies. Instead, they propose using a far more nuanced conception that allows for relative fluidity between what would traditionally have been labeled "women's world" and "men's world." They observe that men and women are both involved in public rituals. Furthermore, men play a supporting, or "instrumental," role in women-only rituals, while women play a similar role in male-dominated rituals. Fernea and Bezirgan further argue that the gender dynamics observed in the rituals are similar to the patterns one would see in other spheres of Middle Eastern society.

In Chapter 11, Lara Z. Deeb studies recent changes in Lebanese Shi'i rituals, which have been brought on by many factors, including urbanization, modernization, and the political ascendancy of Shi'i parties such as Amal and Hezbollah over the past decade or so. The mobilization of the Shi'is as a communal group began in the 1970s under such leaders as Musa Sadr. In recent years a new method of ritual performance has emerged alongside the more traditional rituals. These shifts in ritual practice were influenced by trends in Iran. Proponents of these new ritual practices argue that the newer practices are more "authentic" because they are closer to the original intent of the Karbala narrative. Divergent interpretations of the role of Zaynab in the battle of Karbala are indicative of this discourse. The shift has been toward using Zaynab as a role model for women becoming more directly involved in social and political activism. Women's rituals have slowly transformed in tandem with the broader trends in ritual observance.

Notes

1. This Hadith is reported by the famous Sunni traditionalist Ahmad b. Hanbal in his collection *Mosnad*. This translation is provided by Moojan Momen, *An Introduction to Shi'i Islam* (New Haven, Conn.: Yale University Press, 1985), 14.

2. Ibid., 17.

3. Ibn Kathir, *al-Bidaya wa al-nihaya* (Cairo: Matbaʻah al-Saʻada, 1358 AH). This translation is from Michel M. Mazzaoui, "Shiʻism and Ashura in South Lebanon," in *Taʻziyeh: Ritual and Drama in Iran,* ed. Peter J. Chelkowski (New York: New York University Press, 1979), 231.

4. For detailed analysis of the core basic beliefs associated with the Karbala symbolism, as well as the historical development of these beliefs and practices, see the following two books: Mahmoud Ayoub, *Redemptive Suffering in Islam: A Study of the Devotional Aspects of "Ashura" in Twelver Shiʻism* (New York: Mouton, 1978), and Momen, *Introduction to Shiʻi Islam.*

5. Kashefi's text was a synthesis of a long line of historical accounts of Karbala by religious scholars. He drew material from such famous texts as Saʻid al-Din's *Rowzat al-Eslam* (*The Garden of Islam*) and al-Khwarazmi's *Maqtal nur al-aʼemmeh* (*The Site of the Murder of the Light of the Imams*).

6. For a thorough treatment of the emergence and historical development of *taʻziyeh* rituals from the Safavid through the Qajar period, see Enayatollah Shahidi and Bolukbashi Ali, *Pazhuheshi dar taʻziyeh va taʻziyeh khani az aghaz ta payan-e dowreh-e Qajar dar Tehran* (Tehran: Daftar-e Pazhuhesh-ha-e Farhangi, Komisiyon-e Melli-e Yunesko dar Iran, 2001).

7. *Rowzeh* preachers have traditionally been men, although female orators sometimes give the sermon in private *rowzeh khanis* attended exclusively by women.

8. Jean Calmard, "Le Patronage des Taʻziyeh: Elements pour une Etude Globale," in *Taʻziyeh: Ritual and Drama in Iran,* ed. Peter J. Chelkowski (New York: New York University Press, 1979), 122. For a detailed study of Shiʻi rituals and state patronage leading up to the Safavid period, see Jean Calmard, "Le culte de l'Imam Husayn: Etudes sur la commémoration du Drame de Karbala dans l'Iran pré-safavide" (PhD diss., University of Paris III, 1975).

9. Vernon James Schubel, *Religious Performance in Contemporary Islam: Shiʻi Devotional Rituals in South Asia* (Columbia: University of South Carolina Press, 1993), 110.

10. Juan R. I. Cole, *The Roots of North Indian Shiʻism in Iran and Iraq: Religion and State in Awadh, 1722–1859* (Berkeley and Los Angeles: University of California Press, 1988), 22–27; Sayyed Ali Naqi al-Naqvi, *A Historical Review of the Institution of Azadari for Imam Husain* (Karachi: Peer Mahomed Ebrahim Trust, 1974).

11. See Cole, *The Roots of North Indian Shiʻism in Iran and Iraq,* 22–35; Frank J. Korom, *Hosay Trinidad: Muharram Performances in an Indo-Caribbean Diaspora* (Philadelphia: University of Pennsylvania Press, 2003); al-Naqvi, *A Historical Review.*

12. For detailed discussions of the *taʻziyeh* traditions in Iran, see the following: Peter J. Chelkowski, ed., *Taʻziyeh: Ritual and Drama in Iran* (New York: New York University Press, 1979b); Sadeq Homayuni, *Taʻziyeh dar Iran* (Shirazi, Iran: Entesharat-e Navid, 1989); Shahidi and Ali, *Pazhuheshi dar taʻziyeh va taʻziyeh*; Samuel R. Peterson, ed., *Taʻziyeh: Ritual and Popular Beliefs in Iran* (Hartford, Conn.: Trinity College, Hartford Seminary, 1988); Jaber Anasori, ed., *Shabih khani, kohan olgu-ye nemayeshha-ye Irani* (Tehran: Chapkhaneh-e Ramin, 1992); Mohammad Ebrahim Ayati, *Barresi-e tarikh-e Ashura,* 9th ed. (Tehran: Nashr-e Sadduq, 1996); and Laleh Taqiyan, ed., *Taʻziyeh va teʼatr dar Iran* (Tehran: Nashr-e Markaz, 1995).

13. For Shiʻi rituals outside Iran, see Schubel, *Religious Performance;* Augustus

Richard Norton, *Shi'ism and the Ashura Ritual in Lebanon* (New York: Al-Saqi, 2003); Cole, *The Roots of North Indian Shi'ism in Iran and Iraq;* Yitzhak Nakash, *The Shi'is of Iraq* (Princeton, N.J.: Princeton University Press, 1994); David Pinault, *The Horse of Karbala: Muslim Devotional Life in India* (New York: Palgrave, 2001); David Pinault, *The Shi'ites, Ritual, and Popular Piety in a Muslim Community* (New York: St. Martin Press, 1992b); Frederic Maatouk, *La representation de la mort de l'imam Hussein a Nabatieh* (Beirut: Université libanaise, Institut des sciences sociales, Centre de recherches, 1974); and Waddah Shararah, *Transformations d'une manifestation religieuse dans un village du Liban-Sud (Asura)* (Beirut: al-Jami'ah al-Lubnaniyyah, Ma'had al-'Ulum al-Ijtima'iyah, 1968).

14. The Karbala narrative is an excellent example of what Victor Turner and Stephen Pepper call a "root metaphor" and what Max Black calls a "conceptual archetype." For a discussion of root metaphor see Stephen Pepper, *World Hypotheses* (Los Angeles and Berkeley: University of California Press, 1942), and Victor Turner, *Dramas, Fields, and Metaphors* (Ithaca and London: Cornell University Press, 1974), 25–27. For a discussion of Max Black's conceptual archetypes see his *Models and Metaphors: Studies in Language and Philosophy* (Ithaca, N.Y.: Cornell University Press, 1962), 241. According to these approaches symbolic interpretation is understood as a process of giving meaning to an unknown subject by making reference, either consciously or unconsciously, to a known and familiar conceptual reference point. Therefore, these "key symbols" can provide a set of categories for understanding other aspects of human experience. This reference point can be a historic event, real or imagined, which has a well-developed and articulated meaning in a given society. This process of analogy allows meaning to be derived concerning a contemporary reality that may otherwise cause confusion or even anxiety.

15. See, for example, Hasan Elahi (Butehkar), *Zaynab-e Kobra* (Tehran: Moassaseh-e Farhangi-e Afarineh, 1996), 128–130.

16. Morteza Motahhari, *Hamaseh-e Hosayni,* vols. 1–3 (Tehran and Qom: Sadra Publishers, 1985).

17. Mohammad Mohammadi Eshtehardi, *Sugnameh-e al-e Mohammad* (Qom, Iran: Entesharat-e Naser-e Qom, 1997), 66.

18. Ibid., 344–345. Fatemeh is allowed to speak through Zaynab on the day of Ashura. Zaynab recounts how Fatemeh told her to kiss Hosayn on her (Fatemeh's) behalf as he went onto the battlefield to be martyred.

19. One of the best known works of this type is Allameh Majlesi, *Tarikh-e chahardah ma'sum* (Qom, Iran: Entesharat-e Sorur, 1996).

20. There are many examples of such poems and chants. See Sayyed Rasul Sadeqi, ed., *Naghmeh-e Ashura* (Tehran: Entesharat-e Yasin, 1997), 165. There is also an entire chapter of poetic chants devoted to Fatemeh in the second volume of Morteza Dana'i, ed., *Naghmeh-ha-e Karbala* (Qom, Iran: Entesharat-e Sa'id Novin, 1996), 2:51–70.

21. One of the best collections of these chants is Mohammad Gholami's two-volume work, *Montakhab al-masa'eb, hazrat-e emam Hosayn alayhi al-salam va yaran-e 'u* (Qum: Moassaseh-e Entesharat-e 'Allameh, 1996).

22. *Sima-e zan dar kalam-e Emam* (Tehran: Entesharat-e Vezarat-e Farhang va Ershad-e Eslami, 1992), 58.

23. See Taqiyan, *Ta'ziyeh va te'atr dar Iran*. Many of the chapters are concerned with the *ta'ziyeh* as drama or theatrical performance.

24. For a transcription of the *ta'ziyeh* performance devoted to Hosayn's daughter Roqayyeh, see C. S. L. Pelly, *The Miracle Play of Hasan and Husain, Collected from Oral Tradition* (London, The India Office, 1879), 2:241–257. While Zaynab is in many *ta'ziyeh*, an example is in the same work, pp. 267–285. For additional examples in the original Persian, see Hasan Salehirad, ed., *Majales-e ta'ziyeh* (Tehran: Sorush, 1995).

25. These are sometimes short movies produced by the Iranian government-run television Seda va Sima-e Iran, and are played between programs during the month of Moharram. Other full-length movies, such as *Ruz-e Vaqe'eh*, have been produced in the tradition of *The Message*, a Filmco International movie produced and directed by Moustapha Akkad.

26. For very early examples of this practice see, Lady Sheil, *Glimpses of Life and Manners in Persia* (John Murray, London, 1856), 129. See also Ella Sykes, *Persia and Its People* (London: Methuen and Co. Ltd., 1910), 151.

27. There are of course exceptions to this general rule, such as the work of Mary Hegland, Elizabeth Warnock Fernea, Vernon James Schubel, and Azam Torab.

PART 1

IRAN

CHAPTER 1

Ta'ziyeh
A Twist of History in Everyday Life

NEGAR MOTTAHEDEH

To be sure, only a redeemed mankind receives the fullness of its past—which is to say, only for a redeemed mankind has its past become citable in all its moments. Each moment it has lived becomes a citation á l'ordre du jour— *and that day is Judgement Day.*

WALTER BENJAMIN (1940)

Ta'ziyeh (or *shabih*) is the traditionally accepted term for the "theatrical" performances or dramas that reenact, recount, and recollect the lives of the extended family of the Prophet Mohammad during the month of Moharram. The venerated figures represented in the *ta'ziyeh* are known as the "Fourteen Infallibles" (*chahardah ma'sum*) by Shi'i Muslims.[1] They include the Prophet Mohammad himself, the Twelve Imams, starting with Imam Ali, and the Prophet Mohammad's daughter, the mother of Imams Hasan and Hosayn, known as Fatemeh.[2] In the *ta'ziyeh* drama, these Fourteen Infallibles come alive on the stage of the Iranian "newest days" and take part in the dramatic reenactment of Islam's antiquity—a resurrection, in drama, historically scheduled for Judgment Day. The *ta'ziyehs* enacted during the month of Moharram and sometimes Safar revolve around the tragic death of the Third Imam, Hosayn. They are performed in recollection of the Battle of Karbala, in which Imam Hosayn, his meager army, and members of his family were slaughtered on the plains of Karbala (now in Iraq) by rival claimants to Prophet Mohammad's successorship and the military army of Caliph Yazid.

Moharram Mourning Processions and Early * Taʿziyeh* Performances

John G. Wishard, writing about his life and service as an American medical doctor in Iran at the beginning of the twentieth century, records the following observations about the Moharram mourning ceremonies. On the tenth of Moharram each year, he writes, the city awakens to the commotion on the streets. It is a public holiday and the processions commemorating the murders of Imam Hosayn and his family on the plains of Karbala start early:

> The morning is given up to great processions moving through the streets, composed of men and boys dressed in white, carrying swords, with which they inflict deep gashes into their shaven heads. Others, with bare chests, strike themselves with pieces of chain or with their hands, calling in unison the names of the martyrs. Other bands made up of boys and some men are content to carry banners and cry the names of Hosein and Hassan.[3]

European and American visitors often avoided appearing in public for the duration of the Moharram commemorations because of these acts of self-mutilation. One J. M. Tancoigne, a French officer on duty in Tehran, however, describes a Moharram procession of 1820 in great detail. His description suggests that he recognized that these street processions functioned as ritualized funeral processions; what he describes is typical of the late Safavid and early Qajar dynasties:[4]

> Naked and bleeding men marched behind. . . . They were followed by a long train of camels mounted by men dressed in black, as were female mourners, and an infinity of persons of that sort, who threw ashes and chopped straw on their heads in token of mourning. A more pompous and imposing spectacle suddenly came to variegate these hideous scenes. There appeared two great mosques of gilt wood, carried by more than three hundred men: both were inlaied with mirrors, and surmounted with little minarets: children placed in galleries sang hymns, the soft harmony of which agreeably recompensed the spectators for the frightful shouting they had heard just before.[5]

The modern dramatic forms of the *taʿziyeh* are said to have emerged out of an amalgamation of these ceremonies, which are associated with the mourning processions for Imam Hosayn during the month of Moharram, and the *rowzeh khanis,* or readings of eulogies held in individual homes and public mosques.[6] By the middle of the nineteenth century, the Iranian Shi'is are said to have gathered for the ritual *ta'ziyeh* dramas in the houses of the rich or in *takyehs,*[7] which, according to Comte de Gobineau, a French diplomat writing in 1865, could be found in each quarter.[8] In Tehran, each *takyeh* held between three hundred and three thousand viewers for each performance.

In Isfahan, open-air *takyeh*s seated twenty to thirty thousand viewers per performance.[9] Private residences, too, were opened to the public during the month of Moharram as a way for the well-to-do to offer public and religious service to the community at large.[10] The gatherings were convened so that city dwellers could relive, recollect, and identify with the events of Karbala on the first ten days of the Muslim New Year. In the late nineteenth century, each day a new *ta'ziyeh* drama was performed in the *takyehs,* culminating in the reenactment of the tragedy of Imam Hosayn's murder on the anniversary of his slaughter on the tenth of the month of Moharram (Ashura). In the years of Gobineau's residence in Tehran (1856–1858 and 1861–1864), the *ta'ziyeh* performance was accompanied by a fictive procession to the court of Yazid in Damascus, close behind an effigy of Imam Hosayn's decapitated head mounted on a pole.[11]

In the early years of the Qajar reign, *ta'ziyeh* performances, as culminations of the street processions, were first staged at street intersections and squares, but later moved into courtyards of caravanserais, bazaars, and private homes. "An advantage of smaller sites such as a mosque or a private residence was the *howz,*[12] which, customarily a feature of the courtyard, could easily be converted into a stage by covering it with wooden planks."[13] This stage was left barren except for a few symbolic objects significant to the history of the Karbala tragedy: a basin of water and a tree branch.[14] Whether elaborate or simple, the *ta'ziyeh*'s emphasis on stagecraft and place in a permanent theatre did not culminate until the last five decades of the Qajar reign, according to Johan ter Harr.[15] And even then, little was done in the way of intricate costumes, stage props, and so forth. In the constitution of dramatic meaning, "the public," Matthew Arnold says, "meets the actor halfway."[16] This statement rings true of the early conditions for the staging of the *ta'ziyeh* as well. Tancoigne notes that in 1820, only "the last five representations of the Karbala story were performed on a theatre erected opposite the king's kiosk in the *Golestan* Palace."[17] The remainder, we must assume, took place during the processionals themselves. Such processional *ta'ziyehs,* called "*ta'ziyeh dowreh,*" continued to be performed alongside other stagings of the performance.[18]

The fact is that such transitive performances in squares and open spaces were less responsive to the various prohibitions placed on religious mourning rituals over time. Even under the sternest restrictions on the performance under Pahlavi rule, for example, street performances took place on the morning of Ashura in the Alighapur square in Ardebil. Here the processions and their on-lookers would surround the square as the *ta'ziyeh* players performed scenes from the battle, ending with a moving representation of the flight and capture of the women and children of the Imam's coterie.[19]

Fixing the Space of History

Under the long reign of Naser al-Din Shah Qajar (1848–1896),[20] the *ta'ziyeh* became a sovereign art form; it was given a permanent residence and a royal following. Royal encouragement of individual commemorations of Hosayn's martyrdom for the purpose of patriotic and religious zeal was already an established custom under the Safavid dynasty (1501–1736), whose reign is associated with the formulation of Shi'ism in Iran. Under the Safavids, the pageantry of the Moharram festival achieved extraordinary forms and these celebrations became a unifying force for the country.[21] Naser al-Din Shah, however, would become the monarch known for his frivolous love of the spectacle in the dramatic form of the *ta'ziyeh*. The royal *takyeh* in Tehran was a theatre built for the purpose of *ta'ziyeh* performances under the watchful eye of Naser al-Din Shah. It held several thousand spectators over the course of the month of Moharram.[22] During the other months of the year when the *ta'ziyeh* was not performed, the royal *takyeh* was used instead as a place to house the royal menagerie. Ironically, it became Naser al-Din Shah's temporary burial ground when he was assassinated in May Day 1896.[23] It had been Naser al-Din Shah himself who insisted that this phenomenal brick construction be built in the image of the Royal Albert Hall in London.[24]

The shah was mesmerized by the dome at Albert Hall and was annoyed, shortly after his visit to England in 1873, to find that his staff was unable to create the same spectacular effect at home. It took the intervention of the foreign community to convince him "that the dome he envisioned was physically impossible with the materials available to the Persian builders."[25] Instead the builders devised an ingenious system by which canvas awnings would be stretched across wooden arches that were reinforced by iron braces. Every photograph of a *ta'ziyeh* performance around the country from this period features these marvelous white awnings suspended above a spectacular crowd.[26]

Manufacturing Identity

Under Qajar rule, the theatre that dramatized the antiquity of Islam found a permanent royal home. The royal *takyeh* opened a space of recollection, redemption, and mourning for the Shi'is. Yet, Comte de Gobineau argued that those who attended the spectacle participated without regard to the divergence of religious opinion.[27] Observing the people's enthusiasm for the spectacle, Gobineau claimed that the Persians recognized in this history of brutality the legitimization of their belief in the rightful claimants of the Prophet Mohammad's throne and saw their Shi'i identity revealed in the *ta'ziyehs*. This ebullience would surely explain the palpable fear that kept Sunni followers from attending the performances:

> The Arabians, the Turks, the Afghans—Persia's implacable and hereditary enemies—recognize Yazid as legitimate Caliph; Persia finds therein an excuse for hating them the more and identifies itself with the usurper's victims. It is patriotism therefore, which has taken the form here, of drama to express itself.[28]

The *ta'ziyeh*, then, must be seen as a space in which a phantasmic Shi'i identity could be forged. The annual commemorative events not only offered spiritual renewal for the Twelver Shi'is but also situated the cultural difference of the Qajar subjects vis-à-vis their neighbors. The performances marked their identity as "difference." This difference can be formulated as an identity associated with the meek, but no less victorious, Imam—a validating identity which can be neither robbed nor destroyed by the machinations of the Sunni others.

As anthropologist William Beeman points out, the

> *ta'ziyah* performance offers the opportunity for the spectators ritually to renew their commitment to a religious and ideological order of which they are an integral part. This ideological order does not limit itself strictly to religious dimensions but includes a political and nationalistic dimension as well.[29]

One should observe, however, that this renewal is significantly more historical and more embedded in the changing tides of identity formation in Iran than Beeman here indicates. The *ta'ziyeh* dramas have clearly captured the mythological forces and rationalities that have filtered through various modern institutions and that have animated both personal and collective initiatives at particular times in Iranian history. While at times the structural elements of the * taᶜziyeh* were used to reinforce religious distinctions by casting "the good" as the Imam and his family and "the evil" as the Caliph Yazid and his Sunni adherents, at other times, the *taᶜziyeh* dramatic format was used to hail the people to revolutionary action and to emphasize the role of Iranians as Imam Hosayn's representatives in the world. Literary works, travel narratives, and invocations of various kinds, especially those belonging to the Qajar period, demonstrate the influence of the *taᶜziyeh*.[30] Historical and anthropological evidence from various decades in Iranian history since the years when the *taᶜziyeh* was popular also provides strong support for this argument.

The revolutionary action implanted in the Shiᶜi consciousness by the image of the Imam Hosayn in Karbala demonstrated the strength and value of sacrificial acts, the importance of principled behavior, and the power of communal cooperation against all odds. The vision of Imam Hosayn's revolutionary action, as performed in the *taᶜziyeh* dramas, casts light on the manner in which the populist events of twentieth-century Iran were understood by its participants. For the modern Iranian nation, the Karbala story, told in terms of its revolutionary potential, emphasized that despite the reality of death and suffering, human life could maintain infinite significance and meaning. Imam Hosayn thus represented a life that could and would be remembered for its dynamism of bravery despite all odds.

Mary Hegland, in an anthropological study of an Iranian village before and after the Islamic Revolution in Iran, comments on the changing status of Imam Hosayn in popular Muslim and political discourse. She argues that preceding the revolution Imam Hosayn functioned as intercessor and fulfiller of wishes and selfish prayer directed toward personal salvation and alleviation of individual problems. During the revolution, however, Imam Hosayn functioned as an exemplar for a revolution that was against the oppressor and for the establishment of a just government. According to one informant Hegland interviewed after the 1979 Islamic Revolution, it was only in the last ten years that "the real story" of Imam Hosayn was known.[31] Right before the revolution the role and cooperation of the community in Imam Hosayn's war with Yazid's troops was emphasized. "Greater attention [was] given to his characteristics, attitudes and behavior. For it is what he did and his reasons for doing it that make him worthy of esteem and emulation."[32] Organizational discourse represented Imam Hosayn's attitude as one of cooperation with the community. Hence during the term of the revolutionary struggles, the history of Imam Hosayn's struggle on the plains of Karbala became a lesson in self-reliance and resistance on behalf of the community against an unjust authority. For the Islamic Revolution, the unjust authority took the form of Reza Shah's dynasty. In 1979, after the revolution, the evil Yazid was seen as having been toppled in favor of Hosayn and his community.

Malleable in its archetypal representation of good and evil, the *taʿziyeh* can be seen as more than a popular practice of historical and performative commemoration. The *taʿziyeh* as a popular passion play has left its marks on (and has been marked by) national and religious discourses in various ways throughout the modern period. This influence is evident in the pictorial arts, as well.

Animating Pictorial Arts

At the time of the popularization of the *taʿziyeh* dramas in Qajar Iran, Shiʿi religious scholars were forced, albeit reluctantly, to deliver a decision on the religious performances.[33] The first famous judgment was given by Mirza Abu al-Qasem Ebn-e Hasan Gilani (d. 1815–1816 CE). He was one of the most important religious authorities of the Qajar period and was well respected by the shah and his ministers. In answer to the question of whether it was "lawful on the days of Ashura to play the roles of the Imam or the enemies of the Family of the Prophet in order to induce the people to weep,"[34] Mirza Abu al-Qasem Ebn-e Hasan Gilani issued the following fatwa:

> We say there is no reason to prohibit the representation of [the Fourteen Infallibles] and the generality of the excellence of weeping, causing weeping, and pretending to weep for the Lord of Martyrs and his followers proves this. . . . Sometimes it is supposed that this dishonors the sanctity of religious leaders, but this supposition is invalid because it is not genuine identification, rather an imitation of form, appearance and dress merely to commemorate their misfortune. . . . Thus we answer . . . there is a time when it is among the greatest of religious works.[35]

As a performance that took license with historical materials, *taʿziyeh* was, in the words of one religious thinker, given full range on the condition that it would cause weeping and *pretending* to weep for Imam Hosayn and his family. Such license created the grounds for the emergence of sacred pictorial depictions in Persian popular art during the nineteenth century. For although the Karbala tragedy had been recounted in the tales told by one generation to the next, it was popularly considered sacrilege to represent an animate form. "Once it had been accepted, to the dismay of the orthodox, that the roles of the martyrs and their adversaries were enacted by devout Muslims, the step toward the public's acceptance of religious paintings depicting the same narratives had already been made," Samuel Peterson writes. "After hundreds of years of censure, during the nineteenth century there appear paintings of religious subjects which specifically were intended for the Iranian public at large."[36] The paintings depict the events of Karbala as *a translation* of the *ta'ziyeh* performances into the visual and pictorial arts.

Evidence of this can be seen in the loose relations between these dramatic representations and the *ta'ziyeh*-style Qajar-era depictions of the Karbala massacre that appear on the tile panels in various *takyehs* throughout the country. Covering the walls of the *takyehs*, these tiles cite the *ta'ziyeh*'s performances of Muslim history. In his article on epic theatre, Walter Benjamin conceptualizes such acts of quotation in the dramatic sphere as *literarization*.[37] Citing Brecht's work on theatre, Benjamin uses the term "literarization" to refer to the connections made between the epic stage and other institutions for intellectual activity (a gesture not unlike footnoting the play). Among these connections, Benjamin mentions those between the media (he suggests books) and the epic stage:

> Neher's back-projections for such "turns" are far more like posters than stage decorations. The poster is a constituent element of "literarized" theatre. "Literarizing entails punctuating 'representation' with 'formulation'; gives the theatre the possibility of making contact with other institutions for intellectual activities."[38]

Using material that is already known to the audience, namely historical material, epic theatre like *ta'ziyeh* instructs the actor to transform it, to give it a new twist. The *ta'ziyeh*, as a reenactment of sacred history, cites the past in the context of the present, thus transforming the past in its most minute details. Benjamin writes, "One must, however, expect the dramatist to take a certain amount of license in that he will tend to emphasize not the great decisions which lie along the main line of history but the incommensurable and the singular."[39] The epic actor, like the *ta'ziyeh* performer, thus effects a translation of a known past which brings aspects of the topical and everyday to the fore. The most significant of these "turns" or translations can be seen in the sartorial details of the Karbala paintings of the Qajar period.

Gender Trouble and Women's Performances

When pictorial arts began depicting history in imitation of the actions performed in the *ta'ziyeh,* history lost its essentialized form. The translation of history into the present of the *ta'ziyeh* performance made the usage of veiling arbitrary, by extension, in pictorial form. Historians of the *ta'ziyeh* claim that the introduction of veils into the drama was meant to cover for the fact that only men and children took part in the representation of the Karbala tragedy. Women, in other words, did not participate as actors. So to depict female characters such as Fatemeh, mortal men donned the veil. This minor "twist" has had major consequences for the ancient traditions of painting in Qajar Iran:

> During the last half of the fifteenth century and until the Qajar period, the veil was an exclusive attribute of holy personages and *was not used to cover the faces of women.* However, once it became in *ta'ziyah* productions a standard part of the costume of women—a sign of their modesty . . . it becomes in Kerbela paintings a standard feature of Alid women. No longer used so consistently as the sacred symbol it formerly had been, in Qajar religious painting the veil is ascribed somewhat arbitrarily to holy figures; thus the faces of the Shi'a Imams appear veiled and unveiled.[40]

On the stage itself, the grain of the voice and the tint of the veil determined the gender of the character. Young men with soft voices portrayed female characters and young girls under the age of nine (the age of maturity) performed certain minor roles. One of the early Qajar performers of women's roles, Hajji Molla Hosayn, from Pik Zarand-Saveh, played female characters so well that each year he had to leave his home and farm for the months of Moharram and Safar in order to perform at the royal *takyeh* (*takyeh* Dowlat). Hajji Molla Hosayn and Gholi Khan Shahi were two of the most famous performers of female roles in the late Qajar period and were specifically hired to play the role of Zinat.[41] According to Beiza'i, the male actor would wear a long black shirt which was sometimes decorated with flowers and which reached down to the back of the leg. A second black piece of textile would cover the head, the arms, and the hands. A third would cover the face, so that only the sliver of the eyes and the fingertips of the actor would be visible. The women belonging to Yazid's camp would wear the same costumes but in red.[42]

Western observers of the *ta'ziyeh* during the modern period, those travelers and diplomats used to the European tradition of drama as fictional but historically real entertainment, frequently note the lack of attention paid to the historical accuracy of costumes in the dramatic presentation of the *ta'ziyeh*. Edward G. Browne comments that the performance of the *ta'ziyeh* on the seventh of Moharram 1888 CE was "spoiled in some measure by the introduction of a number of carriages, with pastilions barbarously dressed up in a half-European uniform, in the middle of the piece."[43] He observes that this absurd piece of ostentation seemed typical of Qajar taste.

Writing in the 1860s, Flandin records that the players who represented Europeans on the stage borrowed his troops' triangular hats and (military?) uniforms in order to represent themselves as real *farangis* (foreigners). However, Flandin was moved by the realism, if not the historical accuracy, of the *ta'ziyeh* performance, much like Drouville some thirty years earlier, who could not fathom how the realistic and chaotic battle of four thousand performers left no one hurt or wounded.[44] For Gobineau, the simplicity of clothing seemed appropriate for the production of the *ta'ziyehs*. In order for the spectacle to work, Gobineau maintains, the holy men had to wear turbans and the feminine characters had to wear *the present-day* veils used in Baghdad and Damascus.[45] The *ta'ziyeh* of the Christian girl performed at the shah's Niyavaran palace and then at the royal *takyeh* in Tehran a year later struck Gobineau as one of most powerful *ta'ziyehs* performed in the Moharram sequence. In this performance the clothes of the Christian girl are said to have been based on European paintings, so that in the play, the Christian girl appears as a stereotypical European woman in a straw hat, a fanning skirt, and an apron, performing her part in tall black boots.

This *ta'ziyeh*, which Beiza'i says may be the *ta'ziyeh* known as the "Majles-e zan-e Nasrani," is noteworthy because it is one of the only known *ta'ziyehs* with a female lead character. It is uncharacteristic, too, in that it opens with a curtain around the otherwise open circular stage. The scene is set on the barren plains of Karbala and the coffins bearing the remains of the Imam and his followers are visible. Lit candles above a few of the coffins signify the holiness of the personages within. Weapons are scattered about on the ground, signaling the battle that has just been fought. Gobineau muses that the audience senses it can see both above and below the ground. The girl enters with her entourage, riding a horse. Not knowing where she has arrived, she dismounts and asks her party to put up tents. But with every nail that penetrates the ground, blood gushes out as if from a fountain. Everyone in her party is perturbed. Eventually asleep in one of the upper rooms of the *takyeh*, the girl has a dream. Christ enters and tells the girl about the battle of Karbala. Meanwhile an Arab thief enters the stage and, unaware of the Imam's status, opens his coffin. Looking for weapons and valuables, he attacks the body. The Arab is so evil at heart, Gobineau observes, that he does not notice the candles or the doves that encircle the holy corpse. He is suddenly frightened and then angered by the voice of the martyred Imam who speaks to him. After dismembering the body, the Arab thief leaves the scene. Then all the prophets of the past and the Fourteen Infallibles enter with veiled faces. They walk toward the Imam's corpse. As the performance ends, the Christian girl, moved by the tragic fate of the Imam, converts to Islam.

Though female characters in *taʿziyehs* were rare, their appearance on stage indubitably created the desire among the multitude of female *taʿziyeh* enthusiasts to perform in the *taʿziyeh* and to convene exclusive performances for women. One of the daughters of Fath Ali Shah Qajar (1797–1834), Ghamar al-Saltaneh, arranged to have the full *taʿziyeh* sequence performed at her house to an all-female audience in the first ten days of Moharram each year. The *taʿziyehs* were performed in the evenings following female-only *rowzeh khanis*. In these performances, female *rowzeh khans* such as Molla Nabat, Molla Fatemeh, and Molla Maryam would often take leading roles. The *taʿziyehs* performed in these gatherings, though sometimes selected from among the more traditional scripts, were more often those with female leads. The *taʿziyeh* of Shahbanu, or the wedding of the daughter of Gharish, is among these. Women characters appeared less veiled in these all-women performances. They also appeared as lead male characters in drag, with applied facial hair.

Beiza'i maintains that these performances by and for women were reactions that showed not only women's appreciation of the art form, but also their desire to gain the right to perform women's roles in the larger and more traditional arenas. Women's *taʿziyehs*, however, did not reach the public. Rare, and rarely documented, they were only occasionally performed in larger private spaces, in the homes of the wealthy and powerful, until the mid-1920s.[46]

Messianic Time

Prologues to the *taʿziyeh*, traditionally called "*pish vagheh*," frequently included female characters. In *Religions et les philosophies dans l'Asie Centrale*, Gobineau presents several examples of these. The prologues introducing each *taʿziyeh* provided the audience with a reason to watch the action that was about to take place on the stage. One of those recorded by Gobineau's pen is about the story of Joseph and Jacob. Matthew Arnold in an 1871 talk called "A Persian Passion Play" provides a version of Gobineau's description of this prologue:

> Joseph and his brethren appear on stage, and the old Bible story is transacted. Joseph is thrown in the pit and sold to the merchants, and his blood-stained coat is carried by his brothers to Jacob; Jacob is then left alone, weeping and bewailing himself; the angel Gabriel enters, and reproves him for want of faith and constancy, telling him that what he suffers is not a hundredth part of what [Imam] Ali, [Imam Hosayn] and the children of [Imam Hosayn] will one day suffer. Jacob seems to doubt it; Gabriel, to convince him, orders the angels to perform the *tazya* [*sic*] of what will one day happen at Kerbela. And so the *tazya* commences.[47]

The prologue in its very form captures the measure of time as it appeared in the *ta'ziyeh* performances. Although historically distant, two moments, the suffering of Joseph and the suffering of Mohammad's family, are captured within the time frame of the present, disregarding the temporal impossibility of Gabriel's knowledge of a future event.[48] The present thus captured the antiquity of Islam and the antiquity of the biblical world in one frame. These moments came together in the *ta'ziyeh* to revolutionize the Muslim consciousness of the everyday.

The present moment of the Muslim New Year, as a time filled with the significance of all time, dictated that all the important religious figures who predated and postdated the Karbala tragedy would be added to the repertoire of Moharram dramas.[49] Walter Benjamin recognized this model of the present as a model of messianic time in which the present is the "'time of the now' which is shot through with chips of Messianic time."[50] Benjamin, like the *ta'ziyeh* audience and its makers, understood now-time as a snapshot of all time, a time in which all humanity and its past were redeemed.

As Beeman notes, oratorical skill for the performance of commemorative ceremonies during the month of Moharram involved a similar temporal conception and capacity: "the ability to make the events of [Imam Hosayn's] martyrdom seem immediate and relevant to the audience." Beeman continues:

> One *rowzeh* that was widely distributed on cassette tapes during the fall of 1978 when the [Islamic] revolution in Iran was in full swing, was delivered by Ayatollah Kafi of Mashhad. In this *rowzeh* he calls

Imam Hosayn *on the telephone* and cries out to him to quit the plains of Karbala because the greater enemy is in Iran in the person of the shah's regime. In this he duplicates the kind of telephone conversation that must take place between separated relatives in Iran all the time. The pathos of the plea to Imam [Hosayn] is accentuated by the contemporary setting given to the message.[51]

This sense of the historical significance of the present persistently retold and reenacted in the Moharram passions transforms not only the time of the present into a messianic time filled with possibilities of revolutionary action and redemption, it transforms the stage into a public stage populated with the everyday life and concerns of the masses.

The *ta'ziyeh* representing the historical Fatemeh, the daughter of the Prophet Mohammad and the wife of Imam Ali, is a good example. Fatemeh is shown on stage engaged in the daily routines of the home, washing the clothes of her young sons, Imam Hosayn and Imam Hasan: "As she takes each small piece of clothing out of the washbasin, she identifies it and bemoans the fact that the child who wears it will one day be tortured and killed in the most horrendous way. She ends fainting in grief, her children's clothing spread around her."[52] This engagement of the topical and the historical transforms the stage of the *takyeh* into the site of the everyday recognizable to every woman and man in the audience. The everyday of the *ta'ziyeh* performance reenacts the historical as a *citation á l'ordre du jour*. Judgment Day, the day on which all the Imams of old are promised to reawaken, is played out on the stage of "the most recent days" of the life of the believer.

European witnesses to the *ta'ziyeh* during the mid to late nineteenth century emphasized the public appeal of the *ta'ziyeh* performances in Iran. Writing of his experiences in Tehran during his early travels to Persia between 1887 and 1888, Browne gives a description of the royal *takyeh*, which he visited during the month of Moharram.

The theatre is a large circular building—roofless, but covered during Muharram with an awning. There are boxes (*takches*) all round, which are assigned to the more patrician spectators, one, specially large and highly decorated, being reserved for the Shah. The humbler spectators sit round the central space or arena in serried ranks, the women and children in front. A circular stone platform in the centre constitutes the stage. There is no curtain and no exit for the actors, who when not wanted, simply stand back.[53]

This stage, so undifferentiated from the platform of life, demanded that the actor himself become one of the public when his character was not called for by the unfolding drama.[54] Two or more corridors through the seating area to the back wall of the *takyeh* enabled the bearer of messages, armies, and processions to move through the audience. Actors, in performing their duels, plunged through the audience to gain central stage. Thus even in terms of spatial formality, the *takyeh* was designed to give the participant a sense that he or she was in fact *on* the plains of Karbala and encircled (in the central playing area) by the enemy. Through its spatial form, the *ta'ziyeh* posited the present as the model of messianic time and the crowd as a nation in support of the courageous deeds of the meek Imam.

The royal *takyeh* in Tehran, with its circular brick structure mirroring the British concert hall, was the grandest *takyeh* in Iran during the Qajar reign. It provided a meeting ground, a public sphere, through which contrary discourses of nationalism and dynastic reverence, religious fervor and anti-dogmatic spectacle, the historical and the topical, mingled. Wishard proclaimed the death of the *ta'ziyeh* drama after the 1906 Iranian Constitutional Revolution had passed: "Everywhere these celebrations are becoming less popular, and as education and enlightenment come, we may expect their disappearance."[55] It would seem that the persistent resurrection of Islam's antiquity subsided, at least momentarily, with the forceful coming of modernity.

Epilogue

Under the rule of the Pahlavis (1925–1978), *ta'ziyeh* was forbidden and its image deemed not in keeping with the image of a modern state. After the Festival of Popular Traditions in 1977, attempts were made to lift the government ban on *ta'ziyeh* performances, and the aid of the queen was enlisted:

> She approached her husband on the matter, and he in turn consulted SAVAK. By that point the religious oppositionist fervor leading to the revolutionary events of 1979 had begun to make itself felt, and SAVAK recoiled in horror at the thought of hundreds of *ta'ziyah* performances involving millions of persons being brought to an emotional pitch in a highly moving religious spectacle. Moreover they wished to pacify the conservative mullas opposing the government. Therefore SAVAK sternly advised the shah not to lift the ban and

for the months of Moharram and Safar in 1977 a strict prohibition against *ta'ziyah* performances was again announced.[56]

Though the *ta'ziyeh* has lost the popularity it had under the reign of Naser al-Din Shah, the Islamic Republic has found dramatic performances useful tools for moral and national propaganda. This surprising acceptance of representational art forms that in part transform religious history is no doubt due to the unique efficacy, popularity, and appeal of the *ta'ziyeh* in the previous century.

The tropes of the *ta'ziyeh* and its focus on the recollection of the distant past in the living present seem to appear most forcefully in postrevolutionary Iranian films. The director Bahram Beiza'i, whose earlier work for the theatre was renowned for incorporating indigenous and Eastern dramatic techniques, has introduced some of these elements to his work. A *ta'ziyeh* performance appears, for example, in his *Legend of Tara*, and time folds to awaken the dead for a festive wedding in the film *The Travellers*. Elements of the indigenous theatre also punctuate Beiza'i's other films, such as *Maybe . . . Some Other Time* in articulating a new vision for the postrevolutionary nation.[57] The temporal and spatial tools of the *ta'ziyeh* are used to resurrect a unified sense of the nation and a national identity that embraces Iran's divergent secular and religious histories, including its ethnic multiplicity. For Beiza'i the spatial and temporal tropes of this indigenous religious and nationalistic drama are redeemed in our time, making every moment of time a moment imbued with the images of all time.

Notes

An earlier version of this article was published as Negar Mottahedeh, "Scheduled for Judgement Day: The Ta'ziyeh Performance in Qajar Persia and Walter Benjamin's Dramatic Vision of History," *Theatre Insight* 8:1 (1997). There were numerous editorial omissions and errors in the published article that this chapter attempts to redeem.

1. Twelver Shi'ism is the branch of Islam that is most widely observed in Iran. It features a belief in the familial sucessorship of the Prophet Mohammad by twelve imams. The last of these successors is Abu al-Qasem Mohammad, who according to tradition went into occultation in 874 CE due to the hostility of the enemies of the Imam. The Hidden Imam has many titles, including Mahdi, Saheb al-Zaman, and Qa'em. His return is believed to mark the end of time and the beginning of the reign of peace on earth. On this day, which is the equivalent of the biblical Judgment Day, it is believed that all the past imams will be resurrected.

In contradistinction, the Isma'ilis, or Sevener Shi'is, believe that the Seventh Imam, Isma'il, was to have been the last imam, and later claimed that his son Mohammad al-Tamm would return at the end of the world as the Mahdi (or "divinely guided one"). Ismaʿili doctrine, formulated in the late eighth and ninth centuries, stressed the dual interpretation of the Qurʾan, the esoteric and exoteric, and made a similar distinction between the ordinary Muslim and the initiated Ismaʿili. The Ismaʿili secret was believed to be unlocked through a hierarchical organization headed by the Imam and introduced to the believers through carefully graded levels. Incidentally, the tenth-century major religious and philosophical encyclopedia "Epistle of the Brethren of Purity," which was influenced by Neoplatonism, was said to have been composed in collaboration with a group connected with Ismaʿilism.

2. For a thorough but succinct discussion of the history of Sunni, Shiʿi, and Sufi branches of Islam, consult Wadi Haddad, "Islam: A Brief Overview," in *Taʿziyah: Ritual and Popular Beliefs in Iran,* ed. Milla Riggio, 1–8 (Hartford, Conn.: Trinity College, Hartford Seminary, 1988).

3. John G. Wishard, *Twenty Years in Persia: A Narrative of Life under the Last Three Shahs* (New York: Fleming H. Revell Company, 1908), 158.

4. The Safavid dynasty reigned in Iran between 1501 and 1736. Following the downfall of the Zand dynasty, the Qajars ruled from 1779 to 1925.

5. J. M. Tancoigne, *A Narrative of a Journey into Persia and Residence at Tehran* (London: William Wright, 1820), 196–201.

6. Bahram Beizaʾi, *A Study of Iranian Theatre* (Tehran: Roshangaran and Women's Studies Publishing, 2000), 116.

7. A *takyeh* is a theatre used for the performance of *taʿziyeh.*

8. M. le Comte de Gobineau, *Religions et les philosophies dans l'Asie Centrale* (Paris: Ernest Leroux, 1900), 339–341.

9. Beizaʾi, *A Study of Iranian Theatre,* 122–123.

10. Peter J. Chelkowski, "Taʿziyeh: Indigenous Avant-Garde Theatre of Iran," in *Taʿziyeh: Ritual and Drama in Iran,* ed. Peter J. Chelkowski, 1–11 (New York: New York University, 1979a), 4. Also, Johan ter Haar notes that *taʿziyeh* dramas were performed in more than two hundred locations, each accommodating between three and four hundred spectators in Tehran. See Johan G. J. Ter Haar, "Taʿziye: Ritual Theatre from Shiʿite Iran," in *Theatre Intercontinental: Forms, Functions, Correspondences,* ed. C. C. Barfoot and Cobi Ordewijk, 155–174 (Amsterdam: Rodopi, 1993).

11. For a literary critique of one of these scenes in contemporaneous Persian writing, see Juan R. I. Cole, "I Am All the Prophets: The Poetics of Pluralism in Bahaʾi Texts," *Poetics Today* 14:3 (1993), 447–476.

12. *Howz* is a wading pool.

13. Samuel R. Peterson, "The Tazieh and Related Arts," in *Taʿziyeh: Ritual and Drama in Iran,* ed. Peter J. Chelkowski (New York: New York University Press, 1979), 65.

14. The basin of water was said to represent the Euphrates River, from which Imam Hosayn and his companions were cut off by the troops of Caliph Yazid. The branch of a tree was said to represent a palm grove. See Peter J. Chelkowski, "When Time Is No Time, and Space Is No Space: The Passion Plays of Husayn," in *Taʿziyah: Ritual and Popular Beliefs in Iran,* ed. Milla Riggio (Hartford, Conn.: Trinity College, Hartford Seminary, 1988), 16.

15. Ter Haar, "Taʿziye," 164.

16. Matthew Arnold, "A Persian Passion Play," *Cornhill Magazine* (December 1871), 676.

17. Tancoigne, *Narrative of a Journey into Persia*, 198.

18. Beiza'i, *A Study of Iranian Theatre*, 126.

19. Ibid.

20. For an excellent biography of Naser al-Din Shah, see Abbas Amanat, *Pivot of the Universe: Nasir al-Din Shah Qajar and the Iranian Monarchy, 1831–1896* (Berkeley and Los Angeles: University of California Press, 1997).

21. Peter J. Chelkowski, "Dramatic and Literary Aspects of Taʿziyeh-Khani—Iranian Passion Play," in *Review of National Literatures: Iran*, ed. Javad Haidari (New York: St. John's University Press, 1971), 2:123.

22. Toward the end of the nineteenth century, the performances were extended into the month of Safar, the second month of the Muslim year, in part due to their popularity. It is argued that this extension of the mourning ceremonies was appropriate in that the women of the Holy Family were still imprisoned by the Caliph Yazid during this second month of the Muslim year as well. See Chelkowski, "When Time Is No Time," 14.

23. Peterson, "The Tazieh and Related Arts," 70.

24. He visited London for the first time in 1873. Nasir al-Din Shah describes this visit to the Albert Hall in his travel diary: "Passing through, we came to a place the very picture of paradise. All these corridors, apartments and manufacturies [around the hall] were lighted up in various wonderful manner by jets of gas. The very concert [hall] itself was in an exceedingly spacious enclosure with a roof in shape of a dome were seven tiers of seats all occupied by people, all filled with beauteous women magnificently appareled. . . . Multitudes of gaslights were burning." Nasir Din Shah Qajar, *Diary of the Shah of Persia during His Tour through Europe in 1873*, trans. J. W. Redhouse (London: John Murray, 1874), 165–166.

25. Peterson, "The Tazieh and Related Arts," 64.

26. For an impressive collection of photographs of the *taʿziyeh* in Isfahan, a city known for its superb productions of the *taʿziyeh,* see Jennifer Scarce's review of engineer and amateur photographer Ernst Hoeltzer's collection in Jennifer Scarce, *Isfahan in Camera: Nineteenth-Century Persia through the Photographs of Ernst Hoeltzer* (London: AARP, 1976).

27. de Gobineau, *Religions et les philosophies*, 382.

28. de Gobineau, cited in Arnold, "A Persian Passion Play," 684.

29. William O. Beeman, "A Full Arena: The Development and Meaning of Popular Performance Traditions in Iran," in *Modern Iran: The Dialectics of Continuity and Change*, ed. Michael E. Bonine and Nikki R. Keddie (Albany: State University of New York Press, 1982), 30.

30. The Karbala story and the *taʿziyeh* model influenced the historical representation of one of the most ambitious messianic movements in Qajar Persia, the Babi movement. Several historical texts, among them the works published under the title *Ketab-e Noqtat al-Kaf* (*The New History of Mirza Ali Muhammad the Bab*) and the narratives of the Babi upheavals in Nayriz by Molla Mohammad-Shafi, show a strong reliance on the *taʿziyeh* historical model as a way to validate and justify the messianic and revolutionary acts of their protagonists in relation to a political

and religious system assumed to be outdated, corrupt, and oppressive. For more on this, see Negar Mottahedeh, "Resurrection, Return, Reform: Ta'ziya as Model for Early Babi Historiography," *Iranian Studies* 32:3 (1999b), 387–399.

31. Mary Elaine Hegland, "Two Images of Husain: Accommodation and Revolution in an Iranian Village," in *Religion and Politics in Iran: Shi'ism from Quietism to Revolution,* ed. Nikki R. Keddie (New Haven, Conn.: Yale University Press, 1983c), 226.

32. Ibid., 227.

33. The representation of animate forms in public has traditionally been forbidden, as evidenced even in modern mosques. Flandin comments that the *mollas* were against the *ta'ziyeh* for other reasons, however. They did not approve of the representation of their imams on the dramatic stage. But as Beiza'i argues, the resistance of the clerical class to *ta'ziyeh* performances may have been more professional than ideological: people found in the *ta'ziyeh* an outlet that, though religious, was more palatable than the religious instruction given by the *mollas;* see Beiza'i, *A Study of Iranian Theatre.*

34. Ashura, in the Muslim calendar, are the first ten days of Moharram.

35. Quoted in Mayel Baktash, "Ta'ziyeh and Its Philosophy," in *Ta'ziyeh: Ritual and Drama in Iran,* ed. Peter J. Chelkowski (New York: New York University Press, 1979), 107–108.

36. Peterson, "The Tazieh and Related Arts," 75.

37. Walter Benjamin, "What Is Epic Theatre?" in *Understanding Brecht* (London: Verso, 1992), 7.

38. Ibid., 6–7.

39. Ibid., 7–8.

40. Peterson, "The Tazieh and Related Arts," 79.

41. Beiza'i, *A Study of Iranian Theatre,* 143–144.

42. Ibid., 145.

43. Edward G. Browne, *A Year amongst the Persians, 1887–1888,* 2nd ed. (Cambridge: Cambridge University Press, 1926), 604.

44. Beiza'i, *A Study of Iranian Theatre,* 119–120.

45. de Gobineau, *Religions et les philosophies,* 389.

46. Beiza'i, *A Study of Iranian Theatre,* 151–152.

47. Arnold, "A Persian Passion Play," 673.

48. For another description of the *ta'ziyeh* drama of Joseph, see Chelkowski, "Dramatic and Literary Aspects of Ta'ziyeh-Khani," 126.

49. Chelkowski, "Ta'ziyeh," 4.

50. Walter Benjamin, "Theses on the Philosophy of History," in *Illuminations,* ed. Hannah Arendt (New York: Schocken Books, 1968), 263.

51. Beeman, "A Full Arena," 368.

52. Ibid., 369. In the performance of the "Martyrdom of Ali Akbar," the hero, before going into the battle in which he will be killed, writes a farewell letter to his fiancée in Medina *using a fountain pen,* emphasizing once more the messianic convergence with the topical (Chelkowski, "Dramatic and Literary Aspects of Ta'ziyeh-Khani," 133).

53. Browne, *A Year amongst the Persians,* 603. Browne also notes that it was cus-

tomary for the poor to occupy the special seats reserved for the rich if they were not already occupied.

54. In fact, as Wirth observes, it is not uncommon in *taʿziyeh* performances to see actors on stage drinking tea while waiting their turn to perform; see Andrej Wirth, "Semiological Aspects of the Taʿziyeh," in *Taʿziyeh: Ritual and Drama in Iran*, ed. Peter J. Chelkowski (New York: New York University Press, 1979), 38.

55. Wishard, *Twenty Years in Persia*, 158.

56. Beeman, "A Full Arena," 366–367.

57. For a brief discussion of Beiza'i's work in English, see Hamid Naficy, "Veiled Vision/Powerful Presences: Women in Post-Revolutionary Iranian Cinema," in *In the Eye of the Storm: Women in Post-Revolutionary Iran*, ed. Mahnaz Afkhami and Erika Friedl, 131–150 (Syracuse, N.Y.: Syracuse University Press, 1994), and Najmeh Khalili Mahani, "Bahram Baizai, Iranian Cinema, Feminism, Art Cinema," *Offscreen*, http://www.horschamp.qc.ca/new_offscreen/baizai.html. Also, see my two articles on his work: Negar Mottahedeh, "Bahram Bayza'i's 'Maybe Some Other Time:' The un-Present-able Iran," *Camera Obscura* 43:15.1 (2000), 163–191, and Negar Mottahedeh, "Bahram Bayza'i: Filmography," in *Life and Art: The New Iranian Cinema*, ed. R. Issa and S. Whitaker, 74–82 (London: BFI, 1999a).

CHAPTER 2

The Gender Dynamics of Moharram Symbols and Rituals in the Latter Years of Qajar Rule

KAMRAN SCOT AGHAIE

This chapter explores some of the ways in which Shiʻi women experienced Moharram symbols and rituals in Qajar Iran. It is argued that Iranian women were extremely active in participating in Shiʻi rituals, and that Shiʻi symbols and rituals can be understood as affecting women on multiple, distinct levels. I will restrict the discussion here to four dimensions. First, Shiʻi symbols and rituals served deeply personal functions in the lives of pious Shiʻi women, including psychological, emotional, spiritual, and soteriological aspects. Second, Shiʻi symbolism, which was gender coded in significant ways, served as both a means to articulate gender identities and gender ideals and as a vehicle to pass on gender-specific identities and ideals of behavior from one generation to the next. Third, these symbols and rituals served as one of the more important vehicles for establishing and preserving a variety of social bonds, identities, and relationships, as well as social status. Finally, while these symbols and rituals in certain ways served as a means for reinforcing restrictive social norms for women, at the same time, they provided some opportunities for greater independence, status, influence, and public social participation for some pious women.

On a deeply personal level, pious Shiʻi women in Qajar Iran, like men, looked to the imams for guidance and for intercession. This soteriological aspect of Moharram rituals was arguably the most important for Shiʻi men and women, because it provided a means for expressing piety and working to achieve salvation in the afterlife. Shiʻis have traditionally believed that devotion to the imams is a basis for achieving an exalted place in paradise. While scholars of history tend to ignore the supernatural or metaphysical aspects of these rituals, it would be a mistake to deny their purely spiritual dimensions, which participants usually represent as being the most important aspect of ritual participation. Shiʿi women in Qajar Iran routinely visited tomb shrines of the descendants of the imams, such as the shrine of Imam Reza in Mashhad or of his sister Maʿsumeh in Qom. They also attended ritual sermons, prayed for intercession, made offerings of food or water, and performed a variety of other religious acts in the hope of achieving intercession, blessings, and salvation. Above all, they mourned the tragedy of Karbala and shed tears for the imams.

Pious acts and participation in religious rituals could also bring hope in an otherwise hopeless situation. During the Qajar period, much like today, pious women who took part in these rituals hoped to receive divine blessing, or *shafa*. These women were often deeply concerned or worried about the well-being of their immediate family members. Therefore, when their families faced difficult challenges, they often turned to the imams for guidance and intercession. It was quite common for women, as well as men, to pray for the success or well-being of someone close to them. They may have asked that a sick family member recover from an illness, or for the birth of a healthy child, or for guidance on how to overcome some other hardship or challenge. For many women, this was one of the most important functions of these rituals. This was one reason why women were so heavily involved in ritual offerings, called *nazr*, which involves giving an offering, usually food or water, to the needy, to ritual participants, or to the descendants of the Prophet. It was widely believed that the pious act of making such an offering, especially if the offer was made with pure intention and constituted a personal sacrifice, would be rewarded with divine blessings and good fortune, both in this world and the next.

There may have been many emotional or psychological aspects to ritual participation. As women gathered to mourn, they often exchanged ideas, shared concerns, and confided in each other. They frequently shared with each other the personal difficulties and challenges they faced. This must have allowed them to bond as friends, much as people would in other social settings. In short, these rituals allowed them opportunities to rely on each other for support. While this phenomenon has not yet been studied in detail for the Qajar period, recent research indicates that it is the norm in present-day Iranian society. Crying may also have provided an emotional release of sorts that allowed women to "vent" their negative feelings in a setting in which they felt safe. Many also must have benefited from the practical advice they could receive from their female friends at these ritual events. It is reasonable, therefore, to say that these rituals must have served as both a catharsis and as a support group of sorts. This certainly is the case today.

The moral and ideological values conveyed through the symbolism of Ashura were also very important in the lives of pious women. Shi'i women, like their male counterparts, have traditionally looked to Ashura symbolism as a source of spiritual and moral guidance. Therefore, female characters and gender-coded symbolism in the stories have served to promote certain gender ideals that would then be passed from generation to generation. There are many female characters in Karbala narratives, Rowzeh sermons, and *ta'ziyeh* performances. Va'ez Kashefi, in his book *Rowzat al-shohada*, mentions dozens of female characters, including female members of the Prophet's family, women mentioned in the Qur'an, and other women who end up taking part in the story of Karbala. Similarly, a very large percentage of *ta'ziyehs* had female characters, and sometimes they were main characters, or at least major characters in the stories. For example, Homayuni, who lists over one hundred *ta'ziyehs*, mentions over a dozen that have major female characters.[1] Shahidi and Bolukbashi, similarly, list over two dozen such titles.[2]

The most commonly occurring female characters in Karbala stories and *ta'ziyehs* were Hosayn's immediate female relatives, such as his mother, Fatemeh; his grandmother, Khadijeh; his sisters, Zaynab and Omm Kolsum; his daughters, Kolsum, Sakineh/Sokayneh, Fatemeh (Qasem's bride), and Roqayyeh; and his wife, Omm Layla, or Shahrbanu (the Persian princess). Other prominent female characters included Qasem's mother, the Christian woman, and Omm Salameh, the Prophet's wife, who helped to raise Hasan and Hosayn. The names of women and the details of their involvement in these stories were not always consistent, because different accounts are based on different types of historical documents, and because there are substantial gaps in documentation of the events at Karbala, especially with regard to the women and girls.

Many of these stories focused either on the wedding or the death of these women. There were also several narratives about what took place after Hosayn was killed and the women and children were taken into captivity to Syria. Generally, they all focused on the women's suffering due to oppression, as well as their mourning due to the martyrdom of their husbands, sons, brothers, and fathers. There were also some villainous female characters, such as Hend, who arranged to assassinate the Prophet's uncle, Hamzeh, Yazid's daughter, and other women at Yazid's court; the Qoraysh women who treated Khadijeh and Fatemeh so badly; or even the wife of Abu Lahab from the Qur'anic account. However, these villainous women were the exception rather than the rule, and some of them repented after their acts of malfeasance.

These female characters served as role models; but the rituals were also rich in symbolism that, as a set of symbols, was gender-coded in certain ways. Some symbolic meanings were gender-neutral, while others were coded as either male or female. While some of these gender-coded symbols restricted the social roles of women, others had the opposite effect. Both men and women were represented as having been heavily involved in the Karbala story, and their roles were in some ways similar and in other ways distinct. Throughout these narratives, sermons, and performances, both space and activity were often characterized by gender difference or gender segregation. Men were generally portrayed as warriors, leaders, and martyrs. They usually acted as individuals, by sacrificing themselves directly, or they served the patriarchal function of protecting and maintaining their female relatives. Women were generally portrayed as chaste and secluded, and supportive or nurturing toward their children, brothers, and husbands, whom they ultimately sacrificed for the cause of justice. They also served as the educators of the new generation, and as spokespersons for the cause after the battle was over.

While women and girls were normally portrayed as submitting to "appropriate" male authority (i.e., the Prophet, the imams, and their pious male relatives), they were just as often portrayed as courageously rebelling against "inappropriate" male authority (i.e., Yazid, his men, and other impious men). Women were most often represented as acting "indirectly" through their families, rather than acting directly as individuals. It is only after the males in their families are killed that the women took the offensive, morally challenging their enemies directly. Women also represented the more tragic side of the story in that they were portrayed as victims of humiliation through their captivity, were associated with corpses after the battle, and were shown as mourning the tragedy itself. Therefore, while men were most directly associated with fighting and martyrdom, women were more closely associated with the acts of mourning, burying the dead, sacrificing their loved ones, and enduring suffering, oppression, and humiliation. In general, men were more often portrayed as actors in the story, while women were often acted upon or acted through male intermediaries. The major exceptions to this general tendency are the cases where the women directly confronted and challenged impious men in the story.

Both women and men were represented as possessing gender-neutral characteristics such as good moral conduct, courage, self-sacrifice, and loyalty to the family of the Prophet. Characters such as Fatemeh and Zaynab were portrayed as being unwavering in their loyalty to the Prophet and his family. In the narratives, their loyalty is repeatedly tested, as they are subjected to suffering, humiliation, violence, and the loss of their loved ones. Fatemeh and Ali, who were Hosayn's parents, were portrayed as defending both themselves and the Prophet Mohammad (Fatemeh's father) against persecution. Similarly, Hosayn's sister Zaynab, along with other female characters, such as the old woman Tow'eh, who was said to have given shelter and a hiding place to Hosayn's messenger, Moslem Ebn-e Aqil, were portrayed as uncompromisingly loyal to Hosayn.[3] Zaynab's closeness and loyalty to her brother was a central theme throughout all of these narratives, as was Fatemeh's closeness to the Prophet and to her husband, Ali.

Kashefi, in his seminal book *Rowzat al-shohada,* describes how Moslem Ebn-e Aqil, the imam's messenger to Kufeh, was being chased by Ebn-e Ziyad's men, who had orders to kill him. Moslem met an old woman named Tow'eh, who gave him shelter, food, and water. In supporting him she was portrayed as courageously risking her own life. Both Moslem and Tow'eh were portrayed as loyal, courageous, and self-sacrificing. Loyalty to Hosayn and courage in defending him were presented as central themes in these narratives without being gendered in any significant way. Righteousness and piety have likewise been universally praised as values appropriate for both men and women. There have been countless stories of pious behavior by male and female followers of Hosayn.

One ideal that is clearly stressed in the symbolism of Moharram is the idea that the greatest social status does not derive from wealth and power. The greatest status is represented as being the result of pious conduct and devotion to the mission of the Prophet and his family. For example, Kashefi tells a story in which Fatemeh was invited by some wealthy Qoraysh women to attend a wedding. She was reluctant to attend because the poverty of her family meant that she would not be able to dress in expensive clothes or be attended to by servants. However, the angel Gabriel told the Prophet to instruct her to attend in order to teach the Qorayshi women a lesson. So Fatemeh went to the party despite being dressed in tattered clothes, and without any jewelry or servants. When she entered the room, the whole place lit up and she was attended to by heavenly maidservants. The Qoraysh women thought that they were in the presence of a noblewoman, or royalty. They were mortified when they realized that it was Fatemeh, because some of these women had previously been mocking her state of poverty. The pagan women left immediately, and the remaining women fell all over themselves attending to her. When she was asked what she would like to eat, she stated that her nourishment was devotion to the

Prophet. When they asked her what she wanted, she said that the thing that would make her most happy would be if they all rejected disbelief in favor of faith. Upon hearing this, they all asserted their faith in Islam.

This story represents the victory of a pious woman over women with higher "worldly" status.[4] This theme was also expressed elsewhere in Moharram symbolism. For example, the pious poverty and suffering of the female captives after the battle of Karbala was contrasted with the impious wealth and high worldly status of the women of Yazid's court, and other female Damascenes. For instance, when Hosayn's daughter was tormented by Yazid's daughter and other girls in Damascus because she was poor, her tormentors were shown the error of their ways. This story also stressed that she had infinitely higher status due to her piety and her devotion to her father, Hosayn.[5] In a society (i.e., both seventh-century Arabia and Qajar Iran) where women's status was usually derived from the wealth, power, and worldly status of their closest male relatives, this symbolism established an alternative social status based on piety and devotion to the family of the Prophet and to their divinely ordained mission.

Fighting and martyrdom have historically been portrayed as gendered themes because men have been represented as being the ideal fighters and martyrs, while the ideal woman has been portrayed as sacrificing her loved ones rather than being a martyr herself. According to the narratives, women do not belong on the battlefield at all. Instead, they should lend support nearby. Most sources assert that it was crucial that women accompany Hosayn to Iraq because their participation in the movement was critical to its successful completion. All the adult male followers of Hosayn, except for Ali Ebn-e Hosayn, commonly referred to as Zayn al-Abedin, were killed and their martyrdom was recounted in great detail. Examples include the heroic struggle of Abbas to obtain water for the followers, which eventually led to his death, as well as the struggle of the young and newly married Qasem, who killed many of his opponents in single combat before being killed himself.[6] The martyrdom of Hosayn himself was the climax of the story.[7]

While a few women, and in some cases girls, entered the battlefield, were martyred, or died in a manner that related to the broader struggle of the family of the Prophet, they were few in number, and their stories were not recounted in the same way as those of the male martyrs. An example is the story of the newlywed Vahb and his wife, Haniyeh. In many of these accounts, she lost control out of love for her husband and ran out onto the battlefield to help him. She was called back to the tents by Imam Hosayn, who thereby reinforced the idea that she should not be on the battlefield at all. After repeating her actions, she was eventually martyred, but the story was usually passed over in only a few lines, as opposed to the story of her husband, which was generally given a much more elaborate treatment. Zaynab ran out onto the battlefield as well, which similarly resulted in Hosayn calling her back to the tent area with instructions to care for the women, children, and wounded.

Another good example is the *ta'ziyeh* of Shahrbanu (Hosayn's Persian wife). When she tried to escape to Ray (in northern Iran) on Hosayn's horse and was attacked by the enemy troops, she did not try to challenge them. Ali's ghost then came to clear the way for her escape.[8] It is clear that the ideal of the male warrior and martyr was well developed in the literature, while the female warrior/martyr was not only underdeveloped but was actually discouraged within the narratives. Furthermore, women on the battlefield were called back by Hosayn himself, clearly defining the battlefield as a male space and fighting as a male activity. According to these narratives, women were supposed to lend moral and logistical support to the martyrs from the sidelines during the battle. It should be noted here that under Islamic law it has usually been deemed unlawful for women to fight on the battlefield, except under the most extraordinary circumstances.

There are numerous stories and *ta'ziyehs* based on the death of major female figures, such as Khadijeh, Fatemeh, Zaynab, and Roqayyeh. Their deaths were often portrayed as divinely ordained and predicted by the Prophet, Gabriel, or an Imam. Their deaths were also portrayed as the culmination of endless suffering and oppression at the hands of the opponents of the Prophet and the imams. In fact, they often prayed to God to grant them release from their suffering. In other words, it could almost be said that they were martyred by means of their own grief, which resulted from the suffering they faced when they had to sacrifice their male relatives. As such, their deaths were often represented as a type of martyrdom, although not the same type of martyrdom as that of the males. For example, in Kashefi's text, Fatemeh was portrayed as suffering endlessly following the Prophet's death. She also suffered violence at the hands of the caliph, who confiscated an orchard she had inherited from her father, the Prophet. She mourned endlessly, and in a vision, the Prophet informed her of her impending death.[9] Hosayn's daughter Roqayyeh, who died in Damascus, saw her father in a dream and prayed to be allowed to join him. She too was told of her impending death, and she died shortly thereafter.[10]

Women have generally been presented as being supporters of the martyrs, willing to sacrifice their loved ones. As such, they performed acts of martyrdom through their families, rather than as individuals. For example, the story of Vahb's mother's insistence upon his going out and becoming martyred was a very well developed story, as were countless examples of other female characters who similarly supported the martyrdom of their loved ones. Qasem's bride and Vahb's wife, for instance, were willing to sacrifice their young husbands as martyrs.[11] Such stories were more thoroughly developed and stressed the key theme of women encouraging their loved ones to martyr themselves. Zaynab willingly sacrificed not only her brother Hosayn but also her two sons, and countless other close male relatives.[12] The primary ways in which women were expected to martyr their loved ones was either by encouraging them to do so or by training and educating them during their childhood so that they would aspire to embrace martyrdom later in life. Thus, they were the educators of the future generation of martyrs.

There were many stories of weddings, in which marriage and wedding festivities were contrasted with fighting, martyrdom, and mourning. While weddings were represented as being festive, and marriage was represented as the beginning of a happy life, the fate of the martyrs was represented as the end of worldly life, and the source of sorrow and unhappiness. This juxtaposition served to heighten the tragedy of Karbala, but it also highlighted the willingness of these women to sacrifice their own loved ones and their happiness for the higher divine purpose. In that sense, the stories also served to show how these women "passed the ultimate test" of their piety and devotion to the cause of God and the Prophet's family. One of the more popular ta'ziyehs was the story of Qasem, whom most accounts portray as marrying Hosayn's daughter Fatemeh at Karbala. During the wedding, he was determined to join Hosayn on the battlefield and become a martyr. Even Hosayn could not bring himself to allow such a sacrifice, but he allowed it in the end because of Qasem's determination, combined with his father's posthumous (or miraculous) endorsement of his martyrdom, along with the encouragement of his bride and the other female relatives.[13]

While women generally joined the divine struggle as indirect participants, there was one way in which they joined in as direct participants. Women and girls were represented as enthusiastically joining the men in verbally confronting the enemy and in challenging and condemning impious men for their evil conduct. One of the most salient features of the Karbala stories and performances was the extreme prevalence of sermons and speeches directed at the enemy. These oral rebukes were interspersed throughout every part of the story of Karbala, including times when they were involved in active combat. Once the men were silenced by enemy troops, the women took over as the verbal champions of Hosayn's cause.

The captivity of the female survivors of Karbala is a significant aspect of the story, because the female captives chastised Yazid, his men, and anyone else who stood by and refused to help Hosayn in his hour of need. This part of the story establishes the principle that pious women can and should challenge or criticize impious men, whether they are soldiers, governors, or even the ruling caliph.

The most outspoken critics of Yazid and his men were Zaynab, Omm Kolsum, and Hosayn's four-year-old daughter, Sakineh/Sokayneh. Zaynab is portrayed by Kashefi as criticizing the people of Kufeh, who cried when they saw the tragic scene of the Osara being marched through the city. As the Kufans lined up beside the road to watch the women being taken as captives by Yazid's troops, they mourned the tragedy. This upset Zaynab to the point where she reprimanded them by saying,

> Oh people of Kufeh, you deceptive, fraudulent, lying, and treacherous people; by God, you who have made false promises, and turned your hypocritical faces toward my brother, and sent him deceptive letters . . . and conspired to destroy the household of the Prophet (May God's Peace and Blessing be upon him and his family), and have chosen to give the worst of worldly people authority and power over the best of people, and instead of defending the truth and justice, you simply stood by at a distance, as spectators; now you dare to shed hypocritical tears on our behalf!?!?![14]

She also directly challenged and condemned Yazid's governor, Ebn-e Ziyad, and even the Caliph Yazid himself. When she was brought to face Yazid, she said, "Do you know what you have done!?! You have killed the best household of the Prophet; and you have chopped off the roots and branches of the tree of the garden of his mission."[15] She then went on to condemn and curse him. Sakineh and Omm Koslum had similar confrontations with Yazid and his men. Sakineh's criticisms of these impious men was particularly striking because she was a young girl, not much older than a toddler.

Thus, while men were the primary speakers before the battle, women served the critical function of becoming the spokespeople for the cause once they were taken into captivity to Syria. This is significant because it clearly developed this role as a responsibility for women and assured their centrality to the story and to the overall Shi'i movement. The preservation and spreading of the message was related to the role of women as educators of men and boys. Zaynab coached the believers, and in particular her own sons, on the finer points of the ideology propagated by Hosayn. The message of Hosayn's movement was similarly to be transmitted by women to the next generation of potential male warriors and martyrs. This aspect of the symbolism provided a religious justification for inclusion of women in the process of educating the youth of the next generation.

Another important gendered theme was mourning. While Shi'i men throughout history have definitely been represented as mourning this event, women have generally played a very central, yet somewhat different, role in mourning rituals. Furthermore, there has historically been a hierarchy of involvement in rituals associated with Karbala. Crying has always been portrayed as being worthy of merit, but not exactly the same merit as that associated with martyrdom on the battlefield. Women have often been used as graphic representations of the tragic loss of the martyrs of Karbala. This is closely related to another important gendered theme—the idea of women as victims of humiliation through captivity. Although Zayn al-Abedin was taken captive as well, the stories of women being mistreated and humiliated were much more dominant. These stories stressed disrespect of their status, their humiliation, and the general tragic nature of their being taken into captivity. In such representations, men have usually been the actual martyrs and warriors, while the women have generally been represented as mourning their loss. An excellent example is Figure I.1 (page 4), which depicts the imam's martyrdom by showing his wounded horse surrounded by mourning women and girls. Thus, women become the embodiment of the tragedy by becoming mourners.

Men and women could take on the gender-neutral traits from role models of the opposite sex, while adopting gender-specific traits only from role models of the same sex. These gendered traits were not rigidly exclusive categories but tendencies within a fluid dynamic of interpretation. Like the Prophet Mohammad, Hosayn was used as a role model for both men and women, and in some cases female characters like Zaynab served as role models for both men and women. For example, Zaynab's loyalty and piety could serve as an example for men to emulate. Likewise, women could emulate Hosayn's qualities. Most of the traits attributed to women in the narratives were presented as being acceptable for men as well, whereas the traits attributed to men were not necessarily acceptable for women.

While the symbolism of Karbala in many ways restricted women's social and political roles, it could in other ways provide opportunities for pious women to increase their status and social standing. Under certain circumstances, they could even exert a type of moral authority over some men. This can be seen in four aspects of the symbolism. First, the greatest and most worthy social status for women was supposed to derive from piety, along with devotion to Islam and the family of the Prophet. Second, women had the ability, and the authority to preserve, transmit, and articulate the values of Shiʿism. Third, the precedent was established for women to encourage or even demand that the men in their family conform to religious ideals of behavior. And finally, women were given the right, or even the responsibility, to challenge male authority when a man acted in an impious manner, even if he was the ruling caliph.

The status of most women in Qajar society was based largely on the status, wealth, and power of their fathers, husbands, sons, and brothers. While the ideals imbedded in Karbala symbolism did not negate this basic reality, they did provide some alternative opportunities for pious women to claim authority, higher status, and influence over the behavior of males in their lives. The symbolism provided a precedent for pious women to claim a higher status than women whose husbands were wealthier and more powerful, because it was made clear in the stories that a woman's jewelry, expensive clothing, and so on, were insignificant compared to a woman's moral conduct and piety. Pious women could also stress ideals of right conduct by criticizing or even challenging the impious conduct of the men in their lives. As previously stated, these symbolic ideals did not reverse or negate the dominant patterns of status and power in Qajar society. However, they did provide religious ideals that pious women could potentially use to influence their status within the family and within society. Public and private religious rituals provided similar opportunities.

Shiʿi women have always been heavily involved in Moharram rituals. It is noteworthy that the earliest account of Moharram rituals describes how women appeared in public processions mourning the tragedy of Karbala. In his tenth-century account, Ibn Kathir reports that the Buyid ruler "ordered that the markets be closed, and that the women should wear coarse woolen hair cloth, and that they should go into the markets with their faces uncovered/unveiled and their hair disheveled, beating their faces and wailing over Hussein Ibn Abi Talib."[16] We also have numerous accounts of women participating in these rituals on a large scale throughout the modern and premodern periods. It is clear from these accounts that Moharram rituals played very diverse and significant roles in the lives of these women.

Many Western residents in Tehran during the Qajar period have provided accounts of Iranian women attending these rituals on a large scale, sometimes outnumbering the men. For example, Samuel Benjamin reported in 1887 that Kalians were "smoked by women as well as men. The masculine sex was in but a small minority in the arena; what few men were there stood behind the compact army of women."[17] Furthermore, in police reports compiled in 1885–1887 under the supervision of Count di Monteforte, who was in charge of public security in Tehran, there are hundreds of reports of Moharram rituals in the homes, *takyehs*, and mosques of Tehran in 1886. In most of these ritual events, women are listed as participants.[18] Lady Sheil gives us a brief glimpse of how Iranian women participated in public religious life in large numbers.

> The shah's box was at the top, facing the performers. . . . On his left were the boxes of his mother . . . and his wives; then that of the prime minister's wife, then mine, and next the Russian minister's wife. . . . Part of the pit was appropriated for women of humble condition, who were in great numbers, all however carefully veiled, and all seated on the bare ground.[19]

This account demonstrates well the ways in which the social status of women was reinforced through rituals. Wealthy women usually remained separate and out of sight, while poorer women sat in the "common" or public area. For women, seclusion has generally been one of the primary signs of wealth in most Muslim societies, and *ta'ziyeh* performances were no exception to the rule. Charles James Wills, a Westerner attending a *majles,* wrote in 1883 that "the women having been crowding in from an early hour, the wives of the grandees and officials are accommodated with seats with the princess and her ladies, while the less favoured have the places retained for them in good situations by their servants, and according to rank."[20]

In these rituals, space and activity have generally been gender-coded in certain ways. Most large performances during the Qajar period followed a similar pattern as the royal performance described above. During the Qajar period female participants in public rituals often occupied the second floor, separate rooms, a curtained-off area, the roofs of nearby buildings, or the "pit" in the middle of the *takyeh*. However, practices varied substantially, as did the strictness of enforcement. For example, according to Sven Hedin, who reported on one of the provinces in 1910, enforcement could be rather strict at times: "Here [in the Governor's *takyeh*] a number of spectators, mostly women, had assembled, but the place was cleared at once by the switches of the ferrashes. They have not the slightest respect for ladies."[21] He also reported, "On the flat roofs around the arena women sit wrapped up in their veils, and chattering like jackdaws. Those of higher rank have a white veil before their face with opening for the eyes, just as in the larger towns, but the poorer women have blue veils or rather sack-like wraps which cover the whole head and body. . . . There are certainly as many as 3000 people in the court, and on the roofs around some 340 women have taken their seats."[22] Dorothy De Warzee, H. G. Winter, and other Western travelers to Iran have offered similar reports.[23]

Women were also enthusiastic patrons of rituals, sponsoring women's *majales* and *sofrehs* (ritual dinners), as well as *rowzeh khanis* and *ta'ziyehs*. Women-only rituals were regularly held in private homes, and even in the *takyeh* Dowlat.[24] A typical example was a women's *rowzeh khani* that was held in Reza Qoli Khan's house in Tehran on the fifth of Moharram of 1886. In Safar of the same year, the wife of Mohammad Hosayn Javaheri sponsored a *ta'ziyeh* in the *takyeh* of Melkabad.[25] Other examples of women patrons include Qamar al-Saltaneh, the wife of Mirza Mohammad Khan Sepahsalar, the notable Aziz al-Saltaneh, and at least one of the daughters of Fath Ali Shah.[26] One of the better-known female patrons of such performances was Naser al-Din Shah's sister Ezzat al-Dowleh, who regularly sponsored very elaborate *ta'ziyehs* in her home in Sarcheshmeh.[27] In his memoirs, Abdollah Mostowfi gives a brief account of one of the rituals she sponsored:

> Ezzat od-Dowleh, the sister of Naser ed-Din Shah, provided one such program in her neighborhood. At this time the Princess was on her fourth husband, Mirza Yahya Khan Mo'tamed ol-Molk, the minister of foreign affairs, and the brother of Mirza Hosayn Khan Sepahsalar. This was a very elaborate and beautiful event. The main courtyard of the reception quarters was covered with a three-steeple tent. The large center pool, covered with planks of wood, was converted to a platform and served as the center stage. Three side walls of the courtyard were covered with black cloth. The fourth opened to a large garden. A temporary wooden building with an awning was erected for the season, providing six additional areas to serve as boxes. The interiors of the boxes were elegantly decorated with candelabra and hurricane lamps. Exquisite Persian rugs hung from the walls. The curtains were made of gold and silver brocade. The lower level of this building was designated for the young people, and the upper level for the older guests. . . . Other members of the royal family and aristocracy attended these shows, and were received in the large reception hall by Moshir od-Dowleh himself. The rooms opposite the temporary boxes were for the Princess Ezzat od-Dowleh and her guests. A transparent curtain provided privacy for the ladies. There were three

other rooms on the south side of the courtyard, for the male public, and the courtyard level was for the women. The steel band occupied the porch of the temporary building, or sometimes the roof of the house. The military band, with band director Shokrollah Khan, sat on the front porch. The street served as back stage for the performance, where the animals and crew awaited their turn.

These passion play performances were very elegant and fully equipped. Mo'in ol-Boka and the government cast performed here also. It was a smaller version of the [takyeh Dowlat] productions, but not inferior in any way. The introductory parade of mourners and wailers was limited to a few groups, and they were usually neighborhood organizations of Sartakht and Sarcheshmeh. Lady Ezzat od-Dowleh rewarded the participating groups with a gift of an Amiri shawl tied to the banner on the last day of the performance. Other well-known mourners, such as the Borujerdi group, came to this location during the sermon and preaching sessions only. These functions lasted well into the night, and the public was served tea and water pipes. During the day performances, refreshments and water pipes were limited to the guests who were received inside the quarters.[28]

Women's participation in rituals could at times lead to contention or even conflict, and some men complained. For example, following a noisy outbreak among the women participants in a ritual sermon given in the Sepahsalar mosque, Mirza Lotfollah claimed he would not give any more sermons if women were going to be present in the audience.[29] There are also numerous accounts of fights breaking out among female participants. Lady Sheil recounts:

> Before the curtain drew up, it was ludicrous to witness the contention among these dames for places, which was not always limited to cries and execrations. They often proceeded to blows, striking each other heartily on the head with the iron heel of their slippers, dexterously snatched off the foot for the purpose; and, worse still, tearing off each other's veils; several ferrashes were present to keep the peace, armed with long sticks, with which they unmercifully belaboured these pugnacious devotees.[30]

These fights were usually broken up by servants in charge of the event in question. Some women also got into arguments and physical fights with their husbands because they wanted to attend religious rituals. It was not uncommon during the Qajar period, much like today, for some women to attend these religious rituals either without the husband's permission or in defiance of his instructions that she should not attend.[31]

For example, one of the more interesting police reports from 1887 states:

> Last night the wife of Karim Nam got into a fight with her husband because he would not give her permission to leave the house in order to attend a *ta'ziyeh*, it led to physical fighting between them. Residents in the house calmed them down. Afterwards, this woman ate some opium (i.e., to commit suicide) in order to threaten and punish her husband. She was diagnosed, given help, and recovered . . . in the end her husband was forced to give her permission to go to the *takyehs*.[32]

There are also cases in which women used opium as a threat of suicide in an effort to get their way. Another interesting example of a woman ignoring male authority involved a female slave. "Hajji Mohammad Bazzaz reported to the head of the mahalleh that one female slave left the house to attend a rowzeh khani. She has not returned for two days and is missing . . . as a result of [our] investigation, she was located in the Emamzadeh of Sayyed Esma'il . . . [and was returned to him]."[33] Stories like these give us brief glimpses into the everyday lives of women in Qajar Iran, whose lives would otherwise be little understood by modern scholars.

Women were very active participants in Moharram rituals, which is one of the factors that prompted Ayatollah Khansari (a prominent religious scholar and jurist of the late nineteenth century) to write the following humorous comment:

> It is the consensus of the ulama and is obligatory that women should go anywhere in the streets and markets where there is a *ta'ziyeh*; and it is said, "Woe to any woman, near whom there is a *ta'ziyeh* taking place (within one *farsakh*), but who does not attend it." Furthermore, if a pregnant woman goes into labor and gives birth while attending a *ta'ziyeh* or *rowzeh khani* her child will be considered blessed and should be named Ramadan.[34]

These rituals were also extremely important to women as a means for developing and maintaining a network of friends. Of course, religious rituals were certainly not the only form of socializing in which Iranian women took part. However, among religious Iranian women ritual gatherings have always played an important role. These gatherings have often involved women who were close family or friends, but they could also include distant relations and women with whom they had no previous acquaintance. They also provided an additional source for friendships, both within and outside of family circles. Since men were not allowed to attend some of these religious gatherings, they provided an opportunity for socializing outside the social circles of their male relatives.

Ritual gatherings also provided an opportunity for women and girls, especially those in particularly religious or conservative families who might have encouraged them to stay in seclusion, to enter the public sphere on a broader scale. Visiting the tombs of religious personalities, like Imam Reza and his sister Ma'sumeh, have provided similar opportunities for women. The freedom of mobility associated with public rituals allowed them to spend much of the day and evenings in public areas like mosques, bazaars, neighbors' homes, streets or alleys, and other people's homes. Most Shi'i women in Qajar Iran would have conformed to varying degrees with the ideals of seclusion and gender segregation, in particular upper- and middle-strata women. Although these patterns have changed substantially in recent decades, some conservative religious women, for reasons of personal piety, have continued to minimize the time they spend outside. Young women in particular have often been restricted in their range of activities outside the circle of family supervision, because of the fear that the family might be shamed by gossip or by some unwelcome incident involving the girls. In some cases, the mobility associated with religious rituals has served to empower women to assert their independence and piety. In some extreme cases, this has even led to conflicts between spouses. Sometimes husbands and wives have had arguments when the husband tried to forbid his wife from attending these religious gatherings, and the woman asserted her right to do so.

It is difficult to study women's lives in nineteenth-century Iran due to the lack of detailed accounts of their lives, but the above discussion helps to illustrate how Shi'i symbols and rituals were a dynamic force in the lives of Shi'i women in Qajar Iran. Female characters and gender-coded symbols were widespread in the Karbala narratives, *rowzeh* sermons, and *ta'ziyehs*, and women often served as main characters in these accounts. Furthermore, women were highly active participants in public and private Moharram rituals. While in some ways these symbols and rituals restricted women's social roles and their participation in the public sphere, in other ways they had the opposite effect. Moharram symbols and rituals provided opportunities for pious women and girls to define their gender identities along religious lines, while at the same time asserting direct and indirect influence, expanding their social networks, increasing their social status, and expanding their participation in certain aspects of public life.

Notes

This chapter is based partly on research conducted for my monograph, *The Martyrs of Karbala: Shi'i Symbols and Rituals in Modern Iran* (Seattle: University of Washington Press, 2004).

1. See Sadeq Homayuni, *Ta'ziyeh dar Iran* (Shiraz, Iran: Entesharat-e Navid, 1989), 299–335. The following are some of the *ta'ziyehs* with major female characters, which he lists: Bagh-e Fadak, Dokhtar Nasrani, Shir va Fazzeh, Arusi-e Dokhtar-e Qoraysh, Arusi-e Shahrbanu, Fatemeh Soghra, Mehmani-e Yahud, Nozul-e Zahre (or Arusi-e Zahra), Vorud be Sham, Vorud be Madineh, Vafat-e Hazrat-e Khadijeh, Vafat-e Hazrat-e Roqayyeh, Vafat-e Hazrat-e Zaynab, Vafat-e Hazrat-e Ma'sumeh.

2. See Enayatollah Shahidi and Bolukbashi Ali, *Pazhuheshi dar ta'ziyeh va ta'ziyeh khani az aghaz ta payan-e dowreh-ye Qajar dar Tehran* (Tehran: Daftar-e Pazhuhesh-ha-e Farhangi, Komisiyon-e Melli-e Yunesko dar Iran), 267–322. The following are some of the *ta'ziyehs* with major female characters, which he lists: Anar Avardan-e Jebra'il bara-e Fatemeh (Sham'un-e Yahudi), Taraj-e Khaymeh-ha (Gharat-e Khaymeh-gah), Tavallod-e Zaynab, Jaghali Ferestadan-e Fatemeh-e Soghra (Gol Ferestadan-e Fatemeh-e Soghra), Kharabeh-e Sham (Hendeh va Kharabeh, or Vafat-e Roqayyeh), Khab didan-e dokhtar-e Moslem, Dokhtar-e Nasrani (Zan-e Nasrani, or Takht-e Jebra'il), Dokhtar-e Hendi (Zan-e Hendi, Mard va Namard), Shahadat-e Zan-e Shemr, Shahadat-e Vahb va Arus-e 'U, Shir va Fazzeh, Abdollah va Shahrbanu, Arus-e Qoraysh (Arusi-e Hazrat-e Zahra), Arusi-e Hazrat-e Khadijeh, Arusi-e Hazrat-e Zaynab, Arusi-e Solayman va Belqis, Arusi-e Shahrbanu, Arusi-e Malakeh-e Afaq, Madar-e Saheb al-Amr, Nanpokhtan-e Fatemeh Zahra, Nozul-e Zahreh ya Setareh, Veda'-e Shahrbanu, Vorud beh Madineh, Vafat-e Hazrat-e Zahra, Vafat-e Hazrat-e Zaynab, Vafat-e Khadijeh, Vafat-e Fatemeh-e Soghra, Vafat-e Maryam Madar-e Isa.

3. M. H. Va'ez Kashefi, *Rowzat al-shohada* (Tehran: Chapkhaneh-e Khavar, 1962), 225–227.

4. Ibid., 124–127.

5. See Hasan Salehirad, *Majales-e ta'ziyeh* (Tehran: Soroush Press, 1995), 2:135–152; Lewis Pelly, *The Miracle Play of Hasan and Husain, Collected from Oral Tradition* (London: The India Office, 1879), 2:241–257; and Kashefi, *Rowzat al-Shohada*, 389–390. For a discussion of this story, see David Pinault, "Zaynab Bint Ali and the Place of the Women of the Households of the First Imams in Shi'ite Devotional Narratives," in *Women in the Medieval Islamic World*, ed. Gavin R. G. Hambly (New York: St. Martin's Press, 1998), and Mahmoud Ayoub, *Redemptive Suffering in Islam: A Study of the Devotional Aspects of "Ashura" in Twelver Shi'ism* (New York: Mouton, 1978), 157–158.

6. Kashefi, *Rowzat al-Shohada*, 327–328, and 390. See also Pelly, *Miracle Play*

of Hasan and Husain, 2:1–17. See also Homayuni, *Taʿziyeh dar Iran,* 643–672; for his discussion of the female characters in this *taʿziyeh,* see 684–685.

7. Kashefi, *Rowzat al-Shohada,* 191–210. See also Pelly, *Miracle Play of Hasan and Husain,* 2:81–103.

8. See Pelly, *Miracle Play of Hasan and Husain,* 2:136–151.

9. Kashefi, *Rowzat al-Shohada,* 138–139. See also Pelly, *Miracle Play of Hasan and Husain,* 2:110–132.

10. Kashefi, *Rowzat al-Shohada,* 389–390. See also Salehirad, *Majales-e taʿziyeh,* 2:135–152, and Pelly, *Miracle Play of Hasan and Husain,* 2:241–257.

11. Kashefi, *Rowzat al-Shohada,* 327–328, and 390. See also Pelly, *Miracle Play of Hasan and Husain,* 2:1–17. See also Homayuni, *Taʿziyeh dar Iran,* 643–672; for his discussion of the female characters in this *taʿziyeh,* see 684–685.

12. Salehirad, *Majales-e taʿziyeh,* 2:5–18.

13. Kashefi, *Rowzat al-Shohada,* 327–328, and 390. See also Pelly, *Miracle Play of Hasan and Husain,* 2:1–17. See also Homayuni, *Taʿziyeh dar Iran,* 643–672; for his discussion of the female characters in this *taʿziyeh,* see 684–685.

14. Kashefi, *Rowzat al-Shohada,* 364.

15. Ibid., 366.

16. Ibn Kathir, *al-Bidaya wa al-nihaya* (Cairo: Matbaʿa al-Saʿada, 1358 AH). This translation is from Michel M. Mazzaoui, "Shiʿism and Ashura in South Lebanon," in *Taʿziyeh: Ritual and Drama in Iran,* ed. Peter J. Chelkowski (New York: New York University Press, 1979), 231.

17. Benjamin, cited in Ella Sykes, *Persia and Its People* (London: Methuen, 1910), 150.

18. For a few examples, see Ensiyeh Shaykh Rezaʾi, ed., *Gozaresh-ha-e nazmiy-yeh-e mahallat-e Tehran* (Tehran: Entesharat-e Sazman-e Asnad-e Melli-e Iran, 1998), 197–235.

19. Lady Sheil, *Glimpses of Life and Manners in Persia* (London: John Murray, 1856), 127.

20. C. J. Wills, *In the Land of the Lion and Sun, or Modern Persia* (London: Macmillan, 1883), 281.

21. Sven Hedin reports that "even in such an insignificant place as Chahardeh there is a tekkieh." *Overland to India* (London: Macmillan, 1910), 2:51.

22. Ibid., 43 and 48.

23. Dorothy De Warzee, *Peeps into Persia* (London: Hurst and Blackett Ltd., 1913), 79, and H. G. Winter, *Persian Miniature* (Garden City: Doubleday Page, 1917), 131, 137, and 140.

24. Shahidi and Ali, *Pazhuheshi dar taʿziyeh va taʿziyeh khani,* 110, 204.

25. Rezaʾi, *Gozaresh-ha,* 213 and 248, respectively.

26. Shahidi and Ali, *Pazhuheshi dar taʿziyeh va taʿziyeh khani,* 110.

27. Naser Najmi, *Tehran-e ahd-e Naseri,* 2nd ed. (Tehran: Entesharat-e Attar, 1988), 265.

28. Abdollah Mostowfi, *The Administrative and Social History of the Qajar Period* (Costa Mesa, Calif.: Mazda Publishers), 169–170.

29. Rezaʾi, *Gozaresh-ha,* 731. Ayatollah Khansari similarly criticized women participants, because he believed their enthusiastic participation contradicted the

ideals of modesty and female seclusion. See Molla Aqa Khansari, *Kolsum naneh* (Tehran: Entesharat-e Morvarid, n.d.), 125–126.

30. Sheil, *Glimpses of Life*, 128; see also Reza'i, *Gozaresh-ha*, 201.

31. Reza'i, *Gozaresh-ha*, 154, 164, 178, 184, 664, and 676.

32. Ibid., 178.

33. Ibid., 184.

34. Khansari, *Kolsum naneh*, 125–126.

CHAPTER 3

"Oh, My Heart Is Sad. It Is Moharram, the Month of Zaynab"

The Role of Aesthetics and Women's Mourning Ceremonies in Shiraz

INGVILD FLASKERUD

In women's mourning meetings (*matam majles*) during Moharram and Safar in Shiraz, Iran, the use of aesthetic expressions, such as visual imagery, ritual objects, and elegiac poetry, is so striking that one cannot ignore its potential devotional importance. Clearly, this local display of aesthetics is related to a broader popular Shi'i Islamic tradition, historically and geographically. To develop an understanding of the ritual function of aesthetics, its application must, on the one hand, be related to Shi'i Islamic martyrology and its promise of redemption and intercession and, on the other hand, be related to ritual participants' understanding of the benefits and advantages of applying visual imagery, ritual objects, and elegiac poetry in rituals.

By commemorating the event at Karbala in various forms of mourning rituals during Moharram and Safar, believers can hope for redemption on the Day of Judgment and ask for intercession from holy mediators in this life. I propose that visual imagery, ritual objects, and elegiac poetry serve several functions in achieving these aims. Aesthetics is applied to create the necessary and desirable religious space, creating an emotional environment that can aid participants to mentally cross the threshold of everyday life to participate in mourning rituals. Moreover, the interactive character of poetry recitation provides worshippers with a method for actively expressing sorrow and allegiance to Imam Hosayn and his family. Thus by becoming active performers of lamentation poems, participants conduct a meritorious act, *savab,* which hopefully works to their advantage on the Day of Judgment and promotes their chances of being helped by holy intercession in this life. Constructing ritual objects is likewise perceived as meritorious. Ritual objects and visual imagery are also perceived as suitable offerings (ex-votos), *nazr*, in a prayer-for-help that has been granted by holy mediators. These gifts are believed to transmit blessing, *tabarrok,* to those who come in contact with them. Aesthetics can thus be seen to function as a channel for addressing God's mediators, supporting verbal prayers and supplicants. It can also be seen as a channel for mediating intercession, by spreading God's blessing and grace in the community of believers.

The Concept of Intercession and Redemption in Shi'i Islam

Shi'i Muslims stress the importance of the fourteen *ma'sumeh*, that is, the Prophet Mohammad, his daughter Fatemeh, and the Twelve Imams, as guides to comprehension of the Qur'an and to an Islamic way of life, and as intercessors between God and humanity. Performing rituals is perceived as an effective way of achieving contact with the spiritual world. On a daily basis, communication is channeled through individual and communal prayers, but certain days of the ritual year involve special conditions, such as 'Ayd-e Qorban and Laylat al-Qadr.[1] Celebrating the birthdays and commemorating the deaths of members of the Prophet's household, Ahl al-Bayt, are other important occasions for contact between the mundane and spiritual realms. The annual commemoration of the event at Karbala in 680 AD, when Imam Hosayn and his family members and supporters were overtaken and either killed or taken prisoner by the army of Caliph Yazid, is such an instance. Accordingly, one of the ritual leaders in the present study encouraged participants to engage wholeheartedly in the mourning meeting. She reminded them of the sacrifices of Imam Hosayn and his supporters and pointed out that the ritual was an opportunity for improving living conditions, both at a personal and a communal level. Her remark is related to the common Shi'i perception of the redemptive nature of Imam Hosayn's martyrdom.[2]

The Shi'is understand Hosayn's mission as defending what they recognize as "True Islam" against the unjust ruler of the Muslim community, Caliph Yazid. As a reward for Hosayn's martyrdom, God is believed to have given him the ability to help believers in this life and to act as their mediator on the Day of Judgment. Weeping for Imam Hosayn and members of his holy family, together with concern for the poor, is one way of helping the Imam in his struggle for justice. Such support and mourning is believed to produce personal merit, *savab,* and is hence a source of salvation.[3] Consequently, the imams are not only historical figures, but also meta-historical characters.[4] Their spiritual existence is not bound by historicity, and thus believers can seek their intercession in the present, too. The rituals become occasions for believers to ask for a holy person's intercession to provide help for someone in this life, ask mercy for the soul of dead relatives, and give participants a chance to receive blessings, *tabarrok*. Regarded as the "Prince of Martyrs," Imam Hosayn holds a special place as mediator, but his children are also believed to act as mediators and are frequently addressed in popular rituals.

The Development of an Aesthetic Tradition

This understanding of redemption, mediation, and *savab* has for centuries inspired the Shiʻi Muslim lay public and the development of the Shiʻi tradition. In its many local variations, different rituals have been formed that secure communication between the mundane and spiritual worlds. The use of aesthetic expressions to elicit lamentation and weeping in Moharram rituals is a well-documented phenomenon. The performance of elegies in gatherings for Imam Hosayn appears to be the most widespread aesthetic expression and can be traced back to the Umayyad period (661–750).[5] From the original *maqtal* literature, with collections of martyrdom narratives, two genres of lamentation literature developed. One is the *rowzeh*, a narrative of the sufferings of the imams in general and of the battle at Karbala in particular. The other is the *nowheh*, or lamentation poetry, also known as *marasi*. Examining Moharram rituals that took place during the Safavid period (1501–1722), Calmard observes the use of various dramatic elements such as processions displaying gigantic standards, banners, decorated animals, coffins, and trophies, in addition to the use of sung elegies, storytelling, passion plays, and ritual dance.[6] The same elements were observed across the Shiʻi Islamic world in the twentieth and twenty-first centuries, although with variations between rural and urban communities, between Persian-speaking and Urdu-speaking communities, and between Turks and Arabs.[7] The use of visual imagery is a more recent development in Shiʻi Islamic popular rituals. Inspired by the production of passion plays, *taʻziyeh*, during the Qajar period (1785–1925), narrative paintings produced on canvas with themes from Shiʻi martyrology emerged. A visual element was added to the *rowzeh khani* ritual, or traditional storytelling: a singer, *pardeh dar*, would hang up paintings called *shamayel* or *pardeh*, depicting scenes of the battle at Karbala and then recite the story using a pointer to elucidate the scenes. Later, these narrative paintings were used in ritual buildings such as *hosayniyyeh* (named after Imam Hosayn) and *takyeh* as decorative wall hangings.[8]

Women's Mourning Meetings

Imam Hosayn is supposed to have arrived at the dry plains of Karbala with his party on the first day of Moharram. His camp was surrounded by the army of Caliph Yazid and his people were cut off from a water supply. On the tenth of Moharram (Ashura), Hosayn was beheaded after having seen his friends, supporters, half-brother, and sons being killed. These first ten days of Moharram have become the central focus of the commemoration during which the drama at Karbala is reenacted and mourned all over the Shi'i Islamic world. The women of Shiraz continue these mourning practices today. I was fortunate to be invited to observe several of these rituals, which included mourning meetings performed every morning in a private house, afternoon meetings held in a ritual location called the *zaynabiyyeh*, named after Imam Hosayn's sister, Zaynab, as well as evening meetings in a private courtyard. Mourning also continued throughout Moharram and the following month, Safar, to commemorate the fate of the women and children, left under the protection of Zaynab and Hosayn's only surviving son, Ali Zayn al-Abedin, who were brought as hostages to the caliph in Damascus. One pious woman had picked the eleventh until the twentieth of Safar to host annual mourning meetings for Hosayn's little daughter Roqayyeh in the *hosayniyyeh* attached to her home. Her afternoon meetings also formed part of this study. In all meetings women acted as hosts, leaders, assistants, servants, participants, and economic supporters. Although the rituals took place in Shiraz, they followed traditions from Bushehr, and they attracted women of both Bushehri and Shirazi origin.[9] Furthermore, women from the villages around Shiraz would frequently attend the rituals. Each ritual could last from two to three hours.

Visual Imagery

Upon entering the courtyard and *zaynabiyyeh*, visitors encountered richly decorated interiors. Wall hangings and colorful posters covered the walls. The iconography in these pictorial displays represented central persons in Islam, such as the Prophet Mohammad and the fourth caliph and First Imam, Ali, as well as depicting episodes from the Karbala event. In the

Figure 3.1. Picture of Hosayn from a private courtyard
(Shiraz, 2000). © Ingvild Flaskerud

courtyard a carpet depicting Imam Ali (about 150 × 70 cm) and a poster
representing Imam Hosayn (120 × 75 cm) were placed on each side of the
pulpit, *menbar*. Imam Ali was represented with a dark beard. He had a
green shawl over his head, which was encircled by a nimbus. His gaze was
not directed at the beholder, but turned upward. Visitors to the ritual described it as showing a pious man and as representing Imam Ali. However,
nobody can be sure about the appearance of Ali. Hence, how he looks in
posthumous representations is entirely the product of some believers' visual

imagery. In popular iconography, prototypes are repeated over and over in different pictorial representations to the point that a specific individual, with a specific face and physiognomic attributes, can now be easily identified as a particular imam or holy person. Nevertheless, special attributes and epigraphs are often added to facilitate identification. The most reliable denominators for Ali are his sword, *zu al-feqar*, which in this image was placed below his portrait, and the epigraph "Ali," which was repeated several times. The additional epithet "There is no true hero such as Ali, and no sword like *Zu al-Feqar*. Peace be upon them," can be read as an expression of respect and praise.[10] God, Mohammad, Fatemeh, Hasan, and Abbas were also remembered in this image, through epigraphs, whereas Hosayn was honored by the following words: "Oh Hosayn, The Humiliated" and "Oh Hosayn, Martyr." Similar to the portrait of Imam Ali, Hosayn was represented in a green shawl and had dark hair and beard. However, his gaze appeared different, being sterner. He appeared young and handsome, and his demeanor expressed both strength and determination. He did not have a nimbus around his head, but his face was illuminated from above. Under the portrait it said in Arabic, "His highness Hosayn ibn Ali, Lord of the martyrs, peace be upon him."

Twenty-four appliqué embroideries completely covered the walls of the courtyard. Although Imam Hosayn is the main character of the drama at Karbala, most of these wall hangings referred to his half-brother and standard-bearer, Abu al-Fazl Abbas. According to tradition, Caliph Yazid's army cut off the water supplies to Hosayn's camp. Hosayn's daughter, Sakina, is supposed to have asked Abbas to collect water from the Euphrates. He took up the mission, but he was never able to fulfil his promise. Instead, the caliph's army killed him after having first cut off both his arms. The wall hangings presented variations of the following pictorial program. Abbas was not directly depicted, but referred to by means of symbols and graphics. On the embroideries' right side stood his white horse with his standard on its saddle. Above the horse was written "Oh, His Highness Abbas." The cruel fate of Abbas was alluded to in the description of the horse, with four arrows piercing its body and blood streaming from the wounds. Below and encircling the horse were other items referring to Abbas: his helmet, his cut-off arm, and the water bag, the last two being penetrated by two arrows and water leaking from the bag. Some wall hangings included Imam Hosayn's camp in the pictorial program, others the Euphrates. On the embroideries' left side could be seen a mosque composed of a dome and two minarets. Above there was a calligraphic emblem reading "Oh, Hosayn," alluding to Hosayn's grave-mosque at Karbala, one of

Figure 3.2. A wall hanging showing the horse of Abu al-Fazl Abbas. On the ground is his cut-off arm and the water bag, both pierced with two arrows, and his helmet. In the back is the camp at Karbala, and Abu al-Fazl's grave-mosque at Karbala. From a private courtyard (Shiraz, 2000). © Ingvild Flaskerud

the most popular Shiʿi pilgrimage sites. Only one wall hanging showed a different pictorial program, representing Abbas alive, seated on his horse, holding the standard. In front of him stood Sakina, handing him the water bag.[11]

It may be surprising to encounter such an overwhelmingly Abbas-dominated iconography, but then one should remember that Abbas is regarded as Hosayn's most faithful supporter and friend and that he is one of the most popular intercessors in Shiʿi Islam. Those participating in the rituals described him as Hosayn's attendant, and one woman said, "If Abbas gives you permission, Hosayn will see you." Not only can Abbas act as mediator between a worshipper and Imam Hosayn, he is himself an intercessor and is commonly known as "The gate of desires" (*bab al-havas*). He earned this power to help people after the great sufferings he endured at Karbala. It is further believed that because he failed to fulfil his mission for the thirsty ones in the camp, he is particularly eager to help anyone who asks his assistance. Many visitors recounted stories about how he had helped them, and throughout the year many hosted and attended a ritual called *sofreh-e Abbas*, which is an ex-voto (*nazr*) to Abbas. The Abbas iconography thus recounted the story of Karbala, reminded people of why they had come to the ritual, and helped them cry. What is more, it also indicated a sense of hope that worshippers could put their trust in Abbas.

Another pictorial program referred to the grave-mosques of Imam Hosayn and Abu al-Fazl Abbas at Karbala. They presented a mosque model similar to the one in the Abbas hangings, but their calligraphic emblems referred to God (Allah), Mohammad, Ali, Fatemeh, Hasan, and Hosayn. Most participants seemed to prefer wall hangings with figural iconography, representing humans and animals, rather then calligraphy. They found figural iconography to be more emotional. It was also seen as having a didactic function, and was described as being especially helpful to older women, many of whom were illiterate. The iconography was thought to remind them about the event at Karbala and the purpose of the ritual. In addition, literate women enjoyed reading names of holy persons and poems that were written on the borders of many wall hangings. It inspired them to contemplate the person's character and, as one woman explained, brought her into a mental state of recalling the event at Karbala and contemplating its meaning. To give but one example of a poem on a wall hanging:

Your name comes first on the standard of the kings of the world
The pride of Mostafa's religion,[12] Adornment of God's throne
Let me be your ransom. Oh, Mediator of the Day of Judgment
Pay honor to this beautiful banner, from where your name sways.

In the *zaynabiyyeh,* black fabrics covered the walls, making use of the symbolic significance of black as the mourning color of Moharram. It was said to remind participants of the blood that was shed at Karbala and help them contemplate and cry. On the fabrics were placed posters and wall hangings representing Islam's holy places, such as the mosques in Medina and Mecca and Imam Hosayn's shrine at Karbala. Also on display were portraits representing members of the Ahl al-Bayt. A framed print representing Imam Ali bore resemblance to his portrait in the courtyard mentioned above. However, in this case the picture was not only applied during Moharram but was affixed on a permanent basis. The host explained that she had great respect for Imam Ali. Because he was the ancestor of all the imams, she honored him by always keeping his picture on the wall.

The Prophet Mohammad was represented on a silk cloth (about 150 × 50 cm). Depicted in full figure, he was dressed in a green turban, a green garment covered by a black drapery, and sandals. He had a long black beard and was not looking at the beholder. In one hand he held the Qur'an. The

مرا پیر طریقت جز علی نیست

Figure 3.3. Picture of Ali (Shiraz, 2000). © Ingvild Flaskerud

other arm was raised, and a finger pointed upward. The pointing finger of Mohammad was understood to refer to the dogma of *towhid*, while the Qur'an in his hand informed the beholder that Mohammad is the Messenger of God. The representation can thus be read as the Islamic creed.[13] This interpretation is supported by the Arabic text written above the figure of Mohammad. "In the name of God the Merciful and Compassionate. Mohammad is not your father. He is God's prophet, the last prophet."[14] A large wall hanging depicted the *panjtan* (about 200 × 120 cm). The Prophet is seated with his grandchildren, Hasan and Hosayn, on each of his knees.

Figure 3.4. Tapestry of the Prophet Mohammad hung in a *zaynabiyyeh* (Shiraz, 2000). © Ingvild Flaskerud

On each side sat his daughter Fatemeh and her husband, Imam Ali. Behind the group stood the angel Gabriel. The representation of Mohammad resembles the one described above. He has a black beard, is not looking directly at the beholder, is wearing a turban, a garment, and a mantle. Also, Imam Ali is represented in a way that can be recognized in other images, wearing a green head cover and resting a sword over his knees. Fatemeh is dressed in a brown chador-like garment and has a white veil over her face. The two boys are dressed in red turbans and coats. Although this wall hanging was predominantly red and did not depict scenes from Karbala, the host liked to use it during Moharram because, she said, all the figures represented in it had been informed about what would happen to

Hosayn at Karbala and mourned his martyrdom before it took place. The wall hanging was thus interpreted to point to the meta-historical character of the event at Karbala, although this was not an explicit theme of the image.

All the locations in this study were temporary religious spaces. They were decorated and prepared for visitors on specific days when rituals were being held, and the ritual space thus had to be created anew for each occasion. Visual expressions such as pictures, sculptures, and architectural forms are often used to create religious space.[15] Mosques can be decorated with ornaments and calligraphy, readily interpreted to reflect the doctrine of God's oneness, *towhid*.[16] Such an-iconic decorations do not have any liturgical relevance in rituals, but are used to create a space in which worshippers can transcend their daily existence and focus verbal prayer toward a God who should not be visually represented except in symbolic form. Visual images applied in Moharram and Safar rituals seem to have a similar function as that of ornament and calligraphy. However, they were also intended to connect worshippers to historical figures to whom they should express sympathy and allegiance. It was therefore important that the iconographic and verbal language of visual imagery refer to these persons, be it the Prophet Mohammad, Imam Ali, Imam Hosayn, Abu al-Fazl Abbas, or others, reminding worshippers of the role of these persons and aiding them in mourning.

Posters and wall hangings were also believed to be vehicles for communication between worshippers, mediators, and God. While presenting verbal prayers and supplicants, some women stroked wall hangings and prints with their hand and then stroked their own face or the face of their baby with the same hand. The most common request was protection from illness or cures for disease. It should, however, be noted that the visual imagery was not the object of worship. The pictorial representations were never addressed by *maddahs* during rituals, but individually approached by visitors before, during, and after the meetings. Posters and wall hangings were addressed because worshippers believed they could help them focus their prayer and thereby make it more intense and forceful. A mullah pointed out that pictures could help worshippers to focus on God. He described visual imagery as a way, a *tariqeh*, to God. A *maddah* compared visual imagery to the *mohr*, the piece of clay from Karbala that Shi'i Muslims place their forehead on when prostrating themselves in prayer.[17] The *mohr* is believed to make the distance between God and the worshipper shorter because God loves Hosayn and will accept a prayer from someone who pays him respect. In the same manner, the *maddah* explained, a picture of a holy person brings God and worshippers closer to each other. Consequently, their presence was not believed to contradict the Islamic prohibition against idolatry.[18] Posters and wall hangings were also given the status of ex-votos, *nazr*, a response to prayer-for-help which were believed to have been answered by one of the holy mediators.[19] In general, ex-votos were believed to transmit good fortune, *tabarrok,* to the person, hence adding another reason for worshippers to approach visual images. Contact with these objects, such as touching them and kissing them, was therefore perceived to assist the transmission of a request to God, and to mediate blessing and grace from God.[20]

Ritual Objects

Due to the injustice that Qasem (Hosayn's nephew), Ali Asghar (Hosayn's baby son), and Roqayyeh (Hosayn's little daughter) experienced during and after the event at Karbala, they are included among the mediators, and commemorated and addressed in particular rituals. In the ritual locations discussed here, a pantomime illustrating the marriage between Qasem and Fatemeh was staged on the eighth and ninth of Moharram. Two women, dressed in costumes, acted the roles of the young couple, under the instruction of two assistants (*zaker*). The performance of the wedding then turned into a commemoration of Qasem, who was killed at Karbala on his wedding day. For this particular ritual, a replica of a bridal chamber, *hejleh*, was made. On the same days, the hosts arranged a ritual commemorating Ali Asghar. He was killed by an arrow through his throat when his father brought him to the enemy to ask for water. For this ritual they made a replica of Ali Asghar's cradle. A third object, a replica of Roqayyeh's grave, was erected for mourning meetings taking place in the *hosayniyyeh* during Safar.

A common characteristic of these replicas was that none were permanent in their form, but were constructed for the annual ritual season and dismantled when it was over. The framework for the bridal chamber and the cradle were made of wood. These were decorated with layers of colorful fabrics topped with colored lightbulbs. The base of Roqayyeh's grave was a wooden plate (about 50 × 30 × 5 cm) wrapped in green material. Above it was raised a canopy of fabrics in different colors, also decorated with colorful lightbulbs. Gifts for Roqayyeh were placed inside the canopy but were so plentiful that they also covered a wide space on the floor around the grave and filled up available space in window frames and bookshelves.

A "coffeehouse" painting depicting the return of Hosayn's horse from the battlefield, without its master (in a *hay'at* in Tajrish, in northern Tehran, 1997). © Kamran Scot Aghaie

A large billboard located at the entrance to Behesht-e Zaynab, the martyrs' cemetery in Isfahan. A young mourning girl is shown next to tulips and a goblet, both symbolizing martyrdom—all under the watchful eyes of Khomeini himself (Isfahan, 2001). © Kamran Scot Aghaie

In the background, a poster depicting Fatemeh, holding red tulips symbolizing the male martyrs of her family; in the foreground, a young girl plants
tulips over the graves of the martyrs. Bagh-e Behesht-e Ali (Qom, 2001).
© Kamran Scot Aghaie

Picture of Hosayn from a private courtyard (Shiraz, 2000).
© Ingvild Flaskerud

Picture of Ali (Shiraz, 2000).
© Ingvild Flaskerud

Tapestry of the Prophet Mohammad hung in a *zaynabiyyeh* (Shiraz, 2000).
© Ingvild Flaskerud

Sofreh in honor of Roqayyeh from a *hosayniyyeh*, during Safar (Shiraz, 2000). © Ingvild Flaskerud

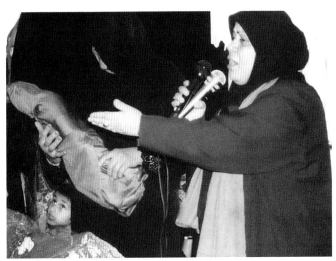

Ceremony for Ali Asghar arranged in a home. In the picture you see a *zaker* holding a doll symbolizing Ali Asghar, and a *maddah* singing. In the front is the cradle of Ali Asghar (Shiraz, 2000). © Ingvild Flaskerud

Women participating in the central procession holding banners with political slogans and shovels for burying the dead (Tehran, 1997). © Kamran Scot Aghaie

Women carrying green flags among the Iraqi immigrants living in Tehran (Tehran, 1997). © Kamran Scot Aghaie

Women in the mass procession in front of the bazaar (Tehran, 1997). © Kamran Scot Aghaie

Procession of women carrying the cradle of Ali Asghar (Tehran, 1997).
© Kamran Scot Aghaie

Figure 3.5. *Sofreh* in honor of Roqayyeh from a *hosayniyyeh*, during Safar (Shiraz, 2000). © Ingvild Flaskerud

The gifts clearly indicated objects that a little girl would appreciate, such as dolls, small cups and plates, and sweets. There were also things Roqayyeh would have needed as a captive of Caliph Yazid. According to the hagiography, Yazid's men forced Roqayyeh to walk barefoot from Karbala to Damascus. This episode motivated many to bring shoes. Further, according to the story, she died in a dark ruin in Damascus, which encouraged visitors to bring candles. All the items used for constructing the replicas and the gifts for Roqayyeh were ex-voto gifts, and as such had to be used. After the replicas were dismantled, some items would be kept for next year's rituals; others would be distributed among those who had visited the rituals and among the poor. This was not done solely to support people materially, but to contribute to the spread of *tabarrok,* blessing.

Many visitors approached the replicas of Qasem's bridal chamber, Ali Asghar's cradle, and Roqayyeh's grave in the same manner as for the visual imagery. Visitors touched the fabrics on a replica and wiped their face, or kissed the replica while making a short individual prayer before, during, or after a ritual. When a mourning meeting was over, many women sat down by Ali Asghar's cradle and Roqayyeh's grave and would touch and kiss each replica. Some put their child inside the cradle or lay it next to the grave, seeking help and protection. Some knitted knots on the fabric covering the bridal chamber, making wishes. The idea was that the wish would be transmitted to the mediators when someone untied the knots when the replica was later dismantled. Typical requests were to bear a child, to have a son or daughter be accepted to university, to cure a drug-addicted son or daughter, to solve a problem with a child's marriage, to have a house, or to cure a sick relative who had been told medical help was useless. The women's approach to the replicas can be described as a minor pilgrimage to a shrine. Their behavior showed parallels with the manner a pilgrim would kiss the gate of a shrine, touch and kiss lattice bars surrounding the sarcophagus in a shrine, tie bits of cloth to the bars, wipe the bars with a cloth, and then wipe their face or bring it home.[21] Replicas were not only approached in individual prayer, but cradle and grave became the center around which one performed the communal ritual flagellation. While standing in circles around the cradle or the grave, women gently hit their chest with one or two hands, a flagellation called *sineh-e sarpay* or *aza-e sarpay,* or they moved counterclockwise while flagellating, called *sineh-e dowr.* The flagellation was accompanied with elegiac poetry, *nowheh.*

The role of visual imagery, replicas, and ex-votos sheds light on a phenomenon indicated by Renard: namely, that not only prayer, but also arts and architecture, are directly related to religious observance.[22] Verbal prayer has a central position in Islamic devotion. It can be of various kinds, such as liturgical prayer, *salat,* and free prayer or supplicatory prayer, *do'a.* The Qur'an is a sourcebook for liturgical prayer, whereas supplications often are chosen from collections attributed to famous persons. Typically, in the mourning meetings in this study, women read prayers from the Qur'an and also selected supplications from *Mafatih al-Jenan* (Keys to the Garden of Heaven), with prayers to be read on particular days of the week, and on holy days. However, the role of visual imagery—the bridal chamber, cradle, and grave—suggests the belief that presentation of verbal prayer and supplications can be aided by honoring and addressing God's mediators and supported by meritorious actions, even outside the scope of the ritual proper. This idea was clearly expressed at the ritual's preparatory stage, when replicas were constructed. It was common for family members, friends, and neighbors to be present for this activity. The host and her assistant examined the items that had been presented as *nazr* and decided how to use them. Then they instructed participants in how to decorate the replicas and were careful to assign the tasks so as to provide participants with the opportunity to perform a meritorious act. In one location, the number of young participants had quite increased from one year to another, some even coming from the villages around Shiraz. The rumor had spread that many who had participated in the previous year had had their wishes fulfilled. Hence, more women came to work for their merit in the hope of being blessed with the fulfillment of a wish.

Elegiac Poetry

One of the most common mourning assemblies among Shi'i Muslims in Iran is the *rowzeh khani,* which is arranged at the celebration of the imams' birthdays or at the commemoration of their deaths, but is also performed at any time of the year as an offering of thanks. A storyteller, *rowzeh khan,* is invited to a mosque, a shrine, a home, a *hosayniyyeh, fatemiyyeh,* or *zaynabiyyeh* to recite stories, *rowzeh,* from the lives of the imams, members of their families, and their supporters.[23] The stories focus on dramatic moments in their lives, such as their suffering and death, and the performance is typically a rather moving moment, the effect being mainly engendered by the emotional power of the storyteller, which can bring many of the listeners literally to tears.

Rowzeh was also performed in the mourning rituals described in this study. However, instead of a *rowzeh khan,* ritual leaders called *maddah* conducted the performance. They were always women, and between two and four of them were invited for each ritual. The primary task of the *maddah* was to engage participants emotionally in order to gradually bring them into the mental state of mourning, where they could express their grief and sorrow for the sufferings of the holy persons in the battle at Karbala. The most common stories were those of Imam Hosayn, Ali Asghar, Ali Akbar,

Qasem, Abu al-Fazl Abbas, Zaynab, Roqayyeh, Moslem, along with his two sons, and Horr. During *rowzeh* the *maddah* performed alone, as a solo singer. Worshippers sat on the floor, weeping, and performed a kind of flagellation called *sineh ru-e pa zadan*, which involves hitting the thighs repeatedly three times, followed by a pause.

After *rowzeh,* there followed the performance of elegies, *nowheh,* which were also intended to engage the heart and feelings of participants and make them weep. In fact, *nowheh* had a more prominent position in these rituals than *rowzeh.* Whereas *rowzeh* could be made brief or sometimes was dropped, a series of elegies was always performed. Elegiac poetry is an old and rich tradition in Islamic literature and has, together with *rowzeh,* been important in the development of the Moharram commemoration. There is reason to believe that the imams, and in particular the Sixth Imam, Jafar al-Sadeq (d. 765 AD), used to bring together their followers to remember the death of Hosayn and invite a poet to recite verses of lamentation and grief.[24] Since then, Sunnis, Shi'is, and Sufis have continued to write lamentation poems about Imam Hosayn and Karbala.[25] Today, small booklets with collections of elegies are available in bookstores in Shiraz. However, each *maddah* in these rituals used a songbook containing a distinct compilation of poems. It was either inherited from someone in the family, with new additions made by the present owner, or consisted of poems collected by the present owner. There were three sources: the personal, the traditional, and the classical. The personal *nowheh* is written by the *maddah.* The traditional is handed down from older *maddahs,* such as the male *maddahs* Bakshu and Elsa Pasir from Bushehr and Qafar-e Asad from Shiraz. The classical type draws from classical literature, for example from Omar al-Khayyam (tenth century), Jalal al-Din Rumi (twelfth century), Hafez (thirteenth century), and Mohsen Fayz Kashani (seventeenth century).[26] *Nowheh* does not have the narrative form of *rowzeh,* but builds around an emotional and symbolic language presented in short sentences, which can be repeated several times. It is a form of responsorial song, alternating between the *maddah* singing one or several lines, and the worshippers presenting stylized answers, repeating lines, or giving replies. While clearly passing on a tradition, several *maddahs* also tried to accommodate the songs for their audience. Some, in order to comply with the taste of the new generation, gave old poems new melodies. In choosing an appropriate melody, they emphasized its emotional temperament and its ability to convey the worshipper's sentiment of love for holy persons who were mentioned and addressed in the songs. This was considered important because the songs worked as vehicles for

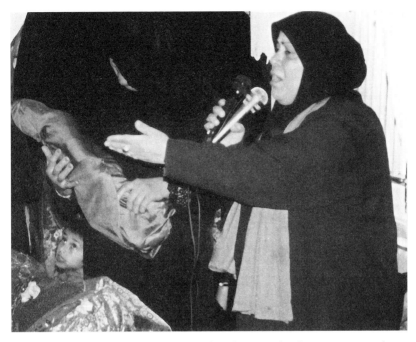

Figure 3.6. Ceremony for Ali Asghar arranged in a home. In the picture you see a *zaker* holding a doll symbolizing Ali Asghar, and a *maddah* singing. In the front is the cradle of Ali Asghar (Shiraz, 2000). © Ingvild Flaskerud

worship. In the same way that worshipping God was considered a meritorious act, composing and performing religious poetry were regarded as meritorious.[27]

Below are some examples of *nowheh* performed at these rituals. The list is not intended to be exhaustive, but was selected to illustrate the variety of form and content of the *nowheh*. Like *rowzeh*, the elegy does not demonstrate concern for historical accuracy. Rather, it is intended to appeal to the feelings of the listeners and engage them in the performance. The themes addressed in *nowheh* deal with the call to go to Karbala, the arrival at Karbala, the battle at Karbala, and its aftermath. However, these events were not necessarily presented in chronological order. Any *nowheh* could be performed at any time. In the Shi'i Islamic tradition it is believed that the Prophet Mohammad was informed about the destiny of Hosayn in a special message from God through the angel Gabriel and that Mohammad subsequently informed his daughter Fatemeh about the future of her son.[28] Some *nowheh* articulate Hosayn's determination to go to Karbala, implying that not only did he know about his destiny, but he was also determined to fulfil it. In the following extract of a *nowheh,* Hosayn is greeting Karbala upon their arrival and asks his followers to unpack the loads on the camels and set up the camp. Because listeners and participants already know the story, the elegy does not need to elaborate on the narrative, but can use symbols and images to hint at it. Addressing the plain of Karbala, Hosayn states his commitment throughout the poem. While simultaneously mentioning Ali Asghar, Abbas, Qasem, and Ali Akbar, he also hints at the high costs of the mission, as if he already knows the outcome of the battle. So does his sister, Zaynab, who is represented mourning the battle even before it takes place. The mentioning of the martyrs' names give the participants an opportunity to address them, and the reference to Zaynab's lamentation allows participants to mourn with her. And indeed they were, accompanying the poem by flagellation called *sineh ruye pasadan,* beating their chests and their thighs. This *nowheh* with flagellation was performed at several of the rituals I attended.

Maddah: Friends, if this is the land of Karbala, unpack the load
Friends, if this is the land of Karbala, unpack the load
Be greeted, land of Karbala. Be greeted, House of God's Light
Answer: Friends, if this is the land of Karbala, unpack the load
Friends, if this is the land of Karbala, unpack the load
Maddah: Be greeted, site of Love. Oh, how beautiful is here the
    smell of Love
Answer: Friends, if this is the land of Karbala, unpack the load
Friends, if this is the land of Karbala, unpack the load
Maddah: Karbala, you are the cradle of Asghar
You are the site of demise of the beautiful Abbas
Answer: Friends, if this is the land of Karbala, unpack the load
Friends, if this is the land of Karbala, unpack the load
Maddah: Oh land, be satisfied. Your king has arrived
Answer: Friends, if this is the land of Karbala, unpack the load
Friends, if this is the land of Karbala, unpack the load
Maddah: Say, where is the bridal chamber of Qasem, where is the
    cypress Ali Akbar
Answer: Friends, if this is the land of Karbala, unpack the load
Friends, if this is the land of Karbala, unpack the load
Maddah: My Zaynab, don't cry next to me, you put my body in
    flames
Unpack the load; unpack the load

Answer: Friends, if this is the land of Karbala, unpack the load
Friends, if this is the land of Karbala, unpack the load[29]

Cut off from water of the Euphrates, the people of Hosayn's camp experienced great suffering. This cruel act by the army of Caliph Yazid was the theme of another *nowheh,* where Hosayn's daughter Sakineh asks her uncle, the standard-bearer Abu al-Fazl Abbas, to bring them water. The poem was accompanied by the sitting flagellation (beating of chest and thigh) and was performed at several rituals.

> *Maddah:* Sad Sakina with wet eyes. Abbas, dear uncle, look at me.
> My lips are dry. The desert is full of water, but I am thirsty
> *Answer:* Sad Sakina with wet eyes. Abbas, dear uncle, look at me.
> My lips are dry

> *Maddah:* I am suffering from thirst
> *Answer:* Sad Sakina with wet eyes. Abbas, dear uncle, look at me.
> My lips are dry
> *Maddah:* My lips are dry, my lips are dry
> *Answer:* Sad Sakina with wet eyes. Abbas, dear uncle, look at me.
> My lips are dry
> *Maddah:* There is not any drop of water in the camp. Without water,
> my dear uncle, I cannot live
> *Answer:* Sad Sakina with wet eyes. Abbas, dear uncle, look at me.
> My lips are dry

The outcome of the request is well known to the participants. Abu al-Fazl Abbas never returned with the water, but was killed in a brutal manner. As previously described, this event was also depicted in various wall hangings on display in the ritual locations. Thirst is a theme also connected to the death of Ali Asghar. When Abu al-Fazl Abbas failed to bring water to the camp, Hosayn brought Ali Asghar to the enemy and asked for water. However, the child was killed by an arrow in the throat, providing another example of the cruelty of Caliph Yazid's army. Although regarded as an exaggeration by some of the visitors to the rituals, the event is elaborated in several elegies. In one of them Omm Layla, the mother of Ali Asghar, presents a lullaby to lament his death. This *nowheh* was performed next to Ali Asghar's cradle on the ninth of Moharram. The *maddah* took out a small, nicely dressed doll, representing Ali Asghar, from the cradle. Playing the part of Omm Layla, she passed the doll around for people to kiss it and present a supplication to Ali Asghar.

Maddah: Oh, my infant Asghar, laye, laye, lay[30]
The infant who died without drinking milk, laye, laye, lay
You are a wanderer, far from Medina, laye, laye, lay
The blood of your throat became your milk, laye, laye lay
The cradle became your grave, laye, laye, lay
Bring your hands to my breast, laye, laye, lay
For how long should I call before you answer? laye, laye, lay

Next, the *maddah* sang another lullaby for Ali Asghar, this time taking the role of Zaynab, who was portrayed as confused, not yet having accepted his death. With this the participants stood up and performed the standing flagellation, *sineh aza-e sarpay,* wailing and slapping their faces. Although the main character of the drama at Karbala is Imam Hosayn, his sister Zaynab has a central role in the story and was often mentioned in *nowheh* performed at the women's rituals. The close relationship between the two is expressed in several elegies. In one Hosayn calls her "the dearest of sisters," in another he asks "the respectful Zaynab" to come and see his face because she shall not see him again. A common theme was Zaynab lamenting the coming death of her brothers and nephews. In one elegy, performed on the ninth and tenth of Moharram, she is described as being depressed about the future prospects, and in the middle of the battle Hosayn finds time to comfort her. He tells her not to cry but also prepares her for what will come:

When comes the night of absence, sister don't cry too much, don't cry
Tomorrow in the desert of Karbala, Zaynab, oh Zaynab
My head will be separated from my body, Zaynab oh Zaynab
When tomorrow comes, I will go to the battle
I will drown in my blood
Tomorrow in the desert of Karbala, Zaynab, oh Zaynab
My head will be separated from my body, Zaynab oh Zaynab
Don't be so sad, you have a great challenge after me
Don't wonder tomorrow (what you should do)

Zaynab's role in the aftermath of the battle is clearly spelled out in a *nowheh* in which Hosayn asks Zaynab to make known the sufferings and injustice that took place at Karbala.

Maddah: When you go to Medina
Answer: Va vayla yahe yave[31]

Maddah: Say to the people of Medina: They killed Hosayn's Akbar
Answer: Va vayla yahe yave
Maddah: Abbas, the standard-bearer
Answer: Va vayla yahe yave
Maddah: The son-in-law of Hosayn
Answer: Va vayla yahe yave
Maddah: Infant Asghar of Hosayn
Answer: Va vayla yahe yave

During this *nowheh* participants performed flagellation while standing in a circle, *sineh aza-e sarpay.* Their answers were loud and many wailed. Their response shows that the mere mentioning of names of the holy persons can elicit strong affection. The participants knew the stories of the holy persons from *rowzeh,* and the hagiographic literature and the elegy functioned like a remembrance. But it was also an important channel for expressing sympathy and mourning. During some *nowheh,* two women faced each other and slapped their own cheeks (*lat*), a mourning gesture also applied for funerals, while crying. This flagellation always became one of the most intense, concentrated, and emotional moments of the mourning meetings.

Historically, the event at Karbala had the dual result of almost eliminating Hosayn's family and establishing Caliph Yazid as the leader of the Muslims, securing the rule of the Islamic Ommat in the hands of the Sunni Muslims, rather than of the Shiʿi Muslims. However, Zaynab survived and had to live with the memory of brothers and nephews who had had their heads and arms cut off. The following *nowheh* expresses her grief, as well as allowing singers to articulate their sympathy with her sorrow and suffering.

Oh, my heart is sad, it is Moharram; it is the month of Zaynab
Oh, my heart is sad, it is Moharram; it is the month of Zaynab
Oh, what injustice, Oh what cruelty
Oh, the people are crying and their eyes are full of tears
Oh, what injustice, Oh what cruelty
Oh, my dear Hosayn, Oh Karbala is close

In another *nowheh* Zaynab's pain is even more directly mentioned

Maddah: Oh, from the heart of Zaynab
Pain flows from the heart of Zaynab
The body of Zaynab was burning
The ruin wasn't acceptable for Zaynab[32]

When this poor place was offered to Zaynab
Answer: Oh, from the heart of Zaynab
Pain from the heart of Zaynab
The body of Zaynab was burning

Maddah: They killed Hosayn with thirsty lips
Answer: Oh, from the heart of Zaynab
Pain from the heart of Zaynab
The body of Zaynab was burning
Maddah: Street to street, city to city
Answer: Oh, from the heart of Zaynab
Pain from the heart of Zaynab
The body of Zaynab was burning
Everybody: Oh God, oh God, oh God, oh God, oh God

Hosayn's suffering and sacrifice have earned him a position as mediator, and participation in rituals commemorating his death is a meritorious act for worshipers seeking help. As I have shown, Hosayn's children are also addressed as mediators. So is Zaynab. After worshippers had commemorated her sufferings through the performance of elegies and expressed sympathy for her situation, a *maddah* presented a supplication to Zaynab:

Zaynab, please ask God to grant our wishes. God, vow to Hosayn, help the families so they don't lose their houses and have to live in the street. God, I entreat you, that some of the youths who are in the net of drug addiction may be cured. God, make this year a nice year for us.

The interactive and engaging character of *nowheh* may explain its popularity among visitors to these rituals. It allowed them to participate with their hearts and minds, expressing sorrow, grief, and allegiance. Further, the poems had a rhyme and a rhythm that made them particularly suitable for accompanying flagellation. Clarke points out that the regular rhythm of lamentation poems had a ritual purpose in men's street processions.[33] Clearly, the regular rhythm of poems, usually with an accompanying drumbeat, facilitated the movements of both the individual and the group in the men's ambulating rituals. In the women's stationary rituals, the rhythm facilitated the community singing of *nowheh*, as well as the performance of flagellation. The sound of hands hitting the chest or the thigh resembled the sound of the drumbeat so characteristic of the men's street processions, and functioned as a method for participating in the sufferings of Hosayn's family.[34]

Concluding Remarks

The importance of the word in Islamic devotion is unquestionable. The Holy Book, the Qur'an, is perceived as the word of God, containing the Truth, and recitation and calligraphy have become sacred arts. The nature of liturgical prayer, performed oriented toward an invisible axis in the direction of Mecca, further strengthens the impression that Islam can do without visual imagery and ritual objects. The idea that Islam prohibits visual representation of figural form, particularly in religious art, has accordingly been stated many times.[35] However, one should be careful to distinguish between a mainly Sunni-Muslim iconoclastic practice and a more tolerant Shiʿi Muslim practice.[36] In Shiʿi Islam there is a strong identification between the word of the Qur'an and the Imams. They are the hidden meaning and personification of the revealed word.[37] As such, they are the active logos (the speaking Qur'an, *nateq*), while the Qur'an is the silent (*samet*), imminent divine logos whose application and understanding is dependent on the Imams. Hosayn occupies a unique place among the Imams. His martyrdom is regarded as the greatest suffering and redemptive act in history. It is believed that participation in the annual commemoration rituals in Moharram, and also in Safar, will be an aid to salvation on the Day of Judgment, as well as being a constant source for seeking help and protection in this life.

The application of aesthetics in Moharram and Safar rituals helped in recreating the event at Karbala. Visual imagery, ritual objects, and the sound of elegiac poetry made the event visible and alive, and thus accessible to worshippers. This visual and oral re-creation brought Karbala alive as memory and hence facilitates commemoration. However, commemoration was not simply about remembering and recollecting the past through seeing, speaking, and hearing. It was about enacting the past and making it present, to allow worshippers to participate in lamentation and mourning together with the survivors of Karbala. In this way, the worshippers renewed their allegiance to the family of the Prophet Mohammad and placed themselves in the potentially rewarding position of addressing holy intercessors. They hoped to improve their life condition at a personal and communal level and to secure their redemption on the Day of Judgment.[38] Visual representations of Imam Ali, Imam Hosayn, and the battle at Karbala; replicas of Qasem's bridal chamber, Ali Asghar's cradle, and the grave of Roqayyeh; and lamentation poetry became the means of this mediation. Worshippers did not approach wall hangings and replicas as objects of prayer but as aids for presenting prayers and supplications and for seeking protection. Presented as offerings of thanks, *nazr,* wall hangings and replicas were believed to transmit blessing and grace. As Jensen remarks, art, as symbol, can act as a bridge between a familiar reality and one that transcends ordinary expression.[39] In the present context, which symbols to apply and approach seemed to be dependent on several criteria, such as how efficiently they could create a mourning mood and how they related to worshippers' life experience and their relation to particular holy persons. For example, women who sought mediation in questions of marriage could visit the bridal chamber of Qasem and Fatemeh, whereas the cradle of Ali Asghar and the grave of Roqayyeh were visited by women who asked for a child or sought protection for their child. The functions of aesthetics in mourning meetings were thus directly related to Shi'i Islamic martyrology and its promise of redemption and intercession. Aesthetics became a necessary instrument functioning as medium or channel for communicating with the spiritual realm.

Notes

The fieldwork on which this paper is based was conducted in 2000 and 2002 as part of a PhD study supported by grants from the Norwegian Research Council.

1. Ayd-e Qorban is celebrated during the pilgrimage to Mecca. Laylat al-Qadr is the night of the revelation of the Qur'an. Both are in the month Zu al-hejjeh.

2. A female *maddah* interviewed by the author in Shiraz (2002). For Shi'is' perception of the redemptive nature of Imam Hosayn's martyrdom, see Mahmoud Ayoub, *Redemptive Suffering in Islam: A Study of the Devotional Aspects of "Ashura" in Twelver Shi'ism* (New York: Mouton, 1978), and Peter J. Chelkowski, "Popular Shi'i Mourning Rituals," *al-Serat* 12 (1986), 209–226.

3. Ayoub, *Redemptive Suffering,* 141–148.

4. Vernon James Schubel, *Religious Performance in Contemporary Islam: Shi'a Devotional Rituals in South Asia* (Columbia: University of South Carolina Press, 1993), 35.

5. Lynda Clarke, "Some Examples of Elegy on Imam Husayn," *al-Serat* 12 (1986), 13–28; Ayoub, *Redemptive Suffering,* 153; Jean Calmard, "Shi'i Rituals and Power: The Consolidation of Safavid Shi'ism: Folklore and Popular Religion," in *Safavid Persia,* ed. Charles Melville (London: I. B. Tauris, 1996), 155; and Chelkowski, "Popular Shi'i Mourning Rituals," 209–226.

6. Calmard, "Shi'i Rituals and Power," 139–190.

7. Peter J. Chelkowski, ed., *Ta'ziyeh: Ritual and Drama in Iran* (New York: New York University Press, 1979b); Chelkowski, "Popular Shi'i Mourning Rituals"; Schubel, *Religious Performance;* David Pinault, *Horse of Karbala: Muslim Devotional Life in India* (New York: Palgrave, 2001); and Ingvild Flaskerud, "Tazia: Shia islamske pasjonspill over et martyrium," *Historie: Populærhistorisk magasin* 1 (2000), 50–57.

8. Peter J. Chelkowski, "Narrative Painting and Painting Recitation in Qajar Iran," in *Muqarnas: An Annual on Islamic Art and Architecture,* ed. Oleg Grabar (Leiden: E. J. Brill, 1989), 98–111.

9. Bushehr is a seaport on the coast of the Persian Gulf to the southwest of Shiraz.

10. Similarly, in Christian iconography, believers can easily identify, without confusion, the Apostles Peter and Paul. St. Peter is represented as an old but vigorous man, with short gray curly hair, balding or tonsured, and a short, usually curly beard, and with broad, rustic features. His special attribute is a key, symbolizing the keys to the Kingdom of Heaven. Other attributes are an upturned cross (his form of martyrdom), a crozier with triple transverses (papal), a book (the gospel), and a cock (his denial). St. Paul is often represented with brown hair, but partly bald, and a long wavy beard. His normal attributes are his sword, which he was executed with, and a book, or a scroll, referring to his authorship of the epistles.

11. Similar wall hangings have been observed by Pinault in Ladakh, India. They are put in *matam-sarai* and shrines where mourning ceremonies are being held. Pinault, *Horse of Karbala,* 203.

12. By "Mustafa's religion" is meant Islam.

13. The symbolism resembles Christian iconography, in which the apostles and Christ are holding scriptures or books in their hands, and the finger gestures convey dogmatic messages.

14. This is a near quotation from Qur'an (33:40).

15. Charles Dillard Collins, *The Iconography and Ritual of Siva at Elephanta* (Albany: State University of New York Press, 1988); Robert E. Fisher, *Buddhist Art and Architecture* (London: Thames and Hudson, 1993); Heather Elgood, *Hinduism and the Religious Arts* (London: Cassell, 1999); and Barbara Daly Metcalf, *Making Muslim Space* (Berkeley and Los Angeles: University of California Press, 1996).

16. Robert Hillenbrand, *Islamic Architecture: Form, Function, and Meaning* (Edinburgh: Edinburgh University Press, 1994), and Martin Frishman and Hasan-Uddin Khan, *The Mosque: History, Architectural Development, and Regional Diversity* (London: Thames and Hudson, 1994).

17. Imam Hussein's blood is supposed to have run into the ground of Karbala. The Shi'is pay him respect by placing their heads on a piece of clay from this ground when they pray.

18. For references to idolatry in the Qur'an, see for example 5:92 and 6:74. See also Oleg Grabar, *The Formation of Islamic Art* (New Haven, Conn.: Yale University Press, 1987), for a discussion of these verses.

19. There is a clear similarity to the application of ex-votos in Catholicism, where images are regarded as effective and adequate vehicles for expressing and giving thanks. See David Freedberg, *The Power of Images* (Chicago: University of Chicago Press, 1989). See also David Morgan, *Visual Piety: A History and Theory of*

Popular Religious Images (Berkeley and Los Angeles: University of California Press, 1998), for a study of visual piety in Christianity.

20. For the use of images in women's *jalaseh*, religious meetings, in Tehran, see Azam Torab, "Neighbourhoods of Piety: Gender and Ritual in South Tehran" (PhD diss., University of London, 1998), 90–91. Here the use of calligraphy as wall decorations is prevalent, but seems to serve no function in the meetings. More generally, they were believed to bring the home grace, have an increasing beneficial effect, and bring protection.

21. Another parallel to the women's minor pilgrimage to replicas is the visitation to a *saqqa-khaneh*, often regarded as a shrine to Abbas. See Chelkowski, "Popular Shi'i Mourning Rituals," 213.

22. John Renard, *Seven Doors to Islam* (Berkeley and Los Angeles: University of California Press, 1996), 35.

23. In male-dominant and gender-mixed meetings, the storyteller was a man, but in women's rituals the storyteller was usually a woman.

24. Ayoub, *Redemptive Suffering*, 158.

25. For Persian religious poetry, see Zahra Eqbal, "Elegy in the Qajar Period," in *Ta'ziyeh: Ritual and Drama*, ed. Peter J. Chelkowski, 193–209 (New York: New York University Press, 1979). For Arabic and Persian poetry, see Clarke, "Some Examples of Elegy." For Persian and Indo-Muslim poetry, see Annemarie Schimmel, "Karbala and the Imam Husayn in Persian and Indo-Muslim Literature," *al-Serat* 12 (1986), 29–39.

26. The practice of combining textual sources can also be found in other Islamic ritual traditions, such as *dhikr* (*zekr*), the mystics' remembrance of God. In Egypt, *munshidin*, who sing during *dhikr*, combine classical Sufi sources such as Ibn al-Farid and al-Arabi with texts drawn from common books of praise and popular Sufi phraseology, in addition to texts written by local shaikhs and the *munshidin* themselves. Sometimes a singer includes material from the secular environment. There is a continuing development of the repertoire, drawing on older sources and adding new material. Earle H. Waugh, ed., *The Munshidin of Egypt: Their World and Their Song* (Columbia: University of South Carolina Press, 1989), 125–136.

27. It is considered particularly meritorious to compose and recite poetry in the memory of Hosayn. Ayoub, *Redemptive Suffering*, 142.

28. Ibid., 70.

29. This, and all subsequent *nowheh*, was registered when performed during the rituals and translated by Mrs. Kamali and the author.

30. Lullaby lyrics are universal, but often are difficult to translate from their local expression. In order to preserve some of the original rhythm and feeling in this lullaby, I have decided to keep the Farsi terms, instead of translating it into "la, la, la," which would be more correct in English.

31. The phrase "*va vayla yahe yave*" is a rhythmical mourning exclamation.

32. Referring to the lodging she was offered as a hostage in Damascus.

33. Clarke, "Some Examples of Elegy," 13–28.

34. The seriousness with which the flagellation was performed was reflected in the large bruises many women had on the inside of their thighs, developed after days of ritual performance.

35. See for example Terry Allen, *Five Essays on Islamic Art* (Manchester, U.K.:

Solipsist Press, 1988); M. S. Ipsirolu, *Das Bild im Islam: Ein Verbot und seine Folge* (Wien and München: Verlag Anton Schroll, 1971); Albert C. Moore, *Iconography of Religions* (London: SCM Press, 1977); and Neal Robinson, *Discovering the Quran* (London: SCM Press, 1996).

36. For exceptions to Sunni iconoclasm, see René A. Bravmann, *Tribal Art in West Africa* (Cambridge: Cambridge University Press, 1980), 35. In West Africa, Bravmann has observed that "mask cults functioned more effectively than available Islamic methods or dealt with a problem for which there was no Quranic solution at all." Anne-Marie Bouttaiux-Ndiaye, in *Senegal behind Glass: Images of Religious and Daily Life* (Munich: Prestel, 1994), presents reverse-glass paintings with religious themes, distributed among Muslims in Senegal. Prints circulating in the Middle East are presented by Sergio Stocchi, *L'Islam nelle Stampe* (Milan: Be-Ma Editrice, 1988), and Pierre Centlivres and Micheline Centlivres-Demont, *Imageries populaires en Islam* (Geneva: Georg Editeur, 1997).

37. Ayoub, *Redemptive Suffering*, 57–58.

38. Although this understanding of the Karbala paradigm relates it to social realities and problems, it does not connect to the ideology of social and political revolution as presented by the Islamic government in its revolutionary indoctrination (particularly between 1978 and 1988). See Haggay Ram, *Myth and Mobilization in Revolutionary Iran: The Use of the Friday Congregational Sermon* (Washington, D.C.: American University Press, 1994).

39. Robin Margaret Jensen, *Understanding Early Christian Art* (London: Routledge, 2000), 6.

CHAPTER 4

The Daughters of Karbala
Images of Women in Popular Shi'i Culture in Iran

FAEGHEH SHIRAZI

Abu Abdallah said: "Whoever recites a couplet about Hosayn (A) and cries and causes others to shed tears, he and they will enter paradise."[1]

Contrary to a popular belief that Islamic tradition and belief do not give an important place to women, women's participation in jihad (i.e., Islamic struggle for a just cause, often war) and their *shahadat* (martyrdom) are central, if often overlooked by scholars. This is perhaps because women's participation is viewed as being more passive than active. However, this form of "passive" support, which is evident in the ritual lamentation chants, the elegies and eulogies of the Ashura poetry and prose, is a very important component of Shi'i popular culture.

Persian literature is filled with information about prominent female Shi'i religious figures, historical facts, and mythology. What is recorded in the history books is often quite different from what is believed by the masses. However, no matter what the recorded history is, the symbolic history in which people believe is the base and core of the popular culture of any society. Keeping this factor in mind, I decided to analyze the literature of the popular culture of Ashura to better understand the portrayal of the images of women.

This study focuses on the images of "holy" females in the Shi'i tradition, for whom countless elegies have been composed. Such elegies are an important component of contemporary rituals during the month of Moharram, especially during the ritual season of Ashura. Manuals containing chants and elegies, which are widely published in Iran, serve as scripts of sorts for the Moharram rituals. Such manuals are readily available to the public and are quite popular. During the rituals, elegies are chanted by the leaders of procession groups and continually recited in religious gatherings, sermons, and lamentation rituals. The importance of such popular religious literature should not be overlooked. The texts of such manuals reveal contemporary popular beliefs and ritual practices.

For this study, I have used numerous Persian manuals of Ashura elegies and eulogies, mostly composed by contemporary authors. The contents of these manuals are quite varied, depending on the personal preferences and religious sentiments of each individual composer. In many instances, a special section or note preceded the main text of the manual to inform the reader about a personal and special spiritual connection of the author to the Prophet Mohammad's household. For a large majority of such authors or editors of Ashura poetry, it is one more way to achieve salvation through their connection with the family of Prophet Mohammad. Mourning is even viewed by many Shi'is as a religious duty or an obligation. The objective of this poetry is to recount the tragic story of Ashura, thereby exposing the villains of the episode while sympathizing with the victims and glorifying the heroic actions of Hosayn and his supporters. Shi'is believe that this pious act will be rewarded on the Day of Judgment and the pious will be brought a step closer to paradise.

The elegies of Ashura were used to bolster support for the cause of the Iran-Iraq War. They were also used to legitimize both the Islamic Revolution of Iran, which resulted in the overthrow of the shah's monarchy in 1978, and the establishment of the Islamic regime that followed. Collectively, the symbolism of Karbala, Moharram, and Ashura have been used to pave the way for social and political transformation in Iran. Imam Hosayn and seventy-two members of his entourage have been endlessly portrayed to remind the population that martyrdom, or *shahadat,* in the name of justice for Islam is a shortcut to the gates of heaven. The idea that the actual experience of martyrdom is wonderful was widely promoted, and martyrs were portrayed as being worthy of envy. There are numerous articles in Iranian daily newspapers during the Iran-Iraq War that revealed the "private" wishes of young soldier boys wanting to be martyred because heaven was awaiting their arrival. Ayatollah Ruhollah Khomeini spoke of martyrs and martyrdom:

Think about the fact that the best people at His own time, His Holiness the Lord of the martyrs [Imam Husayn], Peace be upon Him, and the best youths of Bani-Hashim [the tribe of the Prophet Muhammad and Imam Husayn], and his best followers were martyred, leaving this world through martyrdom. Yet, when the family of Imam Husayn was taken to the evil presence of Yazid, Her Holiness Zaynab [Hosayn's sister], peace be upon her, said: "What we experienced was nothing but beautiful.[2]

Ayatollah Khomeini and the Iranian clergy promoted the idea that the ideal woman is the mother who raises pious children for the Prophet's community. The daughter of the Prophet Mohammad, Fatemeh al-Zahra, who is revered as the most excellent of women, is an important religious figure for Shi'is. Biographical dictionaries and *hadith* collections (i.e., sayings or teachings of Prophet Mohammad) have portrayed Fatemeh as being defined by her marital and maternal functions. As the wife of Imam Ali and mother of Hasan and Hosayn, she is the ideal female image. As the mother of Hosayn, who is popularly known to Shi'is as Sayyed al-Shohada, the Master of Martyrs, Fatemeh occupies a special place in the Shi'i religious hierarchy. Martyrdom is an integral part of Shi'i Islam and Iranian culture.

Shi'is believe that one's entry into paradise will be guaranteed by modeling one's life on the lives of the holy examples and through their martyrdom. Paradise is viewed as a comforting home for those who lost their lives as martyrs for Islam. In the Persian language there are at least three different words that are equivalent to the English word "cemetery": *khakestan, gurestan,* and *qabrestan.* None of these words are inscribed at the cemeteries' entrance signs. Since the Islamic Revolution in 1978, they have been renamed *behesht,* a Persian term for paradise. Nearly all Iranian cemeteries are now named after Shi'i female holy figures. For example, the largest cemetery in Greater Tehran is called Behesht-e Zahra, which literally means "The Paradise of Zahra."

When pious Muslims are buried in any cemetery in Iran, especially those with the honorific title of *shahid,* they take on another symbolic meaning, a cosmological one. In this regard, the holy female figure, after which the cemetery is named, will be viewed as the mother of those who are no longer with us. The martyrs and other deceased are resting at their "mother's home," a safe, comforting place where she will take care of them. In reality, of course, the status of a *shahid* is above the others who are buried in the same cemetery. The lot reserved for *shahids* is an exclusive spot in these *beheshts,* ensuring that on earth their status is remembered by the living. Fatemeh, known as the mistress of all women, has an important role in such cemeteries; she is the mother of the Master of the Martyrs, Hosayn. She constitutes the only direct line of descent to the Prophet of Islam and is considered to be one of his infallible descendants. Fatemeh, or Zahra, as she is most often and popularly known, are two common names used after *behesht.*

Ashura, the tenth day of the month of Moharram, the day of martyrdom for the Shiʿi community, is not a word limited only to a certain location or time.[3] Rather, it is often considered to be timeless and universal in scope. For example, popular posters displayed throughout Iran promoted this idea effectively with the popular Arabic phrase "Kolla yowm(en) Ashura, kollu ard(en) Karbala": Every day is Ashura, Everywhere is Karbala. According to al-Shafeʿi, who authored an Ashura manual, on the fateful day of Ashura the sun did not set at all. Ashura is the axis around which all of history revolves, and Hosayn is an eternal symbol for all of humanity. Al-Shafeʿi further writes with religious passion: "*Ashura* is the symbol of love and life. *Ashura* protects Islam, and safeguards the Qurʾan."[4] He concludes that the human heart without feeling love for Ashura is an empty heart. There have been numerous writings on the importance of Ashura and its significance in terms of humanity, sacrifice, and martyrdom in both classical and contemporary Persian literature. All such documented materials are evidence of the monumental importance of this historical/religious episode for Shiʿi Muslims.

Knowing of the rewards of martyrs in the afterlife, believers celebrate their death. For example, according to Zaynab, the death of Hosayn was an occasion for celebration, not mourning. The concept of celebrating the death of a martyr has been emphasized on numerous occasions by Ayatollah Khomeini:

The departure of a perfect person, the martyrdom of a perfect person is beautiful in the eyes of the saints of God—not because they have fought and have been killed, but because their war has been for the sake of God, because their uprising has been for the sake of God. Regarding martyrdom as a great blessing is not because they are killed. People on the other side also get killed. Their blessing is due to the fact that their motivation is Islam.[5]

The religious duty and obligation that the pious feel to respond to the calling of jihad is an honor. The women of Karbala understood perfectly that the ultimate sacrifice in their lives on earth, which was martyring their loved ones, would be rewarded later in paradise, and that as daughters, wives, sisters, and/or mothers of a *shahid*, they will be treated as martyrs in their own right. The message is clear: the duty is not toward family first. Rather, it is to Islam and the defense of God in the name of justice.

Another author, Hejazi, writes on the earliest existing Persian elegy about Imam Hosayn. He says that the earliest document is from the tenth

Figure 4.1. Women participating in the central procession holding banners with political slogans and shovels for burying the dead (Tehran, 1997). © Kamran Scot Aghaie

century AD. It is the work of the poet Kasaʿi Marwazi, who is considered the first Hosayni poet. He was followed by others such as Nasir Khusru in the eleventh century, Sanaʿi, and later on by Qawami Razi, Anvari, and Zaher Farabi in the twelfth century.[6]

Shiʿi devotional literature of the modern period does not lack female characters. Particular attention is given to the important women who are in one way or another associated with the Ahl Al-Bayt (i.e., the Prophet's family and descendants). Fatemeh, the beloved daughter of the Prophet, is associated with various qualities and is known by various names. Among her honorific titles we are mostly familiar with Fatemeh al-Zahra,[7] the light, the radiant, the fair; Siyyedat al-Nesa, mistress of women; al-Sadiqeh al-Kobra, the great and honest one; al-Shahideh, the martyred lady; and Afzal al-Nesa, the most excellent of ladies.[8]

Alameh Majlesi, one of the most important medieval Shiʿi scholars, devotes an entire chapter to Fatemeh, praising her internal character, her relationship to the Prophet, her marriage to Ali, and her role as a mother. Majlesi describes in detail how Fatemeh should be used as a role model and a symbol of the perfect woman.[9] While this perfect woman's image does not conform neatly to contemporary feminist conceptions of womanhood, it nevertheless plays a major role in the lives of modern Iranian women. Majlesi notes:

Figure 4.2. Women carrying green flags among the Iraqi immigrants living in Tehran (Tehran, 1997). © Kamran Scot Aghaie

Ebn-e Babuyeh according to an authentic *hadith* from Imam Sadeq tells us, Her holiness Fatemeh (peace be upon her) is known to God by nine different names: *Fatemeh, Sadiqeh, Mobarakeh, Tahereh, Zakiyeh, Radhiyeh, Mardhiyeh, Mohadditheh,* and *Zahra* . . . thus do you understand what is the interpretation of Fatemeh? It means the one who is cut off from all the evils.[10]

Majlesi further elaborates that according to this important *hadith,* we must be aware of the position of Fatemeh as the woman above all other women. In a *hadith* attributed to Imam Sadeq, Majlesi informs the reader about three different kinds of lights with differing intensities and colors attributed to Fatemeh:

Why was Fatemeh called Zahra? Imam Sadeq said because three times a day Fatemeh's radiant light shines on Ali. At first during the early morning prayer when people of Medina were still in bed. A white light would shine from the sun, and as it enters the homes of citizens of Medina, this light would make all the walls of homes bright. Thus people of Medina would be running to the Prophet and asking him the source and the reason for this light. He would re-

spond, "Go to the house of my daughter, Fatemeh, so you will understand it." When the people of Medina arrived at Fatemeh's house they
would see her praying and this light is shining upon her. Then they
would learn that the source of the light is her.[11]

Majlesi continues with the description of Fatemeh's radiant light:

During the mid-day, a yellow light would be shining from her chin,
illuminating houses in Medina, coloring every thing in that particular color of yellow. When people asked the Prophet, he would send
them to Fatemeh's house, and they would see that she is praying and
the yellow radiant light is shining from her face.[12]

In describing the third type of light, Majlesi says:

When the day was ending, and sun was going down, her [Fatemeh's]
illuminated face would take the color of red. Thus this red radiant
light would enter the homes of residents of Medina, making every-
thing red. People would be astonished by this event. They would ask
the Prophet about it. The messenger of God would send them to
Fatemeh's house where she would be praying and the radiant red light
would be shining from her chin. Thus the people learnt that the light
was from Fatemeh. The light[13] continually remained on her chin. She
remained illuminated until Imam Hosayn was born. Then her light
was transferred to his chin. This light remains with us and will be
passed from one imam to another imam, until the day of judgement.[14]

Majlesi records other *hadiths* regarding why Fatemeh is called Zahra. One
of the reasons given is that God created her from His own holy light.
Majlesi relates much more regarding Fatemeh and her illumination, but
that is beyond the scope of this chapter.

   In the *Mafatih al-Jenan,* the largest and most widely used collection of
supplications (*do'a*), in the section devoted to a special prayer for Fatemeh
al-Zahra, we learn how she is referred to in relation to the Prophet and
his other male relatives, namely Ali Ebn-e Abi Taleb (her husband) and
Hasan and Hosayn, her sons. The following is a partial section of this special prayer devoted to Fatemeh al-Zahra.

Greetings (peace be upon you) to you O daughter of the Messenger of
   God

Greetings (peace be upon you) to you O daughter of Prophet
Greetings (peace be upon you) to you O daughter of sincere Servant of
    God
Greetings (peace be upon you) to you O daughter of Trusted of God.
    . . .
Greetings (peace be upon you) to you O Mistress of all the women
From the Start to the end of the world. . . .
Greetings (peace be upon you) to you O wife of Ali Ebn-e Abi Taleb,
The second Best next to the Prophet. . . .
Greetings (peace be upon you) to you O mother of Hasan and
    Hosayn,
Master of youths, the people of Paradise. . . .
Greetings (peace be upon you) O you pious, honest martyred lady. . . .
Those who hurt you, hurt the Prophet, those who made you happy,
Made the Prophet happy, those who joined you, joined the Prophet of
    God,
And those who left you, left the Prophet of God and the circle of his
    friends
Because you are a part of Prophet's body and soul,
The Prophet said: by God's graciousness, witnessed by His angels,
That I am happy with those that you (Fatemeh) are happy with,
And I am annoyed with those who annoy you. . . .
Love those whom you love,
And I am kind to those whom you are kind to. . . .[15]

Fatemeh is the sorrowful mother, friend, and compassionate companion
of her husband, Ali, and the beloved daughter of the Prophet of Islam. Examination of lamentation prose, elegies, and popular contemporary Persian
poetry clearly shows that many of the details of the stories are somewhat
ahistorical in that they contradict basic historical facts, events, and time
lines. For example, we know that in 680 AD Fatemeh was no longer living
and therefore was not among Imam Hosayn's entourage as they entered the
desert of Karbala. Yet, numerous elegies refer to her presence at the Battle
of Karbala. The reader must understand that the constraints of time and
space do not apply to God or the holy members of the Prophet's family.
Fatemeh is a central figure in this great episode of Karbala, but she is
present in the form of a nontemporal spirit.

A number of elegies chanted during Moharram relate to events that occurred long before the Battle of Karbala. The birth of Fatemeh has been an
inspirational topic for some of the aforementioned elegies. The following

Figure 4.3. Women in the mass procession in front of the bazaar (Tehran, 1997).
© Kamran Scot Aghaie

poem, from *Masa'eb-e a'emeh-e athar* (The Catastrophe of the Pure [Noble] Imams), is an example of a popular piece chanted during Ashura:

THE BIRTH OF HER HOLINESS ZAHRA (PEACE BE UPON HER)
Glorious happy time arrived
Smell of musk fills the air
I will give this happy news to all the Believers
That mother of two Sons (Hasan and Hosayn)
daughter of the Prophet has arrived (borne)
Her arrival has brought much joy and fortune to our hearts,
The wife of Ali Morteza has arrived
The Mistress of all the women has arrived. . . .
For the benefit of the religion of the Prophet,
the illuminator of the right path, she has arrived,
From her lap leaders are raised
Virtue belongs to her, kindness belongs to her,
honesty belongs to her, greatness belongs to her. . . .
Such a woman is born. . . .
Loyalty belongs to her, love belongs to her, wisdom belongs to her. . . .
May God's kindness be with her

because she belongs to the people of Great Virtues,
She is generous, she is shy, she is born with excellent qualities. . . .
Her broken rib, her shaken frame is caused by her enemy's blow,
May the curse of God be upon her enemy
Her son Mohsen[16] died from the blow to his body, neck and side. . . .
I wish she would be the kind mediator,
asking forgiveness for us on the day of judgement
So our sins will be forgiven
May God have mercy on us,
her birth is like the arrival of new year.[17]

The incident of Fatemeh's broken rib and the injuries inflicted upon her
are further historical facts indicating that there are differences between the
Shi'i and the Sunni traditions. Historically, this incident is referred to as the
Fadak incidence, in which Abu Bakr and Omar wanted to stop Fatemeh
from inheriting the estate of Fadak upon her father's death. "She asserted
that this estate was given to her father unconditionally as his share of the
spoils of Khaybar. Quoting Mohammad's words: We [the Prophets] do not
leave as inheritance what we make through legal alms."[18] Abu Bakr and
Omar went to Fatemeh's house several times, and once she refused to open
the door to them. Apparently, while she was standing behind the closed
door of her house, they kicked open the door, causing fractures and injuries
to her ribs. She was ill for several months and eventually died.[19] According
to Shi'is, her death was caused by Abu Bakr and Omar violently kicking in
the door. Thus, Fatemeh's death is blamed on the supporters of Abu Bakr
and Omar, who also opposed Ali's caliphate.

MARTYRDOM OF ZAHRA
I became like a wingless bird[20]
You [blaming the world] made me motherless
My mother Zahra departed this world
O pity
O my mother you left Zaynab
Wake up and see the wet tearful eyes of Zaynab
Zaynab became motherless
O pity
In your absence, sorrow became Zaynab's companion
Suffering and deprivation became confident friends of Zaynab
You are gone my mother, I became alone

Figure 4.4. Procession of women carrying the cradle of Ali Asghar
(Tehran, 1997). © Kamran Scot Aghaie

O pity
How did your face become black and blue?
Why did your enemies hit your face?
They broke your bones[21]

The lamenting for Zaynab over the death of her mother Zahra is directly
pointing to the physical abuse Fatemeh suffered from the blow to her body,

Figure 4.5. Osara, or prisoners being taken in chains on camels to Damascus (Tehran, 1997). © Kamran Scot Aghaie

the fracture of her ribs, and the blow to her face, which apparently left a bruise. Of course, we should read all such words in the larger religious and cultural context, not as history per se.

The next elegy focuses on remembrance of Fatemeh by Ali, or talking about the sorrow Ali felt as a result of Fatemeh's death. Other forms of elegies dedicated to Fatemeh are generally related to Karbala scenes and the death of her son Hosayn.

AFTER ZAHRA (PEACE BE UPON HER)
Are you aware of what happened to Mowla (Ali) after Zahra's death?
An hour passed like a year
All heard his painful story
The whole world felt the same sorrow. . . .
He did not forget the incidence of her broken bones. . . .
It was a hard and painful day when she passed away
I don't know how Mowla could pass that day
Until Qiyamat (the Day of Judgment) Zhu al-ʿedat[22] cannot forget
All the pain that Sadiqeh Kobra (Fatemeh) endured[23]

Fatemeh is portrayed as a beloved wife missed by her loving husband. Ali is lamenting for her and talking about his unbearable pain and sorrow.

Zaban-e hal, biographical sketches from the perspective of describing one's emotional state, constitutes a group of poems. In the first one, Ali is talking:

ZABAN-E HAL: ALI MOURNING FOR ZAHRA

Oh Zahra, Oh Zahra
One who is murdered by the enemy
Tonight the house without you seems like a prison to me
Tonight I am weeping
My young lady, mother of my children, my flower
My children are crying tonight, I am weeping tonight
My bright moon, the lady of judgement day
With my tearful eyes, I will remain at your graveside tonight
I am weeping tonight
My day became dark like your hair from the sorrow
My eyes are shedding blood instead of tears tonight
I am weeping tonight. . . .
Until the day of judgement I will be in pain
I am weeping tonight[24]

Figure 4.6. Procession of women carrying tents that symbolize the camp of Hosayn's supporters at Karbala. These tents are usually ritually burned at the end of the ritual season, in memory of how Yazid's troops set fire to the camp at Karbala (Tehran, 1997). © Kamran Scot Aghaie

The next *zaban-e hal* poem, composed by the same author, reveals a conversation between Zahra and Ali at her graveside. It seems that the author composed both of these poems at the same time and they are meant to be read together. These poems are followed by a similar set of poems, from Ali to Fatemeh and vice versa. The arrangement in the book suggests that these poems could be read as a conversation between Zahra and Ali telling each other about the sorrow and agonies they are experiencing. Perhaps there is a hint or suggestion by the author to make the reader aware of the loving marital relationship that existed between Fatemeh and Ali.

ZABAN-E HAL: ZAHRA WITH ALI

O my kind cousin, the father of orphans, Oh Ali
King of men, Oh Ali
Forgive me, bless me it is the time to depart, Oh Ali
King of men, Oh Ali
Sit for a minute at my side my dear Ali
There is not much time left before my death, Oh Ali
I leave Hosayn at your care,
O you the king of kings, the kindest of all the sultans, Oh Ali
King of men, Oh Ali
When I depart this world to paradise
Bring our children with you
But be careful so our enemy does not find out
Keep the location of my grave a secret, Oh Ali
King of men, Oh Ali
Oh Ali sit next to my bedside and read the Qur'an
So I can die in peace
Don't shed tears of sorrow and don't weep and cry
Don't break my heart by your broken heart, Oh Ali
King of men, Oh Ali
O God, be kind to all the Shi'i people
Free them in Medina on the graveside of Dear Mustafa (Ali)[25]

This poem shows that Fatemeh al-Zahra was already aware of Ali's death and his gravesite in Medina. She was also aware that a secure place in paradise was reserved for her. She says, "When I depart this world to paradise," and makes sure that when Ali joins her in paradise, he will bring their children along. By addressing the issue of paradise in this particular context, I believe that the author assures the reader of the safe arrival of the

Figure 4.7. Another view of women in the mass procession in front of the bazaar (Tehran, 1997). © Kamran Scot Aghaie

members of the household of the Prophet of Islam to their ultimate place of residence, paradise.[26]

The next most important female figure in the scene of Karbala is Zaynab, sister of Hosayn and daughter of Ali and Fatemeh. Unlike her mother, Zaynab was physically present during the episode at Karbala. The suffering, pain, and humiliation she experienced from the enemy have provided motivations for numerous *zaban-e hal,* or biographical sketches in relation to Ashura. Regardless of Zaynab's role in the tragedy of Karbala, most collections of elegies begin by describing Zaynab's birth. This is very similar to elegies composed for Fatemeh al-Zahra. The birth of any member of the holy descendants of the Prophet is considered a great historical event by Shi'is. The following elegy is dedicated to Zaynab:

THE BIRTH OF HER HOLINESS ZAYNAB
The house and the entire town is bright from the radiant face of the
   girl
Zaynab is shining from the lap of Zahra
The sun became illuminated from her face
Ali and Zahra both are joyous and happy. . . .
Zahra's lap is illuminated from the beauty of Zaynab. . . .

The tower of chastity is lit by the presence of Zaynab
From this light the whole world is illuminated
The Heaven is envious of Zaynab's house. . . .
Happy and content is our Prophet
His lineage will continue. . . .
Happy, happy, happy birthday to the daughter of Zahra[27]

This elegy suggests the idea of illuminated radiant light. As we read earlier in the account of Fatemeh al-Zahra by Alameh Majlesi, the illuminated radiant face was apparently commonly held to be a feature of Fatemeh, and she passed it on to Hosayn, her son. In the above poem, the poet suggests the same idea regarding Zaynab's radiant face, the light that she supposedly inherited from her mother Fatemeh. Belief in this light, popularly called *nur-e Mohammadi,* is shared by both Sunnis and Shiʻis. Legends refer to the Prophet who was born with a radiant light around his head, thus identifying him as a chosen one or a prophet—the one gifted with the light of God. This sacred illumination was then believed to have been inherited by his descendants through Fatemeh al-Zahra.

As the eulogy suggests, this was a very special and happy occasion to be celebrated. The poem describes Zaynab as a special person, illuminated with a special light from birth, radiant like the sun. Her parents were very proud and happy to have her, and she was blessed already by the status of her parents and her lineage from the Prophet. Although the poem is happy, recitation of it during Ashura infuses it with sadness because of the tragic events that were in store for this holy and wonderful baby girl. It is not difficult to understand the religious sentiments regarding Moharram as being associated with bloodshed, injustice, tyranny, and revenge. Thus, even happy poems like this one will be recited in the sad and weeping manner of elegies. The pious will weep sincerely upon hearing these elegies, just as one would weep at a loved one's gravesite. The following elegy testifies to Zaynab's wisdom, knowledge, and talents.

ELEGY OF VIRTUOUSNESS AND WISDOM OF ZAYNAB (1)
Who is the preacher of the Qur'anic message? Who is the guardian of
   children?
Zaynab, Daughter of Morteza (Ali)
Who is the most virtuous of all?
Zaynab, Daughter of Morteza (Ali)
The light of Ali, the loyal Zaynab
The pious one Zaynab

Courageous, patient, Zaynab is the light of Mostafa (Prophet
  Mohammad)
Friend and helpful, the "King" of Karbala, Zaynab
Who is the pure light of God? Who is the protector of orphans?
Zaynab, daughter of Morteza
Don't call her a woman, she is above a man, she is more faithful than
  a man
Don't call her a woman, there is no one more courageous than
  Zaynab
Don't call her a woman, there is no one more knowledgeable than
  Zaynab
In her bravery and wisdom so similar to Haydar Safdar (Ali)
Who is the one with pious knowledge, the protector of women's
  interest?
Zaynab, daughter of Morteza
She shook up the city of Kufa with her pious Qur'anic sermons
With her patience she destroyed the kingdom of tyranny
Her enemies are worried about her now
She reinforced the legacy of her pious belief
through the sacrificial blood of her relatives
Who is the heroine of the time? Who is that shining moon?
Zaynab, Daughter of Morteza
Nabi (the Prophet) taught her lessons in piety and recognizing God's
  existence
From her father she inherited her sacrificial character
From Hasan [her brother] she learned how to be loyal and patient
So she can safeguard the honor of her household
Who is the protector of the orphans? Who is the pure light from God?
Zaynab, Daughter of Morteza
Praises upon her for her loyalty to Hosayn
For motherly care of his children
Her endurance gained the praise of her enemies
Who is the best of all? Who is the shining one?
Zaynab, Daughter of Morteza
No mother gave birth to anyone as eloquent in speech as Zaynab
She memorized the Qur'an at a very young age
Her religious knowledge revived the religion of the Prophet
O you, tyrannous world, you did so much injustice to her
Who is the beloved of God?
Who is the pious source of knowledge for other women?

Zaynab, Daughter of Morteza
She is known to everyone and admired by all
Her holy name Zaynab, is *zinat*,[28] The Jewel of Paradise
She is a representative from Zahra's side for women's welfare
No word can do justice to precisely describe her
Who is the pure light of God? Who is the protector of children?
Zaynab, Daughter of Morteza (Ali)[29]

This portrayal of Zaynab is in some ways unique. Karimi, the author, has introduced a modern and very liberated image of Zaynab. This image corresponds to a contemporary and, one could almost say, a more politically correct representation of women in modern society. She is compared to men in honesty, bravery, loyalty, honor, knowledge of Qur'an, and piety. From a purely feminist perspective, she still is not liberated completely because she walks in the shadow of her male relatives, including her grandfather, the Prophet of Islam, her father, Ali, her brothers, Hasan and Hosayn, and, of course, her sons. Perhaps it is more accurate to say that Zaynab is measured against men or compared to men as being the benchmark. However, it is refreshing to read, for example, that "she is a representative from Zahra's side for women's welfare." This line makes it clear that now two great women of Islam are involved in the welfare of women: Fatemeh al-Zahra as a role model, and Zaynab herself, who supposedly has many of her mother's qualities and is blessed with qualities inherited from important men of the family of Mohammad. While these are closer to modern feminist sensibilities, they still fall short of considering women equal to men.

Don't call her a woman, she is above a man, she is more faithful than
    a man
Don't call her a woman, there is no one more courageous than
    Zaynab
Don't call her a woman, there is no one more knowledgeable than
    Zaynab
In her bravery, and wisdom so similar to Haydar Safdar (Ali)[30]

At this point the reader might be alarmed that the sentence "Don't call her a woman" and the following lines are not actually praise for women. Rather, they praise Zaynab while insulting women as a whole. However, this is still a significant formulation. My understanding is that such poetry would not have been appropriate in past generations. From my readings of

Figure 4.8. Another view of Osara, or prisoners being taken in chains on camels to Damascus; children are often included in these processions (Tehran, 1997). © Kamran Scot Aghaie

more traditional, older elegies, to give such credit to a woman in terms of religious knowledge, bravery, honesty, chastity, and loyalty to family and relatives was relatively rare.

To make my point more specific and clear regarding the modern feminist point of view toward Karimi's poetry, I would like to present one more example from the same collection. The following is a translation of an elegy composed by Karimi in honor of Zaynab:

ELEGY OF VIRTUOUSNESS AND WISDOM OF ZAYNAB (2)
Zaynab, the loyal one, the well spoken one
Daughter of Morteza (Ali), the source of knowledge
Zaynab, the patient one, Zaynab, the lion of Karbala
Praise be upon you for your patience, praise be upon you
You, the unique jewel, the leader of women
Learned one, pious and kind
O you the teacher of virtuousness, the source of bravery
O you the light of the universe, the king of endurance
Zaynab, the pride of two worlds, the light of two worlds Zaynab
Praise be upon you for your patience, praise be upon you
O you the remembrance of Zahra

Pious and dignified, pure light of God
Dignified, eloquent Daughter of *saqi*[31] of the Kowsar
(one of the rivers in Muslim Paradise)
Praise be upon you for your patience, praise be upon you
The sultan of endurance, the capable master
The fountain of virtuousness and chastity
Zaynab the loyal one, daughter of Morteza
Praise be upon you for your patience, praise be upon you
Kufa was agitated by her "Qur'anic" speeches
She revived the religion (Islam) by her bravery
Zaynab O you the conqueror of Sham[32]
O you Zaynab, the mistress of high caliber
Praise be upon you for your patience, praise be upon you
The pride of both worlds
The loyal one, no body can do justice to describe you
The world is amazed by your virtuousness, endurance, and piety
Praise be upon you for your patience, praise be upon you[33]

Again, we read about Zaynab's heroic qualities—her eloquence and knowledge, her care and kindness toward orphans—and Karimi's characterization of her as "the unique jewel, the leader of women." Karimi has composed several other elegies praising Zaynab, all published in a single volume. In addition to elegies devoted to Zaynab, Karimi published a number of poems as a biographical sketch, *zaban-e hal,* in which Hosayn talks to Zaynab. The contents of these are very similar to the elegies for Zaynab already examined above. There are also a few other poems exclusively devoted to Zaynab in other collections, for example, Morteza Dana'i's collection *Naghmeh-ha-e Karbala*[34] (Songs of Karbala), authored by four contemporary poets, mostly praising Zaynab's perseverance and her kindness toward orphans. Nothing is said regarding Zaynab's role as a leader or as an example of a strong woman in the way that Karimi has described her.

After Fatemeh al-Zahra and Zaynab, perhaps the next important female figures of the Karbala are Roqayyeh and Sakineh, daughters of Imam Hosayn, great granddaughters of the Prophet of Islam, and the grandchildren of Fatemeh al-Zahra and Ali.

HER HOLINESS, ROQAYYEH

He arrived, my companion of day and night
The light of my eyes returned from his trip
My father arrived, O my father arrived

Children gather together, we have a guest
Thinking about him occupies my mind
My best friend arrived
Sometimes I kiss his lips, sometimes I smell his face
I said that I am an orphan[35]
He was like my own life, and he returned to me
His head became like the butterfly of candlelight[36]
I circle around his head like a butterfly[37]
His kindness was like a shadow (protection) upon my head
I will tell all my secrets to my father's head
With my rose water tears, I will wash his face
He arrived as a guest to me[38]

This elegy demonstrates the sorrow and sentiments of love of a daughter
for the loss of her father. In this poem there is no reference to any actions of
bravery, as in the poem about Zaynab. The following poem, in the *zaban-e
hal* format, similarly emphasizes Roqqayyeh's male relations and her status
as a victimized orphan:

ZABAN-E HAL: ROQAYYEH (PEACE BE UPON HER)
O you the tyrant, I am daughter of the King of religion[39]
O you the enemy, I am the child of Hosayn
O you the enemy of God, stranger to the Prophet
Be ashamed in front of God, O you miserable infidel
You murdered my father
Yazid! you detached his head from his body
O you tyrant, stop your tyranny, I am a helpless child. . . .

The remaining verses describe how his head was placed on a stick to be
carried off to Syria to the court of Yazid, whom God will punish on the
Day of Judgment for his horrific actions against the family of the prophet
of Islam.[40]
   The next woman of Karbala whose name appears in the elegies of Ashura
is Sakineh, another daughter of Hosayn. Sakineh is portrayed in a fashion
similar to that of Roqayyeh. The following is a sample of an elegy composed
in her honor:

ZABAN-E HAL: SAKINEH (PEACE BE UPON HER)
My father you left me, you decided to depart
My dear, from your longing, I have tearful eyes

Figure 4.9. Women carrying replica of a headless and arrow-riddled corpse of Hosayn (Tehran, 1997). © Kamran Scot Aghaie

My ruined house became a place of my settlement
Look at it my father
After you, Yazid made torments
He did not have mercy on us
My house is vacant, lonely and cold
I am weeping and grieving since my separation from you
I am a broken [child], alone in this world
From the agony and pain of infidels
I cry blood instead of tears
I am in pain from the slanderous remark of our enemies
My face is black and blue from the abuse of this godless group
My father you left us, you decided to depart
My days and nights are spent in pain and weeping
From this ruined corner of the world
They brought pain and agony to your friends and family members
These godless, shameless men
Why did you forget me father?
O you king of infallible
You left to paradise, made me feel like a wingless bird
I can't bare this separation any longer
I remember those sweet nights when my head was resting on your lap

What was your fault except preaching God's message
Is it why your enemies killed your offspring?
You left us and went to another world.[41]

The remaining verses repeat the same idea of lamenting the tragic fate of Sakineh in losing her father and weeping in agony for the torments that Hosayn's surviving family members and friends had to suffer. This poem in its style and content is very similar to two previous elegies in which the pain and suffering of Roqayyeh was illustrated.

Conclusion

Scholars have debated the question of Muslim women's public and social participation in jihad. In recent years, feminist scholarship, resurgence of religious interest, uniting forces of many Islamic groups to revive religious sentiments, and, most importantly, the role of media and accessibility of information and knowledge have collectively been responsible for the re-thinking of the roles and characters of the "daughters and mothers" of the believers.

Martyrdom is viewed by Shiʿis as a duty and as a means to achieve salvation. Moharram, Ashura, and Karbala collectively are associated with the concept of martyrdom and the Master of the Martyrs, Hosayn, the grandson of Prophet Mohammad. Martyrdom is not only the physical sacrifice of one's life, but it is also seen as the mental and psychological anguish of the pious who lose a family member to martyrdom. Women are usually the victims of this psychological form of martyrdom. For the episode of Ashura in the month of Moharram, the importance of contemporary popular manuals written about Karbala lies in the fact that they relate the actual practice of rituals to the chants composed and recited during the ritualistic ceremonies of the *mosibat-e Karbala,* or the tragedy of Karbala.

The social and political history of Shiʿi Islam focuses on two main female characters for their excellence in piety, endurance, and virtue as exemplary women: Fatemeh al-Zahra and Zaynab, respectively the daughter and the granddaughter of the Prophet of Islam, Mohammad. Though both are portrayed as pious and as role models to be imitated, their images are somewhat different from each other in Ashura elegies and poems. As is evident from the elegies devoted to Fatemeh, she is more passive in her actions and is portrayed more as a mother, wife, and daughter. Nevertheless, she is sometimes portrayed as being almost at the level of the prophet. She is the bearer of the light of Mohammad, referred to as *dokhtar-e nur-e Mo-hammadi,* the Daughter of the Mohammad's Light. The importance of the myth of light has been discussed in relation to Fatemeh and the prophet.

Fatemeh's heroic role as a woman is demonstrated through her pain, suffering, patience, and piety. On the other hand, although Zaynab is de-scribed in pious terms and she is praised for endurance and perseverance, she is compared to a brave man, a man of honor, and she is characterized as a fighter whose weapon is her skilled oratory. She is a woman with knowl-edge of the Qur'an. She is a marvelous public speaker, an outspoken per-son, fearless, and at times she is compared to a lion. She is a woman of loyalty and kindness. She is a friend and protector of orphans and one who is genuinely interested in the welfare of all women.

The elegies composed for Roqayyeh and Sakineh, the daughters of Ho-sayn, are different in language, tone, content, and theme from those com-posed for Zaynab and Fatemeh. Both Roqayyeh and Sakineh are presented in more or less the same fashion. They are portrayed as helpless orphans and victims, weeping constantly for the loss of their father. Roqayyeh and Sakineh are portrayed in a more stereotypical manner. There are frequent direct remarks about Yazid and his tyranny, evident from elegies composed for Roqayyeh and Sakineh. In short, they are acted upon, rather than being active agents like Fatemeh and Zaynab.

In conclusion, the Persian contemporary elegies of Ashura have assigned the daughters of Karbala various roles and characteristics. Fatemeh has the highest and most spiritual spot. She has few mundane or ordinary traits that define her character. Rather, she has more spiritual qualities. Zaynab's role, on the other hand, is defined by her more "worldly" heroic actions. The elegies make it clear that she inherited unique and fine qualities from her grandfather, Prophet Mohammad, her mother, Fatemeh al-Zahra, and her father, Ali Ebn-e Abi Taleb. A more passive role is assigned to Roqayyeh and Sakineh. These women are metaphors for various qualities and traits. Collectively they represent the ideals to which a Shi'i woman is encouraged to aspire.

Notes

1. Sayyed Ali Reza Hejazi, "Imam Husain ibn Ali (A) in the Mirror of Poetry," in *Imam Khomeini and the Culture of Ashura,* abstracts of papers presented at the International Congress on Imam Khomeini and the Culture of Ashura (Tehran: The Institute for Compilation and Publication of the Works of Imam Khomeini, Inter-national Affairs Department, 1995), 52.

2. W. T. Workman, *The Social Origins of the Iran-Iraq War* (Boulder, Colo.: Lynne Rienner, 1994), 124.

3. Sayyed Mohammad al-Shafeʻi, *Payramun-e Hamaseh-e Ashura* (Tehran: Markaz-e Chap va Nashr-e Sazman-e Tablighat-e Eslami, 1373 AH), 13.

4. Ibid.

5. Faegheh Shirazi, *Unveiling the Veil: Hijab in Modern Culture* (Gainesville: University Press of Florida, 2001).

6. Hejazi, "Imam Husain ibn Ali," 53.

7. Mohammad Ibn Mokarram Ibn Manzur, *Lisan al-Arab*, 18 vols. (Beirut: Dar Ihyaʼ al-Turath al-ʻArabi, 1988).

8. Ali Shaykh Abbas Qommi, *Kolliyat-e mafatih al-jenan* (Tehran: Chapkhaneh-e Mohammad Ali Elmi, 1964), 571–573.

9. Allameh Majlesi, *Tarikh-e chahardah maʻsum* (Tehran and Qom: Entesharat-e Sorur, 1996). The title of this book translates into English as *The Fourteen Pure/Infallible*. The infallible fourteen people are the twelve Shiʻi imams of the Ithna Ashari branch, the Prophet Mohammad, and his daughter Fatemeh al-Zahra. It should be noted that all of these fourteen pure bodies belong to the same family lineage.

10. Ibid., 162.

11. Ibid., 163.

12. Ibid.

13. I am not clear about which one of the lights the author is referring to here—the white, the yellow, or the red light. I assume the reference is to the red light because Majlesi again refers to her chin as a source of light.

14. Ibid., 163–164.

15. Ibid. For another translation of the same passage, see David Pinault, "Zaynab Bint Ali and the Place of the Women of the Households of the First Imams in Shiʻite Devotional Literature," in *Women in the Medieval Islamic World*, ed. Gavin R. G. Hambly (New York: St. Martin's Press, 1998), 72–73.

16. Mohsen is from the root *h-s-n*, the common root for Hasan and Hosayn. Thus, I interpret Mohsen here as a reference to Husayn, used for maintaining the rhyme.

17. Sohrab Asadi Tsirkani, *Masʻeb-e aʻemeh-e athar* (Tehran: Nashr-e Golfam, 1995), 15–17.

18. S. H. M. Jafri, *The Origins and Early Development of Shiʻa Islam* (London: Libraire de Liban, 1979), 62–63.

19. Some sources indicate that she died within seventy-five days of the Prophet's death, while other sources indicate that she died about six months after the Prophet.

20. The imagery of the motherless child indicates that it is Zaynab, Fatemeh's daughter, who is reciting the poetry.

21. Sadeghi, "Shahadat-e Zahra," in *Naghmeh-ha-e Karbala*, ed. Morteza Danaʼi (Tehran: Entesharat-e Saʻid Novin, 1996), 67.

22. Zhu al-ʻedat is the pen name of the author of this poem.

23. Hasan Farahbaksh (Zhu al-ʻedat) Nayshaburi, *Hamaseh saz-e Ashura* (Tehran: Entesharat-e Bager al-Olum, 1996), 134.

24. Jalil Azadi Ahmad Abadi, *Gol-ha-e ghargh dar khun* (Tehran: Chapkhaneh-e Golbarg, 1996), 7–8.

25. Ibid., 9–10.

26. For other examples of *zaban-e hal* elegies by the same author, see ibid., 10–17, 19, and 22–29.

27. Morteza Dana'i, ed., *Naghmeh-ha-e Karbala* (Tehran: Entesharat-e Sa'id Novin, 1996), 2:128.

28. *Zinat* in Arabic means "adornment," or "jewel."

29. S. Karimi, *Asheghan-e Karbala* (Tehran: Nashr-e Mehrzad, 1996), 90–93.

30. Ibid.

31. *Saqi* in Persian classical poetry is used in various ways; literally it means "the woman who serves wine." In Sufi tradition, the woman who serves wine may be an earthly presentation of the *houri* or *huriyah* (Arabic), defined by Webster's as "one of the beautiful maidens among the pleasures of the Muslim Paradise." If we picture Zaynab as a beautiful pure maiden, then she is serving the purified water of Kawthar to the blessed inhabitants of the Muslim Paradise.

32. A reference to the city of Sham in present-day Iraq.

33. Karimi, *Asheghan-e Karbala*, 94–96.

34. Dana'i, *Naghmeh-ha-e Karbala*, 2:128–137. The contributing poets are Fallah, Mahmudi, Na'imi, and Faraz.

35. Half of this verse appears in Arabic that is not grammatically correct. I have consulted my Arabic-speaking colleagues and followed their suggestion in translation, considering the content of the entire poem.

36. A very common metaphor used in Persian literature. Using the candlelight and the moth or butterfly to express how frantically the butterfly circles around the flame of candle, even though there is a danger of death. It also expresses the agony of one experiencing anticipation or nervousness.

37. This is a reference to Hosayn's head in defeat; it was cut off from his body and traveled with his surviving family members (including Roqayyeh) and friends captured as prisoners of war to Yazid's court in Sham (Syria).

38. Dana'i, *Naghmeh-ha-e Karbala*, 2:125.

39. The tyrant is a reference to Yazid. Here, the king of religion is a reference to Husayn.

40. Karimi, *Asheghan-e Karbala*, 128–130.

41. Ibid., 128–133.

CHAPTER 5

Iconography of the Women of Karbala
Tiles, Murals, Stamps, and Posters

PETER J. CHELKOWSKI

The siege of Karbala and the tragedy of the martyrdom of Imam Hosayn and his companions is considered by Shiʿi Muslims to be the ultimate example of sacrifice and the cornerstone of their faith and culture. Representation of the role of the women of Karbala—the women related to Imam Hosayn and his slaughtered comrades—belongs to one of the most interesting artistic developments in Islam. The dramatic recitation of the heroic stand of the women in *rowzeh khani*[1] evolved into the dramatic action of the *taʿziyeh*[2] performances, which in turn inspired the depiction of these dramas in paintings on canvas and walls. Finally, in recent years, these brave Karbala women have become the subjects of the modern graphic arts. Sadeq Homayuni, one of the greatest authorities on the Karbala rituals, writes:

> Women in Iranian *taʿziyeh* appear in two entirely contrasted countenances: in the good countenance of the protagonists, and in the evil demeanor of the antagonists. In the first category woman is wholesomely good, chaste, pure, innocent, and gentle. She is compassionate and acquainted with pain and suffering. A self-sacrificing devotee, who is ready to endure great hardship for the sake of relatives, friends, and companions, she has no fear of bloody and painful events or the perilous surroundings in which she finds herself. She faces bravely the tempest of calamity and affliction. Her kindness places her at the apex of manifested glory, and her generosity is exemplary.[3]

The antecedent of these sentiments is to be found in the book by Hosayn Vaʾez Kashefi, entitled *The Garden of the Martyrs (Rowzat al-shohada)*.[4] For the last five hundred years, this work has served as a source for the ever growing Karbala rituals and sermons, as well as a rich body of visual and performing arts in Iran and beyond. It has influenced a great number of bards, writers, poets, and performers. A very good example of the influence of *The Garden of Martyrs* on contemporary prose is a book by Dr. Ali Qa'emi entitled *The Role of Women in the Ashura History* (*Naqsh-e Zanan dar Tarikh-e Ashura*).

Qa'emi's work follows in the footsteps of the medieval literary genre known as *maqtalnameh;*[5] it is based not on proven facts, but on the fruits of the author's imagination, which is steeped in myth, legends, and ritual. Qa'emi deftly highlights the remarkable nature of the female relatives and acquaintances of Hosayn. Among the extraordinary group of women at Karbala, Zaynab plays the role of a matriarch. As a daughter of Fatemeh and Imam Ali, a granddaughter of the Prophet Mohammad, and the full sister of Hosayn, she is entitled to that role. It is not only her bloodline, but also her incredible personality, that makes her a leading female protagonist in the Moharram cycle. She is an inexhaustible reserve of physical and psychological strength and energy. Her devotion to her brother Hosayn knows no boundaries. Because Zaynab is Hosayn's beloved sister and not his wife, the affection and love between the siblings is shown in abundance.

There is also a great deal of affection shown between Zaynab and Shahr-banu, the Persian wife of Hosayn. The story of Shahrbanu follows that of Alexander the Great and that of Sasan, the protoplast of the Sasanid dynasty (224–651 CE). Popular legend in Iran holds that Alexander of Macedonia was a Persian king fathered by an Achaemenid ruler. Sasan is believed to have descended in a straight line from the Achaemenid kings (559–330 BC). According to this belief, there was no rupture in the continuity of the Persian royal line from Cyrus the Great until the period of the Arab-Islamic conquest of Iran in 651 CE. This legend survived the conversion of the Iranians to Islam, and, in fact, became even stronger with the adoption of Twelver Shi'ism as the religion of the majority. Iranians place great value on continuity; their appreciation of succession is a reflection of their long history and continuous cultural refinement despite constant foreign invasions. It is commonly believed that Shahrbanu, daughter of the last Sasanid king, Yazdegerd the Third, was taken captive by the Arab conquerors. Eventually, she was given to the family of the Prophet and was married to Hosayn, the grandson of the Prophet. From this union was born the Fourth Imam of the Twelver Shi'is, Ali Ebn-e Hosayn, known as Zayn al-Abedin. In the lineal descent from Sasan to Zayn al-Abedin, the unbroken progression of Iranian heritage can be traced. There is confusion, however, as far as Shahrbanu's children are concerned. In the *ta'ziyeh* repertoire, she is often identified as the mother of all of Hosayn's children. In other cases, Zayn al-Abedin is represented as Shahrbanu's only child and Omm Layla is presented as the mother of Hosayn's other children.

Though Shahrbanu was happy and honored to be the wife of Hosayn, she endured much suffering as a prisoner of war before she became a member of the Prophet's family. This is why Zaynab and the women of Karbala try to help her escape a second captivity under the forces of Yazid. In the *ta'ziyeh* devoted to Shahrbanu, Zaynab expresses her concern for Shahrbanu's well-being in beautiful sentiments filled with compassion and evident fondness.

In accordance with ancient custom in that part of the world, marital affection is not demonstrated in public. That is why in Karbala rituals, and especially in the *ta'ziyeh*, the affection of Hosayn for his wives, and vice versa, is not shown. There are only a few exceptions to this rule. One appears between Hosayn and Shahrbanu. As Shahrbanu is trying to break out of the besieged encampment at Karbala after all but one of the male members of Hosayn's party has been killed, a ghost of the slain Hosayn appears to help her endeavor. Because one of the spouses is dead and there is no possibility of sexual penetration, Hosayn, or rather his ghost, addresses his wife in a very tender, loving way. Another rare instance of demonstrated marital affection on the stage occurs when Qasem, the son of Imam Hasan, leaves Fatemeh—his just-married wife and the daughter of Hosayn—for the battle in which he will die. Because the marriage has not been consummated and he is about to be killed, Qasem and his wife can openly express their love for one another. During this farewell, Fatemeh realizes that her newlywed husband must die and she inquires how she might recognize him at the Day of Judgment. Qasem sings back:

With sorrowful eyes, And sleeves all tattered,
Body ripped open and bones shattered,
With the other martyrs, Abbas and Akbar,
With thirsting lips, still serving your father.[6]

The white burial shroud is then put on his shoulders and he departs for the battlefield. Except for these two scenes and a few others, relationships between men and women at Karbala are delineated only by expressions of respect and admiration. Demonstrations of love and tenderness, which are so important in a dramatic presentation, fall mainly into the hands of Zaynab and Sakineh, the young daughter of Hosayn.

Sakineh is the darling of *ta'ziyeh* and *rowzeh khani* audiences. With her incredulous child's eyes, she sees her friends, cousins, brother, uncle, and, finally, her father, killed one after the other. Her story moves the audience to tears and even rage. In addition to her psychological torment, she suffers a horrible thirst. When Hosayn departs for the battlefield, she throws herself in front of his horse in order to have a few additional moments with her father before he dies. As Hosayn holds her in his lap and lovingly cautions her not to burn her little feet in the hot sand, she begs him not to leave. Despite her young age, Sakineh knows that her pleas are useless and that her father's final battle and death is inevitable.

Qa'emi points out that although the women of Karbala are expected to be exemplars of compassion and kindness, they also assume character traits that are typically more strongly identified with males than females.

There are many attributes, which outwardly one normally expects only to find in men, but in the history of *Ashura*, the same manly qualities are seen in the women. At the same time, these females do not lose their femininity and grace. They never forget the reality of their gender. Zaynab, the daughter of Ali, shared her father's skill in orations and sermons. She learned bravery and eloquence from her father and her brothers Hasan and Hosayn. She learned the maidenly lessons of chastity, purity, and modesty from her mother, who was the daughter of the Prophet. In any case, the blood of the Prophet was flowing in her veins. Zaynab's sister, Kolsum, was of the same mettle. We should not forget that the children of Hasan and Hosayn and the wives of these two Imams were brought up by Zaynab and Kolsum. Their way of life, especially the knowledge of how to confront difficulties and put up with adversity and misfortunes was also dictated by the example of the two sisters. Throughout the Karbala siege, all the women and children listened to Zaynab's commands and followed her counsel.[7]

It can be speculated that Hosayn's death at Karbala was, in part, the result of his decision to take along his household and those of his companions on the journey from Mecca to join his partisans in Kufa. There is no doubt that the presence of women and children slowed down the expedition and its preparation. Their presence also made the caravan much more visible to Hosayn's enemies and their spies. I do not argue that Hosayn would have escaped death had not the women and children been present. The confrontation between Yazid and Hosayn had reached the point where either Hosayn would pay allegiance to Yazid or he would be put to death by Yazid's military might. What I am arguing is that a detachment of armed horsemen could move more swiftly than a household caravan. The speed factor was one thing; the conspicuous aspect of caravan preparation was another. A detachment of horsemen together with the required provisions could be formed easily and could slip out of town without attracting much attention—the caravan could not. There were, no doubt, many spies in Mecca reporting back to Yazid on Hosayn's preparations for a major relocation to Kufa.

Speculation aside, the fact is that Hosayn's women were the eyewitnesses to the horrible massacre at Karbala. In accordance with the *rowzeh khani* and *ta'ziyeh* repertoire, the men did not die together in a swift and overpowering attack by the enemy forces. Their suffering and agony dragged on as each of the seventy-two companions of Hosayn met death and was mourned separately. Hosayn and the women were the helpless observers of this slaughter; as his was the final martyrdom, he watched all the others die before him. Once the men had perished, the women were taken as prisoners and were treated roughly by Yazid's soldiers under the command of the leader of the Syrian troops, Omar ebn-e Sa'd. Finally, the women and their small children underwent tremendous physical and psychological pain as they were forced to accompany the severed heads of their fathers, brothers, husbands, and sons on the way to Yazid in Damascus via Kufa. In turn, these women became part and parcel of the Karbala lore, myth, and rituals, and were elevated to the status of superheroes for their heroic endurance.

Despite this great tribute to the Alid women, they appear physically faceless in *ta'ziyeh* performances. The roles of women in the *ta'ziyeh* have been traditionally performed by men, and in order to disguise their masculinity, veils always cover their faces. Because there has been no obvious characterization of men playing women in a similar manner to Western medieval drama, the protagonist women of the *ta'ziyeh* appear on the stage covered in black from head to toe. Only boys playing the roles of young girls show their faces. As the *ta'ziyeh* gained great popularity in the second quarter of the nineteenth century, a very interesting development took place: the *ta'ziyeh* performance images were transferred by painters from the stage onto canvasses and walls in the form of religious paintings. The women in these paintings were the faithful copies of those on the stage—faceless. This iconographic convention survived until the revolution of 1978–1979. Samuel Peterson writes, "Because of this background, the

religious paintings to appear in nineteenth century Iran which were specifically intended for the public at large represent a phenomenal development
in the history of Islamic arts." He further muses:

> Once it had been publicly accepted, to the general dismay of the
> orthodox, that the roles of the martyrs and their adversaries were
> enacted by devout Muslims, the step toward the public's acceptance
> of paintings depicting the same narratives was not a major one. To
> illustrate that the Qajar genre of Karbala painting was essentially a
> translation of *ta'ziyeh* productions into the visual arts, one need only
> compare the paintings with productions and texts of the dramas.[8]

In order to distance themselves from the characters that they represented, *ta'ziyeh* performers used to hold the texts of their roles in the palms
of their hands, indicating that they were only role carriers and that they did
not assume the personalities of those that they portrayed. This tradition is
almost forgotten today as, thanks to the influence of film and television,
ta'ziyeh performers are more and more likely to embrace the characters
that they represent. The distancing technique is also found in some paintings reflecting the *ta'ziyeh* performances. For example, a *ta'ziyeh* painting

Figure 5.1. A *ta'ziyeh* performance at Hosayniyeh-e Moshir (Shiraz, 1976).
© Peter J. Chelkowski

Figure 5.2. Scene from a *ta'ziyeh* performance at the Takyeh-e Mo'aven al-Molk (Kermanshah, 1999). © Peter J. Chelkowski

on the walls of Emamzadeh-e Shah Zayd in Isfahan identifies each hero in the composition in writing; next to each is the word *shabih*, meaning "likeness."

It is paradoxical that although the veiling of women's heads (including hair) and bodies became compulsory during the Islamic Revolution—and in the Islamic Republic that was established in its wake—the faces of women representing the holy personalities of the Shi'i pantheon have since been depicted with the face veil lifted.

This photograph of a *ta'ziyeh* performance at Hosayniyyeh-e Moshir in Shiraz in 1976 (Figure 5.1) shows three male performers acting as women on a round, central stage. They are totally engulfed from head to toe in black robes, which cover their faces as well. In the pediment that is visible over the audience, the Battle of Karbala is depicted in colorful tiles. It is a perfect example of *ta'ziyeh* tradition because the audience can view the events of Karbala both through the performance on the stage and through the scene portrayed in the tile painting. The women in the painting also appear completely covered.

Pictured here (Figure 5.2) is a scene from the *ta'ziyeh* performance at the Takyeh-e Mo'aven al-Molk in Kermanshah in 1999, on the occasion of the hundredth anniversary of the establishment of this edifice. It provides an intriguing contrast between the performer in a female role—all but his

Figure 5.3. A *ta'ziyeh* performance at the Hosayniyeh-e Moshir
(Shiraz, 1976). © Peter J. Chelkowski

eyes are visible—with the faces of the hundreds of women spectators clad
in chadors in the background.

A *ta'ziyeh* performance of *The Martyrdom of Ali Akbar* at the Hosayniyyeh-e Moshir in Shiraz in 1976 is shown here (Figure 5.3). On the central
stage we see Hosayn, Qasem, and Ali Akbar, as well as the mother of Ali
Akbar, who is played by a male performer totally clad in black robes.

The painting of Ashura, by Mohammad Modabber (Figure 5.4), is a representative example of the *ta'ziyeh* performance cycle and the costumes in
which the performers appear. Women are faceless and in black. The only
difference between the actual performance and the painting is the presence
of haloes of light that appear over the heads of Hosayn and two women—
presumably Zaynab and Kolsum—on the canvas. In the lower left corner,
the wounded horse of Hosayn is shown and behind the tent is the battlefield
strewn with the bodies of the hero's seventy-two martyred companions.

The simple yet convincing painting of the captivity of Hosayn's women
as they carry the severed heads of their male relatives to Damascus (Figure 5.5) appears on the exterior of the Agha Mohammad Boq'eh, or way-
side shrine, in Pincheh Astaneh in the northern province of Gilan. Once
again, the *ta'ziyeh* is transferred from the stage to a wall painting. *Boq'ehs*
in Gilan are usually painted on their outer walls with scenes from the Karbala tragedy. The women are garbed in black with their faces hidden as
usual.

A tile painting of the Battle of Ali Akbar on the walls of the Takyeh-e

Mo'aven al-Molk in Kermanshah (Figure 5.6) is yet another example of the *ta'ziyeh* technique of concealing the masculinity of an actor in a female role. Young Ali Akbar is gallantly fighting an entire detachment of enemy forces while his veiled mother observes his struggle at a distance from the entrance to her tent.

The Islamic Republican Party (Hezb-e Jomhuri-e Eslami) issued a poster (Figure 5.7) on the occasion of the anniversary of Zaynab's death. The text in the lower right corner reads: "O Zaynab, the tongue of Ali in pursuit," referring to the great oratorical skills that Zaynab inherited from her father, Ali. Dr. Qa'emi notes that

> there was no other more eloquent woman than Zaynab; when she spoke, men held their breath. One person who heard her speak said, "I swear to God that I have never heard a woman with such lucid, clear, and accurate language and such logical rhetoric in my life . . . the fiery tongue of Ali could be heard in her speech."[9]

Two crowds of women appear in this poster. The first group is composed of women in white chadors (symbolically representing shrouds and readiness for martyrdom) who ride camels while holding in their arms the severed heads of their martyred male relatives. The camels are chained together to

Figure 5.4. A painting of Ashura. © Peter J. Chelkowski

Figure 5.5. Painting depicting the captivity of Hosayn's female
relatives (Gilan). © Peter J. Chelkowski

symbolize captivity. In the second group is a multitude of women wearing black chadors with clenched fists stretching away to the horizon. The
women wearing white chadors represent the courageous captive women of
Karbala being taken from the battlefield to Damascus. According to tradition, the resolute stand of these women transformed their captivity into a
defeat for Yazid and a victory for Zaynab and her companions. The black-
chadored women represent contemporary Iranian females supporting the
war efforts against Iraqi aggression. A large silhouetted woman in a white
chador looms out of the crowd of contemporary women and smashes the

Ommayyad/Pahlavi crown with her fist. According to Shi'i tradition, the Karbala tragedy transcends the confines of time and space; as one proverb says: "Every day is Ashura and every place is Karbala." The woman in the white chador links the past and present with her timeless expression of defiance in the face of tyranny and injustice.

The graphic artist Mostafa Gudarzi simplified this message in his poster (Figure 5.8) entitled *The Heirs of Zaynab* (*Varesan-e Zaynab*), by portraying a black chador–clad woman carrying a gun. She appears in front of a tiled wall that serves as a mirror in which a crowd of black chador–clad women is reflected. Her face displays grim determination. Under Islamic law, women are not expected to be active military combatants. However, during the war with Iraq they played an extraordinary role in daily activities and appeared in graphic arts representations bearing arms. The participation of women in street rallies and marches, while organized, was genuinely spontaneous. Many Iranian women identified with Zaynab: although they were bereft and heartbroken, like Zaynab, they did not lose their combative spirit. Dr. Qa'emi explains,

> On the Ashura Day, one could see many women who went to the battlefield and nobody could prevent this. For example, Abdullah Kalbi tried as best he could to keep his wife from entering the battle-

Figure 5.6. A tile painting of the Battle of Ali Akbar (Kermanshah). © Peter J. Chelkowski

Figure 5.7. Poster commemorating Zaynab's death. © Peter J. Chelkowski

ground, but to no avail. She kept saying, "I must go with you and die together with you." Only when the Imam ordered her to return to the tents, did she reluctantly leave her husband.[10]

During the war with Iraq, the birthday of Zaynab was observed as "Nurses' Day," and posters and postage stamps were issued for that occasion. One such stamp (Figure 5.9) shows a white-clad nurse caring for a wounded young soldier. To many, she is not just a nurse discharging her duties on the celebration of Zaynab's birthday; she is Zaynab herself. This identification of the historical Zaynab with the graphic images of women produced on the anniversaries of her birth and death is not an isolated or occasional occurrence. On my trip to Iran for a *taʿziyeh* conference in the year 2000, any Iranian woman to whom I showed a graphic depiction of a heroic female immediately identified the unnamed woman as Zaynab or Fatemeh Zahra.

In the poster (Figure 5.10) entitled *Guards of the Realm of Light*, by Kazem Chalipa, a couple standing under the protective gaze of a picture of

Figure 5.8. Poster entitled *The Heirs of Zaynab (Varesan-e Zaynab)*.
© Peter J. Chelkowski

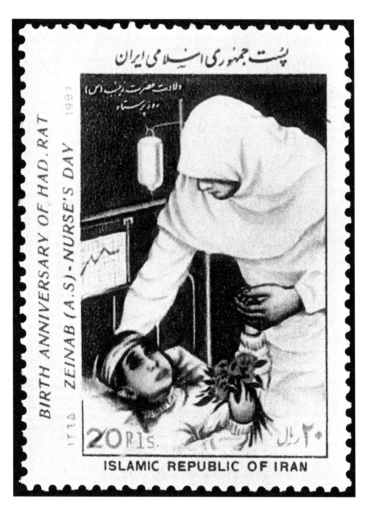

Figure 5.9. Postage stamp commemorating Zaynab's birthday.
© Peter J. Chelkowski

the revolutionary leader encourages their child to take part in the revolution. A woman clad in proper Islamic attire steers her son, carrying a grenade in one hand and a Molotov cocktail in the other, toward the enemy. Dr. Qa'emi explains, "These women with their own hands sent to the battlefield their sons, husbands, and brothers. . . ."[11] Qa'emi's work and Chalipa's image both recall Zaynab, who sent her two young sons into the battle at Karbala to be martyred. In the *ta'ziyeh,* when Zaynab offers her children as a sacrifice, Hosayn is horrified and asks how she can bear to give up her sons. She explains,

As long as you remain, I have no need of sons. Except for you, I require no light for my sight. These two children of mine who will precede you into the fight, are both your slaves, by God. I, whose eyes weep tears for your sake, am your handmaiden if you accept my service.

Deeply moved, Hosayn gathers her to himself, saying, "You are not my handmaiden; you are my precious one. You are my honored and grieved sister. Don't weep further; don't be sad. Your children have permission to go to battle."[12]

Figure 5.10. Poster entitled *Guards of the Realm of Light.* © Peter J. Chelkowski

This poster also recalls the sacrifice of the mother of young Qasem, who sent her just-married son to the killing fields before he was even able to consummate his marriage to his new bride.

Fatemeh, the daughter of the Prophet Mohammad and his first wife Khadijeh, is known as Zahra ("shining serene"). In the eyes of Shiʿis, she is the "embodiment of all that is divine in womanhood—the noblest ideal of human conception."[13] Her marriage to Ali produced Hasan and Hosayn, as well as Zaynab and Omm Kolsum. Although Fatemeh died some forty-seven years before the tragedy of Karbala, she belongs indirectly to the Karbala cycle. One of the ten chapters of *The Garden of the Martyrs* is devoted to her. There are several *taʿziyeh* plays that take her life and death as their subject. She is known to the average Iranian through *rowzeh khani*, *taʿziyeh*, and other popular rituals. Her ghost appears in several *taʿziyehs*, but especially in the *taʿziyeh* entitled *The Martyrdom of Hosayn:*

Fatima: May I be offered for thy wounded defaced body! Tell me, what dost thou wish thy mother to do now for thee?
Husayn: I am now, dear mother, at the point of death. The ark of life is going to be cast on shore, mother. It is time that my soul should leave my body. Come close my eyes with thy kind hand.
Fatima: O Lord, how difficult for a mother to see her dear child dying! I am Zahra who am making this sad noise, because I have to close the eyes of my son Husayn, who is on the point of death. Oh, tell me if thou hast any desire long cherished in thy heart, for I am distressed in mind owing to thy sad sighs![14]

In the same spirit, her ghost appears in the poster by Hamid Qaderiyan (Figure 5.11) representing a group of mourning Iranian women at the cemetery which bears her name, "Zahra's Paradise" (Behesht-e Zahra). She is shown as a shimmering white image that brings consolation to the grieving women at the grave of a martyred hero of the Iraqi War. More often, however, she is depicted as a combative woman leading other women, as in the poster by Mohammad Khaza'i (Figure 5.12), in which she hovers over a crowd of black-chadored women, inspiring and energizing them. In her red chador, with her hand lifted high in a mingled gesture of exhortation and direction, she urges the others forward. One of the flags flying in the background bears the words, "O Zahra!" and a rifle barrel is seen over her shoulder to highlight the revolutionary aspect of her presence. A marching woman carries a portrait of Ayatollah Khomeini in which he, too, raises his hand to incite his followers. Another woman carries a written quotation

Figure 5.11. Poster by Hamid Qaderiyan depicting the ghost of Zahra.
© Peter J. Chelkowski

of Khomeini's that could be directly applied to Zahra: "A man ascends to heaven from woman's lap."

In the transmission of the Karbala events from one generation to the next, new methods have been developed to consistently move and inspire Iranian audiences by reminding them of Hosayn's timeless sacrifice. Thus, from the oral recitations of the *rowzeh khanis* to the mass-produced imagery of contemporary graphic arts, runs a thread of relevance which not only links one art form to the next, but also unites spectators past and present. The emotional and historical bonds forged by these dramatic presentations—whether staged, painted, printed, or recited—of the Karbala tragedy have had lasting implications for the faith, culture, and politics of the Iranians. The human representation of the most holy personalities in Shi'i history has impacted deeply the way Iranians view themselves and their society. Nowhere is this more apparent than in the iconography of women in the arts. Although traditionally women have been largely faceless and voiceless in Iranian society, the women of the *rowzeh khani* and the *ta'ziyeh* are presented as valiant heroines whose qualities of compassion and courage are held up as exemplars for all persons—male and female—to emulate. Certain characters are identified so strongly with specific virtues that they continue to be role models for modern Iranians. Therefore, a nurse is not

Figure 5.12. Poster by Mohammad Khaza'i depicting Fatemeh Zahra.
© Peter J. Chelkowski

a nurse, but Zaynab, and an anonymous woman inciting others to courage and resistance is not unknown, but is Zahra. The resilience, devotion, and aspirations of the women of Karbala are now reflected in the women of contemporary Iran. Through various artistic and dramatic media, the ideals of one generation have crossed the ages to become the ideals of every generation.

Notes

1. The *rowzeh khani* is the Shiʿi Iranian mourning ritual commemorating the suffering and martyrdom of Imam Hosayn. The name of this public lamentation is derived from the title of M. H. Vaʾez Kashefi's literary masterpiece, *Rowzat al-shohada* (*The Garden of the Martyrs*) (Tehran: Chapkhaneh-e Khavar, 1962). *Rowzeh khani* literally means "recitation from *The Garden [of the Martyrs]*," and is popularly called just "*rowzeh.*" The art of *rowzeh khani* depends on the ability of the *rowzeh khan* to manipulate the assembled crowd, using his (or her, if the gathering is entirely female) choice of episodes of the Karbala tragedy to bring the audience to a state of frenzy in which they identify with the suffering of Hosayn and the other martyrs. See Peter J. Chelkowski, "Rawda-Khwani," in *The Encyclopedia of Islam*, ed. E. van Donzel, C. E. Bosworth, W. P. Heinrichs, and G. Lecomte, vol. 8 (Leiden: E. J. Brill, 1993).

2. The Shiʿi passion play called *taʿziyeh* is the only serious drama ever developed in the Islamic world, with the exception of contemporary Western theatre productions. See Peter J. Chelkowski, ed., *Taʿziyeh: Ritual and Drama in Iran* (New York: New York University Press, 1979b). For a brief account of *taʿziyeh*, see Peter J. Chelkowski, "Taʿziyeh," in *The Oxford Encyclopedia of the Modern Islamic World*, ed. John L. Esposito et al., 4:200–202 (New York: Oxford University Press, 1995).

3. Sadeq Homayuni, "Zan dar Taʿziyeh-ha-e Irani," *Faslnameh-e Honar* 40 (1999), 46.

4. Vaʾez Kashefi was born in the first half of the ninth century AH in the town of Sabzavar and died in 910 AH in Heart. Seyyed Mirza, the son-in-law of Soltan Hosayn Bayqara, commissioned Kashefi to write a *maqtalnameh* about Imam Hosayn's passion and death at Karbala. Kashefi completed the task in 908 AH (1502–1503 CE) and entitled the book *Rowzat al-shohada* (*The Garden of Martyrs*). The composition of the book coincided with the ascension of the Safavid shahs to the Persian throne in 907 AH (1501 CE) and their establishment of Twelver Shiʿism as the state religion. Since Iran at the time was primarily Sunni in orientation, *Rowzat al-shohada* became a very important tool in the Shiʿi propagation of faith. *The Garden of Martyrs* bears the Arabic title, but is written in flowing Persian.

5. *Maqtalnameh:* a literary genre that has flourished in the Muslim world for the last thirteen centuries; first in Arabic, then Persian, and finally in Turkish and Urdu.

6. Chelkowski, *Taʿziyeh*, 17.

7. Ali Qaʾemi, *Naqsh-e Zanan dar Tarikh-e Ashura* (Qom, Iran: n.p., n.d.), 19.

8. Samuel R. Peterson, "Shiʿism and Late Iranian Arts" (PhD diss., New York University, 1981), 64–65.

9. Qaʾemi, *Naqsh-e Zanan*, 93.

10. Ibid., 62.

11. Ibid.

12. Rebecca Ansary Pettys, "The Taʿziyeh Ritual of Renewal in Persia" (PhD diss., Indiana University, 1982), 296.

13. Fatemeh, the daughter of the Prophet Mohammad, born at Mecca probably about the year 605 CE, who married Ali after the Battle of Badr (or in some ac-

counts after the Battle of Ohod). She died in 633 CE. See H. Lammens, "Fatima," in *Concise Encyclopedia of Islam*, ed. H. A. R. Gibb and J. H. Kramers, 101–102 (Boston: Brill, 2001).

14. Colonel Sir Lewis Pelly, *The Miracle Play of Hasan and Husain, Collected from Oral Tradition* (London: The India Office, 1879), 2:102.

PART 2

THE ARAB WORLD, SOUTH ASIA, AND THE UNITED STATES OF AMERICA

CHAPTER 6

Sakineh, The Narrator of Karbala
An Ethnographic Description of a
Women's Majles *Ritual in Pakistan*

SHEMEEM BURNEY ABBAS

This chapter consists of an ethnographic account of a women's *majles* (plural *majales*) in Pakistan. The *majles* will be explored here as a communicative speech event where members of a speech community congregate and participate in an event based on common beliefs, values, and attitudes.[1] The *majles* will be investigated as an event where speakers and listeners share the knowledge of rules for the conduct and interpretation of speech.[2] The purpose of this essay is to provide a sociolinguistic mapping of the women *nowheh*-chanters' discourse in the Pakistani languages using Hymes' model of the ethnography of speaking and how ritual speaking is done in a cultural system.[3] Communicative conduct within a community comprises determinate patterns of speech activity wherein the communicative competence of persons constitutes knowledge with regard to such patterns. I will discuss ways of speaking especially in regard to the Sakineh narratives, focusing on the relationships among speech events, acts, and styles, on the one hand, and personal abilities and rules, contexts and institutions, and beliefs, values, and attitudes, on the other.[4] This is demonstrated through transliteration, translation, and linguistic representation of the order of a women's *majles*. The transliterations represent the social interactional processes of the *majles* and the competence of the female *nowheh khans* (chanters). Because of the transliteration methodology, an analytical discussion of the political aspects of these rituals is not given, though these dimensions are manifest in the *nowheh* texts themselves and the highly politicized opposition that the poetic discourse generates based on the shared rules of performance among the speakers and the listeners. The transliterations are intended to provide the reader with a clearer under-

Figure 6.1. Girl dressed as Sakineh, holding Hazrat Abbas' *alam*, or standard. Abbas is considered the protector of children (Rawalpindi, 2000). © Shemeem Burney Abbas

standing of the basic structure and style of a women's *majles*, which is fairly representative of the rituals analyzed in the other chapters.

This account demonstrates how Sakineh serves as the narrator of Karbala in the *nowhehs*, or mourning songs and chants, at these Shiʿi *majales*, which are held during the annual Moharram celebrations in Pakistan. The Sakineh myth is concerned with the structural properties of the Karbala story and how it is narrated in the *majales*.[5] I focus on the dynamic structure of the Sakineh texts by analyzing the stories in relationship to the contexts in which they are performed, in terms of the potential for openness of interpretation and in terms of the ways in which this potential is exploited during Moharram performance and the emotions generated therein.[6] Sakineh is Imam Hosayn's daughter; she survived the tragedy of Karbala along with her paternal aunt, Sayyedeh Zaynab. Sakineh's age is not known with any real certainty, but she was a girl-child whose age was probably between five and twelve years. Many of her discourses in the oral tradition are addressed to her sister Soghra, who, according to some *hadith*, was left behind in Medina due to illness. Thus, while Sakineh is the speaker in the stories, Soghra is sometimes the listener to whom the stories are addressed. The *nowheh*, a song of lament, can be sung as a dyadic unit in which two parties take turns in advancing the story, or it can be chanted as a monologue. Both women and men have participated in the tradition of chanting *nowhehs*. In a two- to three-hour *majles*, at least an hour is allocated to reciting *nowhehs*. Thus, in the chanting of the Sakineh *nowhehs*, there is a long tradition of mutually understood speech between speaker, hearer, and that which is spoken about, including the political dimensions of the discourse. The mutually shared speech is elaborated in communication theory, linguistics, semiotics, literary criticism, and sociology in various ways.[7]

The *nowhehs* that are transliterated and translated here, along with the photos provided, were collected during fieldwork in Pakistan during Moharram in 2000. Sakineh embodies grief and evokes a sense of tragic empathy in the assembly of mourners when the *nowhehs* are chanted in this girl-child's voice. This is a special emotional feature of a Shi'i *majles*, according to Hymes' model. Sakineh as a survivor of Karbala tells many stories in the aftermath of her father's death. Girl-children are trained to reenact the stories of Sakineh at Shi'i *majales* in Pakistan during ritual Moharram celebrations.[8] These rituals are characterized by the ritualized speech form of *nowhehs*, which involve linguistic play based on code-switching.[9] Furthermore, the *nowhehs* have strongly embedded political references: the binaries of a high moral and ethical order versus expediency and moral corruption that led to the Battle of Karbala. Between speakers and listeners in the shared codes of communicative competence the references are mutually shared and interpreted.

The first ten days of Moharram constitute a period of ritual mourning among Shi'is in Pakistan. *Majales* are held to lament the martyrdom of Hazrat Imam Hosayn in the battle of Karbala in 680 AD. During the Moharram celebrations, *majales* are either held in public Shi'i *emambarehs*, which are supported through community funds, or in the private *emam-*

Figure 6.2. The *zakereh* opens the *majles* with rhetorical discourse in prose (Rawalpindi, 2000). © Shemeem Burney Abbas

barehs that the well-to-do have in their homes in the cities and in rural areas. An *emambareh* is a public or private space in a Shi'i community for performing sacred rituals such as prayers, *majales*, and birth and death rites. The wealthy *sayyeds*, who are descendants of the prophet Mohammed and typically owners of large landholdings, have private *emambarehs* in which rituals are enacted in an elaborate manner.[10] Generally, the pattern of the ten-day celebrations in the Moharram *majales* is as follows:

First to fifth of Moharram: reenactment of events on a day-to-day basis according to the Karbala tragedy, accompanied with ritual lamentations and self-flagellation (*matam*).

Sixth of Moharram: narratives about Karbala and enhanced *matam*.

Seventh of Moharram: new rituals are introduced, such as carrying a replica of Ali Asghar's cradle, Qasem's henna ceremony, and Sakineh's *nowhehs*.[11]

Eighth of Moharram: Hazrat Abbas' *alam*, or standard, raised with the *panjatan*.[12]

Ninth of Moharram: general intense mourning with narratives from Karbala.

Tenth of Moharram: Ashura—the day of Imam Hosayn's martyrdom. Pakistani Shiʿis fast on this day, breaking the fast in the late afternoon after noontime prayers. The final activity is the Sham-e Ghariban ritual, which commemorates the act of trying to find the corpses of the fallen martyrs.[13]

After Ashura and Sham-e Ghariban rituals, the following are observed:

Sevvom: *Majales* are held on the third day after Ashura and Sham-e Ghariban. These *majales* celebrate the martyrdom of Hazrat Imam Hosayn, his family, and his companions.

Chehelom: *Majales* are held for the same reason on the fortieth day after Ashura.[14]

In between the Sevvom and the Chehelom, *majales* are held in the *emambarehs* according to the schedule of the caretakers. However, there is no set pattern. The period of mourning during Moharram is called *azadari*.[15] The mourners are *azadars*. During this period a part of the home in a Shiʿi household may be temporarily converted into mourning space for the purpose of *azadari*. The mourning area is called an *azakhaneh*.

The women's *majales* rituals this researcher observed at *emambarehs* in Rawalpindi, Wah, and Lahore inform this ethnographic account of speaking as a cultural system. However, the rituals documented here are based on a ritual observed on the seventh of Moharram, 2000, in the Baji Sabira ka *emambareh* in Chowk Marir Hasan in Rawalpindi, which is popularly referred to as the *zaynabiyyeh*.[16] This *emambareh* is named after its owner,

Figure 6.3. Ali Asghar's cradle and Moharram emblems in the *emambareh* at the *zaynabiyyeh*. Rituals are performed around emblems on the seventh and eighth of Moharram (Rawalpindi, 2000). © Shemeem Burney Abbas

Ms. Sabira Zaidi, who is an émigré from North India and who speaks chaste Urdu.[17] The *majales* in this *emambareh* follow the elaborate pattern of Lucknow *majales*.[18]

The *zaynabiyyeh* was a 50 × 50 foot square structure built at the far end of Ms. Sabira Zaidi's home. The *emambareh*, compared with the rest of the house, was a newer structure and was carefully crafted after the design of Iranian mosques with arched windows and a handcrafted wooden door with intricate floral filigree carved on it. Inside the *emambareh* was a large crystal chandelier, perhaps of Turkish or Iranian origin. Outside the *emambareh* was a large courtyard lined with black marble for women *azadars* (i.e., the mourners or ritual participants) to sit when there were more attending, especially on the seventh, eighth, and ninth of Moharram. The courtyard was covered with *catais* (rush mats) or *duris* (thick cotton mats) during the *majales* for the *azadars* to sit on. Across the courtyard was a verandah where there were two bathrooms and a row of faucets for women *azadars* to perform ablution. The *nazr-niyaz* (ritual food offering for the sake of the *emam*), which were distributed after the *majales* and which were typically contributed by the *azadars*, were set up in the verandah.

Ms. Sabira Zaidi, who had been recently widowed, looked after the upkeep of the *emambareh* herself. Ms. Zaidi and her daughters worked to keep the *emambareh* clean for the *azadars*. Ms. Zaidi called herself the *kaniz*, or the handmaiden of the *emambareh*. This was evident in the well-maintained environment of the *emambareh*, as well as the owner's hospitality toward the *azadars* who had come for the *majales*. Inside the vast space of the *emambareh* there were large white sheets for the *azadars* that covered the carpeting on the floor. The white sheets radiated expansiveness in the space in addition to making the female mourners feel they were welcome in the *majles*. During Moharram, the white sheets were replaced every day.

Women *azadars* who participated in the ritual *majales* were mainly Shi'i. However, there were also Sunni participants, called *molais*, there because they sympathized with Imam Hosayn's cause. Participants at the *majles* consisted mostly of working-class women such as laborers, maids, factory workers, or housewives from low- or middle-income groups. Among the mourners were also some professionals such as doctors, professors, and bank executives. Since the *emambareh* was in the army quarters and was centrally located, wives of Shi'i army officers were also well represented. Ms. Sabira Zaidi's *emambareh* has assumed a high stature due to the sophistication of the *majales* format and its diverse participants.

In this chapter I apply Hymes' mnemonic speaking model to the women's *majles* proceedings as recorded at the Rawalpindi *emambareh*.[19]

Figure 6.4. Girls training at chanting *nowhehs* for Sakineh (Rawalpindi, 2000).
© Shemeem Burney Abbas

The sociolinguistic, social interactional model involves the following components:

Setting: *emambareh*; public or private; morning, afternoon, or evening.

Participants: *zakereh* (narrator of key sermon), *nowheh-khans* (chanters), hostess, spokeswomen, female audience.

Ends: lamentation, communication, messaging, demonstration, protest.

Act sequence: story, narratives, responses-ratification, interpretation.

Key: mournfully, grieving, passionately, seriously.

Instrumentalities: rhetorical Arabic, Persian, Urdu; chanted Panjabi and Urdu *nowhehs*.

Norm of interaction: rhetorical discourse and response; poetic discourse and response.

Genre: *majles*.

The women's *majles* reported here was a mutually achieved, mutually ratified speech event between speakers and listeners, performers and audiences. Various speakers took the floor according to a pattern of turn taking. The forms of speech—rhetorical, lament and *nowheh* chanting, *darud* (prayer for the dead), *salam* (blessings), and *salavat*—were adjacent to each other and within the smaller units of talk, where speakers used the pattern of the adjacency pair as demonstrated in Erving Goffman's work on speech.[20] Briefly, Goffman posits that speech constitutes small units of talk; that talk is socially organized, not merely in terms of who speaks to whom in what language, but as a little system of mutually ratified and ritually governed face-to-face action, a social encounter. Accordingly, the performers of this *majles* who enacted the lamentation rituals participated on various levels, the highest being the *zakereh,* who initiated the *majles* proceedings with a well-researched rhetorical discourse about the moral, political, and ethical issues that led Hazrat Imam Hosayn to oppose Yazid.

The *zakereh* initiated her speech with a verse in Arabic from the Qur'an, followed by the *hadith*, which are the sayings of the Prophet Mohammad or his family. The *zakereh* was a trained rhetorician and had been inducted into the discourse traditions from childhood. She patterned her moral and political arguments after Sayyedeh Zaynab, who led Hosayn's family after the Battle of Karbala. Sayyedeh Zaynab is said to have been a highly effective orator in Yazid's court, where she articulated the ethical, moral, and politi-

Figure 6.5. These women are performing *nowhehs*—chants at Qasem's henna ritual on the seventh of Moharram. Women in the background are holding trays of fruits and sweets (Rawalpindi, 2000). © Shemeem Burney Abbas

cal polarities that led to the conflict in Karbala. Thus, the *zakereh* at a Shi'i *majles* often reenacts Zaynab's oratory, reaffirming Levi-Strauss' approach to analyzing myths across societies and his assertion that such myths or stories have an identifiable underlying or abstract structure.[21] The *zakereh*'s speech invariably referred to the girl-child Sakineh and her infant brother, Ali Asghar, who was martyred in Karbala.[22] The discourse of the entire

Figure 6.6. The hostess of the *zaynabiyyeh* leading the *matam* ritual in the center while *nowhehs* are being chanted (Rawalpindi, 2000). © Shemeem Burney Abbas

majles, both the prose of the speakers and the poetry of the *nowheh* chanters, was loaded with political metaphors; the outcome of Hosayn's moral stance was the martyrdom at Karbala. The transliterations demonstrate the political tensions of the conflict: Hosayn's rejection of accepting Yazid's caliphate on moral grounds leading to his own death and the death of his supporters, who were male family members and loyal companions. Here one may also draw on Levi-Strauss' symbols of life and death, young and old, and men and women.[23] Each *nowheh* narrative was immersed in political protest articulated through the subtle chanting of the *nowheh-khans.* The participants were assumed to know the underlying nuances of the discourse, the deeply rooted metaphors that a *nowheh* pointed toward, such as a male member like Qasem or Ali Asghar. The participants had grown and matured in the oral Shi'i traditions; they understood the signification. Thus, while chanting with the *nowheh-khans* or chanters, the participants were able to infuse an emotion into the assembly that resulted in intense lamentation, expressed through chest beating, or *matam.* The *matam* is a form of political protest.

During the *majles* proceedings at the *zaynabiyyeh,* the *zakereh*'s speech was prompted by the hostess, Ms. Sabira Zaidi, who sat close to the *menbar,* or pulpit, at the feet of the *zakereh.* The hostess continuously ratified the *zakereh*'s speech. Sometimes she ratified it with the *salavat,* or blessings upon the Prophet Mohammad and his family, in Arabic; sometimes she ratified the speaker's discourse with continued lament through her own weeping and utterances like *"hai, hai."* This was particularly so during emotionally expressive outbursts devoted to Sakineh and the theme of Ali Asghar's thirst at Karbala. Again, one may draw upon Levi-Strauss: historical events or fables are transformed through abstract structures. The performers and participants themselves "posit underlying structures or meanings in the

Figure 6.7. Children reenacting performances related to Sakineh (Rawalpindi, 2000).
© Shemeem Burney Abbas

form of interpretations of the symbolism of the text and its message and—the most important point—they do so as part of its very performance, for an audience to hear, learn from and criticize." Lamentation was communicated at many levels in the *majles*.[24]

In addition to the *zakereh* and the weeping hostess, the key performers of this *majles* were the *nowheh-khans*, whose communicative competence was demonstrated in their ability to chant the *nowheh* with an emotion that brought their listeners to tears. The chanters accomplished this through ritual speech, drama, and vibrant body language, beating their chests in rhythm as they chanted the poetry of the *nowheh*. The chest beating had percussion qualities that brought out the emotion in the assembly; these elements, put together as text and context, created the *majles*. The assembled listeners, too, performed their function by ratifying every utterance, every move; they were the ones who understood the ritual-ceremonial discourse of Karbala and who understood the linguistic variety involved.[25]

The women's *majles* ritual at Ms. Sabira Zaidi's *emambareh* lasted for more than two hours. The speech event constituted the speakers, listeners and participants, and rhetorical and poetic narratives about Karbala. The speech event was a mutually ratified, social interactional context that used text and narratives and the relationships of the linguistic and emotional components. Its basic linguistic and communicative structure was as follows:

Salavat. Opening of the *majles* with recital of the *darud* by Ms. Sabira Zaidi, the hostess of the *majles:* "Allah homma salli ala Mohammad va al-e Mohammad." (O God, may thy blessings be on Mohammad and his family). The participants repeated the *salavat* after the hostess.

Zakereh. Rhetorical prose *majles* discourse or sermon, which lasted for thirty-five to forty minutes. It started with an Arabic quote from the Qur'an. The *zakereh*'s speech was patterned on philosophical discourses related to religious, ethical, social, and political issues.

Salavat. "Allah homma Salli ala Mohammad va al-e Mohammad."

Darud. "O God may thy blessings be on Mohammad and his family." The *darud*, which was frequently repeated at key points in the discourse, was led by the hostess throughout the *zakereh*'s speech.

Nowhehs. Panjabi or Urdu chants about Karbala, often in Sakineh's voice.[26]

Matam. Passionate chest beating for lament, accompanied by *nowhehs*.[27]

Salam. Prayers and eulogy in Arabic, Persian, Urdu, and Panjabi for the Prophet Mohammad, his family, and the martyrs of Karbala. There was always a reference to Sakineh.

Ziyarat. Invocation and closure in Arabic, Persian, Urdu, and Panjabi for the Prophet Mohammad, his family, and the martyrs of Karbala, again with a reference to Sakineh.

On this particular occasion, which was the seventh of Moharram, 2000, Baji Sabira Zaidi had chosen to dedicate the *majles* to Qasem, Imam Hasan's adolescent son who was about to be married. Thus, on 7 Moharram, the groom's (i.e., Qasem's) henna ceremony was celebrated. The ritual was a celebration as well as a lament for Qasem. After the *zakereh* completed her rhetorical speech and the recitation of the *salvat* and *darud* that the hostess initiated and that the participants repeated after her, the *nowheh-khans* moved to the center of the *emambareh*, creating a little circle for themselves with the hostess among them. The assembly of participating mourners stood around the group of chanters, ready to join the ritual chanting and the *matam*. The *nowheh-khans* chanted the key lines and the assembly repeated the lines after them, establishing the communicative mode. The following Panjabi *nowhehs*, which have been transcribed and translated, demonstrate the communicative competence of the *nowheh-khans*, who are inducted into these oral linguistic traditions from childhood. Girl-children chanters took the floor immediately after the women *nowheh-khans* as a part of their training. The group of women who chanted these *nowhehs* spoke in the voice of a scribe, probably Sakineh, who writes a letter from Karbala to her sister Soghra in Medina:[28]

1	*Karbal tun peya likhda*	from Karbala the scribe writes
2	*hun vaqt reha koi nahin*	now time left none there is
3	*men keya, men likhan*	I what, what can I write?
4	*mere Awn-o Mohammad te*	my Awn and Mohammad[29]
5	*Asghar te javan jeha koi nahin*	and Asghar's youth none matches
6	*men keya, men likhan*	I what, what can I write?
7	*Karbal tun peya likhda*	from Karbala the scribe writes
8	*mor vaqt reha koi nahin*	return, time will not

(Next, lines 6–8 are repeated; followed by lines 3–5; followed by lines 6, 8, and 6)

The *nowheh*-chanters continued to beat their chests to create rhythm with the poetic text:

9	*Qasem da je nahin likhiya*	Qasem's news none is written
(Repeat line 9)		
10	*hun banara bana betha*	now has adorned himself the groom
11	*khod sehre saja betha*	himself a crown of flowers has festooned
12	*khod sagan manan betha*	himself celebrated his own ritual
(Repeat lines 11–12)		
13	*mere hun hathan te*	mine now on the hands
14	*hun rang reha koi nahin*	now henna there is none
(Repeat lines 6–8)		
15	*hun ki men likhan*	now what I can write?

The *nowheh*-chanters continued to sing the elegy, in Sakineh's voice in Panjabi, thereby symbolically becoming Sakineh themselves. The audiences ratified the chanting by repeating the *nowheh* text, line by line after the chanters. The girl-children in the assembly chanted significantly as they beat their chests in harmony with the women, taking the floor independently as performers during a part of the chanting. They sang in Panjabi, leading the performance:

16	*jag nagar gai ujri*[30]	in the world destroyed
17	*hun kiyun dukh khani*[31] *tun*	now why grief you swallow?
(Repeat lines 16–17)		
18	*ommat ne hai aj lutiya*[32]	the followers have today looted
19	*Akbar di javani nun*	Akbar's youth[33]
(Repeat lines 18–19)		
20	*phupian te mavan vala*	paternal aunts and mothers him to claim
21	*churche de siva koi nahin*	publicity only there is and nothing else remains[34]
22	*men kiya men likhan*	I what, what can I write?
(Repeat lines 20–22)		
23	*meri behnan de hatan hun*	on my sisters' hand now
24	*rang koi reha nahin*	henna none remains
25	*hun ki men likhan*	now what can I write?
26	*Karabal tun peya likhda*	from Karbala the scribe writes
27	*hun vaqt reha koi nahin*	now time left none there is
28	*hun ki men likhan*	now what can I write?

The chanters at the *zaynabiyyeh* sang another *nowheh* in Panjabi using Sakineh's voice:

29   *manzur kiyun na hoiyan*   Why were they not accepted?
30   *ujri*[35] *di an do'avan*   My prayers, I the shattered one
(Repeat lines 29–30)
31   *kuch bol munh hon Akbar*   Move thy lips and say something
                                             O Akbar!
32   *Soghra nun ja bulavan*   Shall I go and call Soghra?
(Repeat lines 29–30)
33   *Sarvar de dil di halat*   The state of Hosayn's heart[36]
34   *bas rab hi janda he*   Only God alone is aware of
35   *manzur kiyun na hoiyan*   Why were they not accepted?
36   *Zaynab da dil he aza*   Zaynab's heart is in lament
37   *qutbe men parh sunavan*   Shall I read an elegy of it?
(Repeat lines 29–30)
38   *Saidanian te barish*   On the *sayyedanis*[37] is wreaked
39   *pathran di ho rahi he*   The thunder of stones
(Repeat line 36)
40   *Ghazi nun ja bulavan*   Shall I go and call Abbas the
                                             Ghazi[38]
41   *qesmat ne jad milaya*   If fortune favors us and we meet
42   *Soghra gila kare gi*   Soghra will complain
(Repeat line 36)
43   *Akbar nun sehra lavan*   Shall I put the crown of flowers on
                                             Akbar?

(Repeat lines 29–30)

The Panjabi *nowhehs* at the *majles*, accompanied by the *matam*, were followed by another general *matam* led by the hostess, Ms. Sabira Zaidi. The communicative patterns of the speech event are illustrated through the following transliteration. This second *matam* was in Urdu and was characterized by a call-and-response pattern:[39]

H: Hosayn Hosayn   P: Hosayn Hosayn
/th /th /th th/ (repeating pattern)   /th /th /th th/ (repeating pattern)
H: Hosayn Hosayn   P: Hosayn Hosayn
H: Ali Mowla   P: Ali Mowla
H: Ali Mowla   P: Ali Mowla
H: Vali Mowla   P: Vali Mowla
H: Ya Abbas   P: Shir Abbas[40]
H: Hai Sakineh   P: Hai Pias[41]
H: Hai Sakineh   P: Hai Pias
H: Hosayn Hosayn Hosayn

The communicative dimensions of the *majles* were evident as I could hear the voices of the girl-children in the background repeating "Hosayn" after the hostess. The text and context established its own relationship on many levels within the same time frame. The ritual chanting with lamentation, like jazz, was cyclical and not linear; there was much in the performance that was repetitive and generated emotion through linguistic play and verbal art on several simultaneous levels. Following the general lament transliterated above, the participants chanted another *nowheh* in Urdu, this time using Sayyedeh Zaynab as the mythical narrator. The passion was at its peak in the assembly and weeping could be heard in the background; the hostess, Ms. Sabira Zaidi, wept the loudest, her face covered with a white handkerchief. The social interactions were within the established frames of speech and the speech event:[42]

> *ro ro karti*[43] *Zaynab beyn piyasa mar lia*
> (Zaynab wept and lamented, "Thirsty they killed,")
> *ro ro kati Zaynab beyn piyasa mar lia*
> (Zaynab wept and lamented, "Thirsty they killed,")
> *ya Nabi Kufion ne Hosayn piyasa mar lia*
> ("O Prophet, the Kufis killed a thirsty Hosayn,")
> *mera bhai Hosayn piyasa mar lia*
> ("My brother Hosayn, thirsty they killed")

Intense, emotional *matam* followed the chanting of this *nowheh*, which was led by the hostess. Then there was a liturgy of Hosayn *matam* in which the participants chanted: "Hosayn Hosayn Hosayn" for several minutes, beating their chests in a group self-flagellation ritual. Throughout this *matam*, I could hear the loud lament and weeping of the hostess, now in the background. She was exhausted and had moved to the back of the assembly; she sat with her back resting against the wall. A different *zakereh* took over the proceedings in order to recite the *salam* (blessings), which was a prelude to the end of the *majles*. A calm descended on the participants as the *zakereh* recited the following *salam* in poetic narrative in Arabic, Persian, and Urdu.[44] Below are excerpts from this *salam*, or *ziyarat*.[45]

al-salam-o alaykom ya Fatema al-Zahra	Peace be upon you O Fatemeh, the bold
al-salam-o alaykom ya ebn-e Mo'meneen	Peace be upon you O son of Ali
al-salam-o alaykom shams o shakur	Peace be upon you o sun and sunshine

al-salam-o alaykom al-aman   Peace be upon you, may there be
al-aman   peace, grace and mercy
al-salam-o alaykom Ahl-e Bayt-e   Peace be upon you O family of
Haram   Mohammad

The *zakereh* recited the *salavat/darud:*

Allah homma Salli Ala Mohammad   O God, may thy blessings be on
va al-e Mohammad   Mohammad and his family
Ya Nabi asl-salam-o alaykom   Peace be upon you, O Prophet

The *salavat* was followed by a recital of the opening chapter of the Qur'an.[46]
The *zakereh* led the *ziyarat* and *do'a* for the assembly in Urdu:[47]

Ya Khoda	O God
Is qowm ka daman gham-e Shabir se bhur de	Fill this nation's lap with grief for Hosayn[48]
Valvala Awn o Mohammad de	Give this nation the valor of Awn and Mohammad
Maon ko mile sani-e Zahra ka saliqah	May mothers have the skills of Zaynab[49]
Behnon ko Sakineh ki do'aon ka asr de	May sisters have the powers of Sakineh's prayers
Mowla tujhe Zaynab ki asiri ki qasam he	O God for the sake of Zaynab's imprisonment
Be jorm yatimon ko rehai ki khabar de	To innocent orphans in prisons, may there be news of freedom[50]
Mowla koi gham na dena de seva gham e Shabir	O God give no other grief except grief for Hosayn

For three minutes, the *zakereh* recited the prayers in Urdu. After the closure of the *majles*, *nazr* (food offerings) was distributed among the participants. The Pakistani *majles* described in this chapter reveals that much of the oral history of Karbala tragedy is reenacted in Sakineh's voice. The *nowhehs* sung in Sakineh's voice at this *majales* created "*riqat*," or ritualized grief, among the female participants. *Riqat* was created through descriptions of the events at Karbala, from this girl-child's perspective, and in her voice. Both male and female *nowheh-khans* commonly use this method for emotional effect. Sakineh therefore is a metaphor of grief in the folklore built around Karbala. As a vulnerable young girl, Sakineh serves as a highly sympathetic character in the context of the ethical and political issues that led to the Karbala tragedy. Thus, in accordance with Hymes' model, Sakineh serves as the frame for the ethnography of speaking at a Shi'i *majles* during the Moharram lamentations.

Notes

1. Dell Hymes, *Foundations in Sociolinguistics: An Ethnographic Approach* (Philadelphia: University of Pennsylvania Press, 1974), 45–46.

2. Ibid., 51.

3. Dell Hymes, "Toward Ethnographies of Communication: The Analysis of Communicative Events." In *Language and Social Context,* ed. Pier Paolo Giglioli (New York: Penguin Books, 1972), 21–44.

4. Ibid., 45.

5. Adapted from Joel Sherzer, *Language in Use: Readings in Sociolinguistics,* ed. John Baugh and Joel Sherzer (Englewood Cliffs, N.J.: Prentice-Hall, 1984a), 195.

6. Ibid.

7. Hymes, *Foundations in Sociolinguistics,* 54.

8. Albert B. Lord, *The Singer of Tales* (Cambridge: Harvard University Press, 1960), 21–26. The training of *nowheh*-chanters in Shi'i *majales* is similar to the one that Lord describes among the Muslim *guslars* in Yugoslavia during Ramadan.

9. Collected during a Moharram *majles* in Pakistan. I apply theoretical and methodological approaches from Richard Bauman, *Verbal Art as Performance* (Austin: University of Texas Press, 1977), and Hymes, "Toward Ethnographies of Communication."

10. For instance, the Gilani and Gardezi *sayyeds* in Multan and the Makhdooms in Sind.

11. Ali Asghar, infant son of Imam Hosayn, was slain at Karbala. Ali Asghar's cradle becomes a focal point of lament during Moharram rituals. Qasem was the adolescent son of Imam Hasan and a nephew of Imam Hosayn. Qasem was about to be married when he was killed at Karbala. Qasem's henna ceremony is celebrated among Shi'i female mourners in the subcontinent during Moharram *majales.* All *nowhehs* may not necessarily be in Sakineh's voice, but a large majority of them are sung as if she were the narrator. Sakineh's narrative creates a passionate lament in the *majles* assembly.

12. Hazrat Abbas, a half-brother of Imam Hosayn, is believed to have inherited Ali ibn Abi Talib's valor. Abbas was martyred at Karbala as he carried the standard of Hosayn's forces while attempting to bring water back to the camp from the Euphrates. The flags were green. At the top of flagpoles, there were metal replicas of a human hand, called a *panjatan,* with each finger representing one of the five most holy persons for Shi'is. The *panjatan* include Mohammad the Prophet; his son-in-law, Ali; the Prophet's daughter, Sayyedeh Fatemeh Zahra; and the Prophet's grandsons, Imams Hasan and Hosayn. Hazrat Abbas is called upon as a protector of children in the Moharram *majles.*

13. W. and P. Japp Beach, "Storyfying as Time-Travelling: The Knowledgeable Use of Temporally-Structured Discourse," in *Communication Yearbook 7,* ed. R. Bo-

strom (New Brunswick, N.J.: Transaction Books-ICA, 1983); and A. L. Ryave, "On the Achievement of a Series of Stories," in *Studies in the Organization of Conversational Interaction*, ed. Jim Schenkein (New York: Academic Press, 1978). Accordingly, in time travel, it was at *zohr*, the late afternoon, when all of Hosayn's forces were eliminated. Hosayn's horse, Zuljenah, returned riderless to the camp. Thus, as part of lament rituals in Pakistan, Zuljenah processions are led by Shi'i mourners to a local Karbala in the city on Ashura. The evening of Ashura is when the women and children were left alone in the camp with Hosayn's ailing son, Ali Zayn al-Abedin. The women's camps were said to have been looted. The evening of Ashura is called the Sham-e Ghariban, or Evening of the Oppressed. According to *hadith*, Imam Hosayn's sister, Sayyedeh Zaynab, was left to assume responsibility for the survivors, including the girl-child Sakineh.

14. In Shi'i households in Pakistan, Karbala is mourned for fifty days.

15. From the word *aza,* which means "to mourn." The word can also mean "condolence."

16. Named after Sayyedeh Zaynab.

17. Out of respect for her grace, the *azadars* address Ms. Sabira Zaidi as "Baji," an intimate term for an elder sister. "Baji Sabira ka Emambareh" means "*emambareh* belonging to Baji Sabira."

18. Meer Hasan Ali, *Observations on the Mussalmans of India* (Karachi: Civil and Military Press, 1973 [1832]), and Abdul Halim Sharar, *Lucknow: The Last Phase of an Oriental Culture*, trans. E. S. Harcourt and Fakhir Husayn (Bolder, Colo.: Westview Press, 1975).

19. Hymes cited in Joel Sherzer, "Strategies in Text and Context: Kuna kaa kwento," in *Language in Use: Readings in Sociolinguistics*, ed. John Baugh and Joel Sherzer, 183–197 (Englewood Cliffs, N.J.: Prentice-Hall, 1984b).

20. Erving Goffman, "The Neglected Situation," in *Language and Social Context*, ed. Pier Paola Giglioli (New York: Penguin Books, 1972), 61–66. Goffman's theory is that talk is based on small units of speech; utterances and sentences are placed adjacent to each other as speakers take turns to talk. This is demonstrated in some of the transliterations here, e.g., the hostess leading the *matam* and the assembly of mourners responding with chants of "Hosayn, Hosayn." It is also evident in the photograph of the hostess, Ms. Sabira Zaidi, leading the *matam* proceedings. This is also observed in the "hai, hai," utterance that the hostess prompts during the narration of a Sakineh story.

21. Levi-Strauss, cited in Sherzer, "Strategies in Text and Context"; Aisha Bint al-Shati Mistri, *Karbala ki Sher Dil Khatoon*, trans. Muhammad Abbas (Lahore: Maktaba-e Imamia Trust, 1996).

22. The *zakereh* uses texts like the following to write her narrative, which she delivers from memory at the *majles*: Ayub Naqvi Abadi, *Tarjuman-e Karbala: Zaynab Bint e-Ali* (Karachi: Aliya Publications, 1999), and Ibrahimi Ameeni, *Fatima Zehra: Islam ki Misali Khatoon,* trans. Akhtar Abbas (Lahore: Shafaq Publishers, 1405 AH).

23. In Sherzer, "Strategies in Text and Context," 195.

24. I adapt this argument from Joel Sherzer's study of the Kuna Indians of Panama; "Strategies in Text and Context," 195.

25. Ibid., 189.

26. In Pakistan, *nowhehs* are sung in languages such as Pashto, Balti, Sindhi, Siraiki, Baluchi, and regional dialects according to the speech communities.

27. Catherine Lutz and Lila Abu-Lughod, eds., *Language and the Politics of Emotion* (Cambridge: Cambridge University Press, 1990), and Erving Goffman, *Frame Analysis* (New York: Harper and Row, 1974). Theoretical approaches from these authors are used to interpret the data.

28. According to belief, Soghra, a daughter of Imam Hosayn, was left behind in Medina because she was ill and could not travel. The women who chanted the *nowheh* beat their breasts as they sang. The *nowheh* can be sung as a dyadic unit in which two parties take turns in the storytelling process. The *nowheh* can also be chanted as a monologue. The participants stand in a circle for chanting *nowhehs* and doing *matam.*

29. Sons of Sayyedeh Zaynab killed in the Battle of Karbala.

30. This is the feminine form of the word meaning "one who is devastated."

31. This is the feminine form of the word meaning "one who swallows."

32. *Ommat* means "sect, people of the same religion."

33. Akbar was Imam Hosayn's adolescent son.

34. Could also mean "notoriety" in terms of the opposing forces of Yazid.

35. The repetitive use of *"ujri,"* or the devastated female Sakineh, is significant.

36. Imam Hosayn is called Sarvar here. *Sarvar* means "leader" or a "chief."

37. Female descendants of the Prophet Mohammad's family.

38. One who fights against infidels, a conqueror, a living hero. Ghazi is embedded in the Islamic concept of jihad, or fight against falsehood.

39. Jim Schenkein, *Studies in the Organization of Conversational Interaction* (New York: Academic Press, 1978), and Harvey Sacks, Emmanuel Schegloff, and Gail Jefferson, "A Simplest Systemics for the Organization of Turn-Taking in Conversation," *Language* 50:4 (1974), 696–735. The transcription is based on an adaptation of the conversational analysis system of Sacks, Schegloff, and Jeffersen, also documented in Schenkein.

40. Abbas, the Lion, known for his valor.

41. A reference to Sakineh's thirst.

42. Goffman, *Frame Analysis.*

43. Feminine verb form of "to do."

44. The terms are intralingual.

45. Framing of the *majles* proceedings in this part by the weeping of the hostess in the background.

46. The opening verse of the Qur'an is also recited for the dead.

47. *Ziyarat* is a pilgrimage or visit. The hostess continued to weep as the *majles* was reaching closure through the prayers. The entire ritual was framed in the hostess' weeping and lament, which the participants responded to. *Do'a* is a prayer that can be said in Arabic, as well as in an indigenous code such as Urdu or Panjabi.

48. Fondly called "Shabir," which means a tiger or lion.

49. Also called "Zahra" or "Fatemeh the second" for her boldness and oratorical skills.

50. A political reference to current prisoners of conscience in the country.

CHAPTER 7

Sayyedeh Zaynab
The Conqueror of Damascus and Beyond

SYED AKBAR HYDER

O God! Answer our prayers for the sake of Zaynab,
The patient and wounded woman of Karbala,
Those who are ill, hasten to cure them,
Deliver us from envy and mischief,
Intercede on our behalf, O Sorrowful Zaynab![1]

A majestically solemn shrine awaits the pilgrim-visitor who walks through the raucous markets of southeast Damascus. As one enters the arched gate of the shrine of Sayyedeh Zaynab, the gilded dome, the ceilings and walls glittering with mirrors, and the tear-filled eyes of the pilgrims all reflect the reverence and love that is accorded to this granddaughter of the Prophet Mohammad, the older daughter of Fatemeh Zahra and Ali Ebn-e Abi Taleb. Pilgrims from diverse ethnic backgrounds and nationalities recite the prayers, such as the one quoted above. Many travel to the shrine not only to reaffirm their commitment to the cause of Islam, for which Zaynab gallantly fought, but also to atone for their sins and ask for Zaynab's intercession in their "this-worldly" as well as "other-worldly" lives. Few pilgrims who come to the shrine of Sayyedeh Zaynab remain untouched by the intensity of devotional acts that incrementally manifest themselves as one moves closer to the sepulchre of the Prophet Mohammad's granddaughter.

The modes of invoking Zaynab are as diverse as the ethnic backgrounds of thousands of pilgrims who converge at this shrine, ranging from reading the tributary Arabic prayers, *ziyarat*, that salute the trials and tribulations of Fatemeh's daughter to reciting moving Urdu elegies that recount her courage and remarkable vivacity. During my 1996 visit to Damascus, one of the things that struck me most was the use of tape recorders by several South Asian pilgrims who played Urdu elegies and sermons in honor of Zaynab, resonating the symbiosis between modern technology and premodern history. In this chapter, I explore the mapping of Zaynab as a rhetorically deployed trope in such Urdu sermons and elegies from twentieth-century South Asian Shiʿi oral and written traditions. First, I examine Rashid Torabi's (d. 1973) treatment of Zaynab. Torabi is one of the leading Shiʿi orators (zaker) of South Asia. Then, I discuss the invocation of Zaynab in modern Urdu poetry.

Setting the Stage for Zaynab

The commemoration of Karbala for more than 15 million South Asian Shiʿis, as for millions of other Muslims in South Asia and beyond, is the cornerstone of spirituality. In the Indo-Pakistani subcontinent, Karbala is ritualistically mourned by Shiʿis for two months and eight days (ayyam-e aza) each year. During these mourning assemblies, or majales, Shiʿis reinforce their religious identity and historical validity by situating Karbala in the history of Islam. Through the rituals of mourning, Shiʿis bridge the historical and cultural divides between themselves and the martyrs of Karbala as if to say, "had we been in Karbala, we too would have fought with you, O Hosayn!" When it comes to having an enduring impact on Shiʿi piety, few people from the subcontinent can be considered on a par with Rashid Torabi, a leading conductor of majales for many years.

Born in Hyderabad, India, Torabi studied philosophy and Islamic theology in Allahabad and Lucknow. A fervent supporter of the creation of Pakistan, he left Hyderabad after the partition and rapidly gained popularity as one of the foremost orators of Pakistan. Once the medium of radio became widespread in the 1960s, his speeches were broadcast on Radio Pakistan. The rapid growth of radio, television, and audiotape has not only gained Torabi renown throughout the Urdu-speaking world, but has also kept his memory alive for more than twenty-five years after his death. His tapes are still the favorites of those Shiʿis who have limited physical access to centers of commemoration—for example, those living in U.S. cities like College Station, Texas, or Ithaca, New York. When I asked members of his large following why his majales are still cherished today, most of them had the same response: He proves the cause of the Prophet's household not only through the verses of the Holy Qurʾan, but also through quoting Sunni historical sources. So closely is Torabi identified with Moharram oratory that he has been referred to as menbar ka dusra nam, or "the pulpit's second name." I heard Torabi's voice in Damascus during the months of Moharram and Safar. To me, the echoes of his sermons were an eerie reminder that much like the martyrs of Karbala and Sayyedeh Zaynab, Rashid Torabi had also proceeded to live on in death—through the medium of the audiotape!

The sermon that I heard in Damascus on the first day of the Islamic month of Safar was perhaps one of Rashid Torabi's most powerful. This sermon, in many ways, is a continuation of the earlier Torabi sermons that established Zaynab as the co-hero of Karbala, along with her brother, the martyred Imam Hosayn. Although Zaynab has remained a central character throughout the story of Karbala—from the time Imam Hosayn left Medina for Kufa to the time he was martyred on the plains of Karbala—her pivotal role became unmistakable on the night of the tenth day of Moharram, the day of Ashura.

As the day of Ashura drew to a close, the last surviving grandson of the Prophet had been murdered by those who claimed to be the Prophet's followers. Legend has it that so blighting was this incident to God's creation that the sun was eclipsed, the earth quaked, and the clouds wept tears of blood. The desert of Karbala then witnessed the arrival of night, Sham-e Ghariban, or the night of the dispossessed. It was at this time that Zaynab took charge of her desolated household. The *majales* commemorating this evening are usually held (among South Asian Shi'is everywhere) in very little light. In the late 1960s and early 1970s, it was this *majles* of Rashid Torabi that was broadcast around South Asia from Karachi. Torabi's prose narration of Zaynab's endurance in the face of such sorrows would be followed by Sayyed Ali Reza's powerful farewell *salam* (eulogy) that saluted Zaynab:

We convey greetings to our princess [Zaynab]
To whom the King [Hosayn] entrusted the house in his dying
 moments
Her journey reduced her to such straits of helplessness
That despite sacrificing her children
She was unable to save her brother
Shackled, encircled by the Syrians
She has to teach the way of Hosayn
In the manner of Ali![2]

The focus of Shi'i commemorations shifts to Zaynab at dusk on Ashura. For the rest of the commemoration period (almost two months), no gathering is likely to be void of Zaynab's mention. Prior to the tenth of Moharram, Zaynab has been Hosayn's strongest supporter. She leaves her husband behind in Medina in order to accompany her brother. Al-Hosayn is deferential to his sister, and her significance is underscored by the greatest Urdu elegy writer, Mir Anis (1804–1874):

> From her elders the rose of Zahra [Fatemeh's title] inherited
> Fatemeh's character and the majesty of God's Lion [Ali]
> Hosayn, the Oppressed King, recognized the rank of the second
>   Zahra
> And considered her a second mother[3]

So, Zaynab was the second Fatemeh Zahra. Moreover, she had the majesty of Ali, the Lion of God. Imam Hosayn treated his sister accordingly. Ali Akbar, the Imam's own son, was raised by Zaynab. She herself had two sons whom she allowed to fight for their uncle, in spite of the Imam's insistence that they should not fight. When the forces of Yazid went on to plunder the tents of the Prophet's family, Zaynab stood guard over the survivors. Within hours the women of the household, led by Zaynab, and Hosayn's only surviving son Ali (Zayn al-Abedin), were taken as captives, first to the court of Ebn-e Ziyad in Kufa and then to the palace of Yazid in Damascus. Along the way, both Zaynab and Ali b. Hosayn gave eloquent sermons in support of the cause of those who were murdered at Karbala. Finally, on the first day of Safar, Zaynab, with strength and vigor, confronted Yazid to redeem her family's suffering and to tell the world the reasons for which Hosayn and his companions suffered.

Zaynab in the Court of Yazid

When recounting the events of this solemn day, the first of Safar, Rashid Torabi compares it to Ashura: "For me, this day is not less in significance than the day of *ashura.*"[4] "My God! The revolution of time! This household of Mohammad and this treatment [of the household] by his community."[5] Torabi is quick to remind his audience of the oft-cited words of the Prophet to his community: "Certainly, for you, I am leaving two valuable things behind—the Book of God, and my progeny, my household. If you stay faithful to them then you will never be led astray. After me, these two will never be separated. They will meet me by the fountain of Kausar."[6] On this day of Ashura, the progeny of the Prophet, led by his granddaughter Zaynab and his great-grandson Ali b. al-Hosayn, both well versed in the Book that was revealed to their forefather and abiding by its commands at the cost of immense personal sacrifice, are to face Yazid. This *majles* is a commemoration of the confrontation between Zaynab and Yazid. It is repeated year after year, says Torabi, so the world does not fear *yazidiyyat*, or Yazidism. The minority must not be intimidated by the majority.[7] Thus *hosayniyyat*, the way of Hosayn, can remain the model for generations to come.

Torabi's narration of this event proceeds as follows: Along with the captured family of the Prophet, the heads of the martyrs are also taken into Yazid's presence. Yazid first asks the identity of each of the martyrs and then turns to the captives. Among the captives, Yazid notices a woman who is encircled by other women and whose very demeanor signifies defiance. Yazid lashes out, asking, "Who is this arrogant woman?" A surreal silence envelops the court. Responding to this question, this "defiant" woman rises and makes her way through the women who surround her. Having come face to face with Yazid, she retorts: "Why are you asking them [the women]? Ask me. I'll tell you [who I am.] I am Mohammad's granddaughter. I am Fatemeh's daughter. Ask me, Yazid." The entire court is awestruck with this introduction of Zaynab as she begins her *khotbeh* (sermon) with the praise of God:

In the name of Allah, the most gracious, the most merciful. All praise is due to Allah, the Lord of the worlds. May praise and salutations be upon my grandfather, the Leader of Allah's Messengers, and upon his progeny.[8]

Torabi reminds his audience that three *khotbeh*s in history are memorable: those of Fatemeh, those of Ali, and those of Zaynab. If Fatemeh's *khotbeh* was incomplete, Ali completed it. If Ali's *khotbeh* was incomplete, then Zaynab completed it. Fatemeh's *khotbeh* had also been in the court, says Torabi, carefully sidestepping the name of the ruler in whose court the *khotbeh* was given.[9] Torabi does not need to mention this name, for his Shi'i audiences know very well that the court was that of the first caliph, Abu Bakr. Fatemeh had argued with Abu Bakr over her inheritance, which the Prophet had left for her at Fadak, but to no avail.[10]

Speaking for the cause of justice had been the vocation of the Prophet's family and it was in this very spirit that Ali, too, had come to Abu Bakr's court—in order to claim the caliphate for himself. Again, Torabi does not need to name the forces that opposed Ali. Ali's Shi'is know that Ali pleaded his case (for being the most deserving successor to the Prophet) in Abu Bakr's presence, in the sermon of *shaqshaqiyyeh*; again, to no avail. By alluding to the *khotbehs* of Ali and Fatemeh, Torabi intertwines Karbala and its aftermath with the injustices that had befallen the Prophet's family after his death. Karbala thus becomes a culmination, the pinnacle of sacrifices in the cause of Islam. Through this medium, an alternative Islamic history is invoked.

Now, with the martyrdom of Hosayn, Torabi tells his audience, the names of the enemies of the Prophet's family no longer need to be suppressed in carefully crafted, ambiguous texts. The Muslim community as a whole hardly needs any justification for chastising Yazid. It is up to Zaynab to proclaim the message of her parents and brothers loudly and clearly. At the same time, it is up to the *zaker*, the likes of Torabi, to proclaim the antecedents of injustices that had been the lot of the Prophet's family.

The interest of the audience is heightened as Torabi once again speaks the language of Zaynab, which has now become the language of the Qur'an. The Prophet's granddaughter, after sacrificing her family in the way of God, is now speaking through the language of God to a tyrant who is gloating at his "victory":

O Yazid! Have you forgotten the words of God: "Let not those who disbelieve think that our giving them respite is good for their selves; We only give respite to them that they may increase in sins, and for them is a disgraceful chastisement."[11]

After uttering these words from the Qur'an, Zaynab lashes out at the vices of Yazid and his forefathers, especially his grandmother:

What else could I have expected from the progeny of he whose forefathers have eaten the liver of my forefathers? This blood (of my forefathers) runs in theirs and the martyrs' blood has nurtured their flesh. What else could I have expected from such a progeny?[12]

Torabi reflects on Zaynab's words as follows:

Have you seen this? This is an oppressor's court. This is a tyrant's court. This is a despot's court. This is a murderer's court and that is the daughter of the Lion of God [Ali]. It is this sermon of Zaynab that has preserved these houses [Shi'i houses] for centuries.[13]

Through the words of Zaynab, Torabi invokes those "historical" events that privilege the Prophet's family at the expense of Yazid's. Zaynab is quick to point out the not-so-illustrious ancestry of Yazid: his grandmother, after all, had gnawed on the liver of the Prophet's uncle after the Battle of Badr, thereby securing for herself the title *jigarkhar-ha*, the liver eater. It was also in the Battle of Badr that the Meccan aristocracy, comprising Yazid's Umayyad ancestors, was defeated by the Prophet's forces and Yazid's grandfather, Abu Sufyan, was taken captive. When Abu Sufyan was taken to Mohammad, he fell at the Prophet's feet as an act of apology, and the Prophet freed him. Zaynab reminds Yazid of this family's debt to her own family:

O progeny of the freedman of the Prophet! Is this your justice? Your daughters, your slave girls, your dear women are all sitting behind the curtain and the daughters of the Prophet, in shackles, unveiled, stand before you.[14]

Veiling, to Torabi as to many others, signifies honor and privacy. Fadwa El Guindi captures the historical significance of veiling in Islamic societies so well:

In general, veiling by women or men communicates, not subordinated gender status or the shame of sexuality, but the group status of the individual, the identity of the group and the sacredness of privacy. Whether it is the Prophet entering Makka in victory or A'isha in public political speech, veiling becomes a device to formalize communication and a means to ceremonialize one's status and one's group identity. But when the two sexes are together joined in sacred time and space to worship God the central spatial object of the pilgrimage, the Ka'ba, itself veiled, becomes the metaphor of sacred privacy in public.[15]

One of the accusations made against Yazid and his subordinates is that they forcefully took the veils from the Prophet's family and dishonored them by making them walk, unveiled, in the streets, markets, and palaces of Kufa and Damascus. As Zaynab's sermon clearly attests, this attempt at dishonor fails miserably. Zaynab gains honor and respect not on account of her gender, nor because of the presence or absence of her veil, but through her discourse. Zaynab proceeds in her sermon:

I swear by Him who has bestowed prophecy upon our house and who has honored us with His book. I swear by Him who has selected us. I swear by Him who has given us good fortune. O Yazid! You will not be able to efface our account nor will you be able to comprehend our intentions, our goals and the mystery of Hosayn's murder. Begone! I don't expect any such thing from you.

Torabi continues in the present tense: "The deluge of tears is sweeping the durbar audiences into the feet of Zaynab." Rashid Torabi has elsewhere compared this sermon of Zaynab to that of the Prophet when he defeated the armies of Yazid's grandfather: "When Mecca was conquered, the Messenger gave a sermon. Now, having conquered Syria, Zaynab is giving a sermon."[16] The Prophet, in his sermon, had freed Yazid's grandfather, Abu Sufyan. Zaynab, today, is reminding Yazid of that freedom as she implicates him in the destruction of Islam. She is exposing the hypocrisy that has, through might or sheer brutality, assumed power. She is underscoring the insignificance of such worldly power—the wrath that awaits those who ride on wealth and arrogance. Her grandfather had completed the cycle of messages that were revealed by God. Her mother and father had stood steadfast and confronted the ruling authority of the time (Abu Bakr.) Her brother had sacrificed his own life and that of his family to preserve the message of God. All these deeds needed to be brought to light, and for that, God had chosen Zaynab. Zaynab was truly her mother's daughter, and her mother was the Prophet's daughter. It did not matter that no son of the Prophet survived, says Torabi. His beloved daughter, Fatemeh, survived him. To Torabi, Fatemeh is the *waris* (heir) to the legacies of all the Prophets.[17] Torabi's *majles* has as its subject the daughter of Fatemeh, the honor of the Prophet's house. This is not because she is a woman rather than a man, nor because she is in public instead of being behind the veil, but because she carries the benefaction of God's messengers and saints, of her parents and of her brothers, a benefaction consisting of virtue, justice, patience, motherhood, sisterhood, sacrifice, love, swordless war, dishonored honor, and so much more. Who in human history, whether man or woman, could carry all of this with such grace and fortitude? When Torabi constantly refers to her as "princess," it is not because she is entitled to such a title on a worldly level, but because she is the princess of God's kingdom, of the hereafter, of a realm in which worldly glory fades into nonexistence. That Zaynab's centrality in the readings of Karbala has an important bearing on the gendered dimension of this struggle can be gleaned from the discourses of other South Asian Shiʿi authorities, such as Sayyed Ali Naqi al-Naqvi:

> While looking at the merits and circumstances of Zaynab the Great, may Allah's peace be upon her, can any person hesitate to say that the stations that she passed [the obstacles she overcame] were more difficult than that station that was crossed by the friends of the Prince of Martyrs [Hosayn]? Having observed the historical conditions, can any person claim that in those forceful and trying moments, Zaynab's tongue had any knots, her heart any intimidation, or that she herself had any fear or dread? . . . —She is the voice of truth in the face of a tyrannical government and an oppressive sultanate—Can there be any doubt that each and ever sentence of [Zaynab's] speech was more brutal for Yazid than the wounds wrought by thousands of swords and spears? Can it be refuted that this sermon and many more sermons like this, some reaching us through history and others not, were such powerful weapons that they overturned the ruling throne of Yazid and the Umayyads and rendered them non-existent?[18]

In Naqvi's reading of Karbala—which is quite similar to many a Torabi sermon dealing with Zaynab—not only did Zaynab complete Hosayn's battle, but she became the medium through which Karbala would survive into posterity. She would become the inspirational rallying cry for the overthrow of the Umayyads that would take place within the next few decades.[19] Karbala is thus as much a man's war as it is a woman's. Hosayn and Zaynab, seen through this angle, become co-heroes of this battle.

It is imperative at this point to mention the projection of Zaynab among South Asian Shiʿi authorities as a site of the cultural construction of gender. Zaynab's intervention in Islamic history is evinced through the narrative of femininity. Zaynab can ratify the cause of Hosayn by reproaching Yazid in his own palace. The obeisance of the entire durbar to this woman of the Prophet's house is somehow surreal. Yazid can arrogate to himself the status of the ruler of the Islamic world, he can gloat over his temporal victories, but it is left to Zaynab to provide the counter to Yazid's reading of his own authority, to set straight the historical record. Zaynab's sermons would soon ring out to the world, inspiring all to rise for the sake of justice. Even though she was physically shackled, her message could not be contained in the palace of Yazid or the prison of Damascus. The tradition of *majles* that she invented would live on for at least a millennium, if not longer.

Zaynab in Modern Urdu Poetry

The invocation of Zaynab in twentieth-century Urdu poetry follows the patterns of commemorative prose narratives that I have discussed in the past few pages. The three poets I will discuss in this section are Iftikhar Arif (b. 1943), Parvin Shakir (d. 1996), and Vahid Akhtar (d. 1996). Iftikhar Arif, who presently lives in Great Britain, is one of the finest living poets composing devotional verses in honor of the martyrs of Karbala. He has also done much to enhance the cause of Urdu in Great Britain as an active member of the Third World Foundation's Urdu Markaz in London, an organization that furthers the literary appreciation of this language through such activities as the organization of *moshairahs*, or poetry gatherings. The importance of the imagery of suffering in Arif's poetry, especially the suffering of the Imam Hosayn, is attested to by the commentators of his works.[20] Along with Hosayn's suffering, Arif sees Karbala as a testimony to Zaynab's courage. One of his most famous poems regarding this topic merits our attention:

BEAR WITNESS, O KARBALA
Bear witness, O Karbala
Fatemeh's daughter
Transformed her father's courage
Through patience.
Compensated for her brother's friendship
In what a manner!
Bear witness, O Karbala.
From the gate of the city of wisdom
Till the tents of victory
Till the assembly of martyrdom
How many names were heard!
How many wondrous stations were traversed!
Those who thought the companionship of truth
To be a duty

Were disposed on the path of the truth.
And Zaynab was with them at every step
Bear witness, O Karbala
Then came that evening,
When the sister was alone,
One journey ended.
On the scorching sands of the place of martyrdom,
A few unshrouded corpses,
Of brothers and nephews,
Of those nurtured in laps,
Of fellow travelers,
Of companions,
A few burnt tents,
A few scared kids,
Their refuge, Zaynab
Their courage, Zaynab.
Bear witness, O Karbala.
From the sacred spot of martyrdom,
A new journey commences
One of its destinations, Syria
Syria, the Syria of the oppressed
And that sermon of Zaynab
Then the world stretching from the durbar
Began to ask
In the story of oppression
Till where do the margins
Of legends extend
The world began to think
Till where do the chains
Of the beautiful pulpits extend
Those who have sacrificed their houses
In order to guard the good
Till where does their courage go
Time bore witness
In the face of compulsion
The lesson of patience, Zaynab
The last page
Of the book of martyrdom, Zaynab
This pain which stands strong
This too is a testimony

This eye which is wet
This too is a testimony
This ground upon which lamenting exists
This too is a testimony.[21]

For Arif, Karbala must be constructed by the inclusion of Zaynab. Zaynab is produced symbolically as the one who has the transformative role in Karbala—the bravery and strength so closely associated with her father are given a new meaning through Zaynab's patient struggle, wherein physical battles are replaced by the battle of words. She leads Islam on a new path by accomplishing in the palaces of Kufa and Damascus a nonviolent victory. Tear-filled eyes testify to the resilience of the traditions of commemoration that Zaynab began. Zaynab's struggle begins where Hosayn's ends—during the dark night after the massacre at Karbala, popularly known as Sham-e Ghariban, or the Night of the Dispossessed.

Having witnessed the merciless slaughter of her family, Zaynab took over the banner of Islam from her brother. Thus, Sham-e Ghariban, although a sorrowful moment in the life of the Prophet's household, should be seen, so the poet tells us, as the revivification of Hosayn's cause. Even though Hosayn was killed during the day, his cause passed from his hands to those of his sister. The day belonged to Hosayn; the night to Zaynab.

For the Harvard-educated Parvin Shakir, one of the most famous of the contemporary female Urdu poets, Zaynab's fight for the cause of justice can also be seen as a paradigm for those women who still combat oppression in various forms. She speaks of Zaynab's plight through the deliberate absence of Zaynab's name, in universal terms:

HELP ME!
From the tent of innocence
As soon as I proceeded towards the city of justice
From their ambush
My killers also emerged
With ready to shoot bows, with targeted arrows, with loaded pistols
While giving the arrow shooters on the scaffold command
To be ready
Having grasped the thirsty spears on the highways
The mischievous ones, row by row—
In the city square, the city's judge armed with a dagger
Streets dotted with daggers hidden in sleeves

Osara, a reenactment of prisoners being taken in chains on camels to Damascus (Tehran, 1997). © Kamran Scot Aghaie

Another view of women in the mass procession in front of the bazaar (Tehran, 1997). © Kamran Scot Aghaie

Procession of women carrying tents that symbolize the camp of Hosayn's supporters at Karbala. These tents are usually ritually burned at the end of the ritual season, in memory of how Yazid's troops set fire to the camp at Karbala (Tehran, 1997). © Kamran Scot Aghaie

Another view of Osara, a reenactment of prisoners being taken in chains on camels to Damascus; children are often included in these processions (Tehran, 1997). © Kamran Scot Aghaie

Women carrying replica of a headless and arrow-riddled corpse of Hosayn (Tehran, 1997). © Kamran Scot Aghaie

A *ta'ziyeh* performance at Hosayniyeh-e Moshir (Shiraz, 1976). © Peter J. Chelkowski

Scene from a *ta'ziyeh* performance at the Takyeh-e Mo'aven al-Molk (Kermanshah, 1999). © Peter J. Chelkowski

A painting of Ashura. © Peter J. Chelkowski

Poster entitled *The Heirs of Zaynab* (*Varesan-e Zaynab*). © Peter J. Chelkowski

Poster entitled *Guards of the Realm of Light.* © Peter J. Chelkowski

Poster by Mohammad Khaza'i depicting Fatemeh Zahra. © Peter J. Chelkowski

Every resident of the city in mayhem
Listening to the sounds of my lonely litter
The spiders of ingenuity, webbing the webs around me
Someone desirous of my banner
Someone wanting my head
And someone wanting to steal my veil,
Is about to snatch [it]
The circle of the enemy is about to be fortified
The last battle with death is about to happen
In the Kufah of love
My helplessness
Covering the face with its hair
Folding its hands
Bowing its head
Uttering only one noun on its lips
O Forgiving and Merciful One!
O Forgiving and Merciful One![22]

The markets and palaces of Kufa were the first ones through which Zaynab passed after her brother's martyrdom. Kufa was the capital of Ali and the city from which Hosayn had received invitations. Zaynab had to make the painful passage through the city before she arrived in Damascus, Yazid's capital. Traditional accounts have presented the most heart-wrenching images of Zaynab's suffering in this city: her veil, the attire of honor for a woman of that time, was snatched mercilessly and she was forced to cover her face with her hair. In the face of all this, she invoked the name of the Merciful at every step.

This poem, however, is written in the first-person mode with no mention of the name "Zaynab." It is as though the poet herself is retracing her steps in history and reading her own struggle into that of Zaynab. As Gopichand Narang, a leading critic of Urdu literature points out, through such words Parvin Shakir "speaks" Zaynab's language, thereby "erasing the distance of centuries."[23]

Zaynab's struggle is seen in the context of not only the struggles of women before her, but also those who followed her. Thus, the suffering of Zaynab is resurrected through the poet's own suffering. However, this time around, Shakir gives the impression that the suffering might actually be more severe than that which befell Zaynab. One of Ali's epithets is *mush-kilkusha,* or the "knot-opener of difficulties." Even when the Prophet encountered difficulties, Shiʿi lore has it, he sought assistance from Ali. In one of her poems addressed to Ali, Shakir describes the "spell" of Ali's name, which has saved the cause of virtue in the most trying circumstances, including those through which the Prophet's family suffered in Kufa and Syria. In her own age, this spell has lost its charm.

O CONQUEROR OF KHAYBER!
Once again move your hands
We have been defeated by our wretched egos
O Cup bearer of Kausar!
Once again raise your eyes
Look. For your followers,
Have sacrificed such a Euphrates for a little bit of thirst.[24]

In spite of being deprived of the water of the Euphrates, Ali's son Hosayn and Ali's daughter Zaynab continued their fight for the righteous cause. With all their sacrifices, Hosayn and Zaynab caused a more majestic river than the Euphrates to flow. The followers of Ali, unable to bear the discomfort of relatively little thirst, sacrificed this greater Euphrates at the threshold of their fleeting desires. Shakir just hopes to remain steadfast— like those who were martyred at Karbala and those who survived in order to keep alive the martyrs' cause—in such thirst:

May I remain steadfast in the thirst of many an hour
May the soul grant me the strength of Karbala in the desert of affliction.[25]

Vahid Akhtar, a powerful poet and philosopher, as well as the chair of the philosophy department at Aligarh Muslim University in the early 1990s,[26] further elaborates the contributions of Zaynab to the cause of justice. In the preface to his elegy commemorating Zaynab, Akhtar writes:

The tongue of Zaynab accomplished a greater task than the swords of Husayn and Abbas. In the market of Kufah, in Ibn Ziyad's court, throughout the patience-testing journey till Syria, among the crowds of Damascus, among the throngs of the world at the court of kingship, and in the face of Yazid's insults—at all these instances if there was a sword that was raised and then struck the heads of oppression and falsehood, it was either the sword of Zaynab's sermons or the miracle of the tongue of the Fourth Imam.[27]

Zaynab, for Akhtar, is the combination of all the heroes of Islam and is inextricably bound not only to the cause of Hosayn but to the overall cause of the Prophet of Islam:

Fragrance is not separate from the rose
Nor is the rose separate from the rose garden
Sorrow is not separate from the soul
Nor is the soul separate from the body
Blood is not separate from the heart
Nor is the heart separate from the heartbeat
Neither poetry from the poet
Nor the poet from the art is separate
Truth is from the Qur'an,
The Qur'an from the Messenger of God
Karbala is from the martyrs
The martyrs from Zaynab.

Just as the name of Islam is with the name of Mohammad
The names of Zaynab and Shabbir cannot be separated
She is the noblest of women, he is the leader of the caravan of truth
With him martyrdom begins and with her it ends
The purpose of life of Zaynab and Shabbir is one
The volumes are two, but the style of writing & the meaning of what
     is written is one.[28]

Zaynab's authority, in the eyes of Vahid Akhtar, is also enhanced because she begins to pen a "new history"[29] by supporting Hosayn's cause after his martyrdom. She becomes the guardian of the two most precious things the Prophet has left behind, his progeny and the Qur'an:

Patience is restless to guide Zaynab
Only she remains to guard the Prophet's family and the Qur'an
She is the shade protecting the candle of the imamate
She has been created in order to propagate the cause of the Prophecy
Ask the son of Zahra how the head shall be forsaken
Ask Zaynab's heart what the magnitude of patience is.[30]

Patience, through Zaynab, is lifted up to the same lofty station as courage. Hosayn sacrifices his head to resurrect Islam and it is left to Zaynab to protect and articulate this Islam.[31]

In the poetry of Vahid Akhtar, as in the poetry of Parvin Shakir and Ifti-khar Arif, and of course in the sermons of Rashid Torabi, Zaynab becomes the signifier of an everlasting Karbala. She is, so to speak, bound to the aesthetic of preservation. The narrative landscape of Karbala needs a repository in which the remnants of the battle fought on the Euphrates can be preserved; this is Zaynab's womb, which nurtures future Hosayns. Through her sword-like sermons, she rallies people to Hosayn's cause in order to fill the void left by the murder of the Prophet's grandson. By commencing the tradition of commemoration, she preserves the invaluable message of Islam for perpetuity.

The figuration of Zaynab in this narrative landscape also evinces the need for this story to have a feminine dimension. The individuals we have discussed in this chapter take it as axiomatic that women can complement the struggle of men through the waging of their own war. While this battle may be fought without a sword, it can be just as forceful, through moving oratory and with patience. In order for Karbala to be a model for an ideal life, it needs to articulate both masculine and feminine ideals. Thus, Karbala is not constructed through the exclusion of the feminine, but with the feminine as an integral component. After all, reforming the worlds of women has been an age-old concern for many a reformer and poet for, if nothing else, these worlds were cradles for future men. In Zaynab's war, too, we see the accommodation of her reformist agenda within her overall role as the caretaker of the Prophet's family. She is emplotted discursively as a model of Islamic femininity while retaining her signification as a challenge to the most formidable of unjust male authorities. She is simultaneously a warrior and a woman. Her gendered presence becomes subservient to her agency as the spokesperson of Islam. In short, she constitutes an interface between womanhood and warrior. Thus, Zaynab is neither rhetorically excluded from the constitution of this trope nor is her physical presence and gendered inscription an oversight. By advancing Islam in a tyrant's court, she bestows on her devotees an imagination that sanctifies the "woman warrior." Additionally, she becomes the first one to displace Karbala geographically by continuing to wage her brother's battle in Kufa and in Syria. Through invoking Zaynab, her devotees endorse and commemorate her struggle everywhere. She is memorialized and cherished in South Asian literary traditions just as she is in ornate Syrian architecture, or via thousands of audiotapes and compact discs—containing eulogies and elegies in her honor—that circulate the world over.

Notes

1. Sayyed Anis Jahan Haydari, *Guldasteh-e morad* (Bombay: Kaidari Khutub Khana, n.d.), 131.
2. Sayyed Al-e Ahmad, "Salam-e akhar," in *Suz-e Karbala,* ed. Sayyed Hasan Abbas Zaydi (Karachi: Ahmad Book Depot, 1983), 350. The original Urdu is as follows:

salam bhejte hain apni shahzadi par
ke jis ko sonp gae marte vaqt ghar sarvar
musafirat ne jise be basi ye dikhlai
nisar kar die bachche na bach saka bhai
asir ho ke jise Shamion ke narghe men
Hosayniat hai sikhana Ali ke lahje men

3. Mir Anis, *Marsiyeh dar hal-e sani-ye Zahra hazrat Zaynab Kobra* (Hyderabad: Aijaz Printing Press, n.d.), 3. The original is as follows:

gul-e zahra ne buzorgon se yeh virsa paya
sirat-e Fatemeh aur dabdabah-e sher-e khuda
martaba Sani-e Zahra ka jo pehchante the
Shah-e mazlum unhen man ki jagah jante the

4. Rashid Torabi, *Majales-e Torabi,* ed. Sayyed Zulfeqar Hosayn Hosni, 3 vols. (Karachi: Mahfuz Book Agency, 1991), 2:244.
5. Ibid., 2:243.
6. Ibid., 2:223.
7. Ibid., 1:159.
8. Ibid., 3:66.
9. Ibid.
10. The Shiʿis in the subcontinent are a minority community, and because of this they feel the need to exercise discretion so as not to offend the sensibilities of the majority Sunnis. For Sunnis, the four caliphs after the Prophet are "rightly guided." Hence casting aspersions on their character is simply unacceptable. Shiʿi-Sunni controversies in the subcontinent have raged on for years over the issue of *tabarra,* or the condemning of the enemies of the Prophet, which to many a Shiʿa is a doctrinal component of religion. Members of the Sunni community have accused Shiʿis of cursing the first three caliphs even in the forum of the *majles.* Sunnis have reacted to such vilification with praises of the companions (*madh-e sahaba*), which infuriates Shiʿas, for this, in Shiʿa opinion, is tantamount to calling the Karbala tragedy an aberration in the history of Islam.
11. Torabi, *Majales-e Torabi,* 3:68.
12. Ibid., 3:67.
13. Ibid.
14. Ibid., 3:68.
15. Fadwa El Guindi, *Veil: Modesty, Privacy and Resistance* (Oxford: Berg, 1999), 126.
16. Torabi, *Majalis-e Torabi,* 2:249.
17. Ibid., 3:102.

18. Sayyed Ali Naqi al-Naqvi, *Mujahida-ye Karbala* (Lucknow, India: Sarfaraz Qaumi Press, n.d.), 332–341.

19. Ibid., 341–342.

20. Faiz Ahmad Faiz and Gopichand Narang have both commented on Arif's fondness for the trope of Karbala. See Iftikhar Arif, *Mehr-e do nim* (Karachi: Danyal, 1983), 5–10 and 23.

21. Ibid., 67. The original is as follows:

Karbala gavahi de
Karbala gavahi de
Fatemeh ki beti ne
bap ki shujaat ko
sabr se badal dala
bhai ki rifaqat ka
haqq ada kiya kaisa
Karbala gavahi de
bab-e shahr-e hikmat se
khaimagah-e nusrat tak
mahzar-e shahadat tak
kaise kaise nam ae
kya ajab maqam ae
haqq ki pasdari ko
farz janne vale
rah-e haqq men kam ae
sath sath thi Zaynab
Karbala gavahi de
phir vo sham bhi ai
jab bahan akeli thi
ek safar hua anjam
reg-e garm-e maqtal par
chand be kafan lashe
bhaion bhatijon ke
godyon ke palon ke
sath chalne valon ke
sath dene valon ke
kuch jale hue khaime
kuch dare hue bachche
jin ka asra Zaynab
jin ka hausla Zaynab
Karbala gavahi de
mashhad-e muqaddas se
ek naya safar aghaz
jis ki ek manzil sham
sham sham-e mazlumi
aur vo Khotbehe Zaynab
phir to bar sar-e darbar
puchne lagi dunya

zulm ki kahani men
dastan saraon ke
hashiye kahan tak hain
sochne lagi dunya
minbar-e saloni ke
silsile kahan tak hain
khair ke tahaffuz par
ghar lutane valon ke
hausle kahan tak hain
vaqt ne gavahi di
jabr ke maqabil men
sabr ka sabaq Zaynab
mushaf-e shahadat ka
akhari varaq Zaynab
ye jo dard mahkam hai
ye bhi ek gavahi hai
ye jo ankh pur nam hai
ye bhi ek gavahi hai
ye jo farsh-e matam hai
ye bhi ek gavahi hai

22. Parvin Shakir, "Sadbarg," in *Mah-e tamam* (Delhi: Educational Publishing House, 1995), 131–132. The original is as follows:

Adrikni
khaimae be gunahi men
shahr-e insaf ki simt junh barh
apni apni kamingah se
mere qatil bhi nikle
kamanen kase tir jore tamanche charhae
machanon pa navak badaston ko tayyar rahne ke ahkam dete hue
shahrahon men pyasi sinanen liye fitnagar saf ba saf
chauk par qazi-e shahar khanjar bakaf
raste dushne dar astin
ghat men shahar ka har makan
mere tanha kujave ki ahat ko sunte hue
ankabut hunar mere charon taraf jal bunte hue
koi mere sar ka khwahan
to koi rida ka tamanna ban kar
jhipatne ko hai
halqae dushmanan tang hone ko hai
maut se akhar jang hone ko hai
Kufae ishq men
meri becharagi
apne balon se chehra chupae hue
hath bandhe hue
sar jhukae hue

zer-e lab ek h ism parht
Ya Ghafur ur-Rahim
Ya Ghafur ur-Rahim

23. Gopichand Narang, *Sanaha-e Karbala bataur Sheri Isteara* (Delhi: Educational Publishing House, 1986), 85.
24. Shakir, "Sadbarg," 134. The original is as follows:

Fatah-e Khaibar!
apne hathon ko phir junbish de
ham apni na murad ana se har chuke
Saqi-e Kausar!
ek dafa nazren to utha
dekh ke tere manne vale
zara si pyas pe kaise Farat ko var chuke

25. Mahdi Nazmi, *Reg-i Surkh* (New Delhi: Abu Talib Academy, 1984), 201. The original is as follows:

pahron ki tishnagi men bhi sabit qadam rahun
dasht-e bala men ruh mujhe Karbalai de

26. Vahid Akhtar has also noted similarities between the Islamic Revolution of Iran and the uprising of Imam Hosayn at Karbala. Akhtar was inspired by the pivotal figures of this revolution, including Ali Shariati, Mortada Motaharri, and Ruhollah Khomeini. He credits Ayatollah Khomeini for safeguarding the legacy of Karbala: "But the main inspiration [for the Islamic Revolution of Iran] came from Imam Khumayni's interpretation of the true spirit of Karbala, which in his view, is not a battle limited to any particular period of time but a continuing struggle in the 'Eternal Now.' By the means of Muharram ceremonies he revitalized and re-energized the downtrodden Muslims to fight courageously, fearlessly, and selflessly unarmed against the most heavily armed regimes in the region which enjoyed total support of a superpower like the U.S. He brought about a metamorphosis of the Iranian ethos and, as a result, there emerged from the fire of Phoenix a revolutionary nation of free men and women. Freedom is the core of Imam Husayn's message." Sayyid Vahid Akhtar, "Karbala, an Enduring Paradigm of Islamic Revivalism," *al-Tawhid* 13 (1996), 113-125.
27. Vahid Akhtar, *Karbala ta Karbala* (Aligarh: Vahid Akhtar, 1991), 158-159.
28. Ibid., 168. The original is as follows:

bu alag gul se nahin gul nahin gulshan se juda
gham nahin jan se alag jan nahin tan se juda
khun nahin dil se alag, dil nahin dharkan se juda
sher shair se na shair hai kabhi fan se juda
haqq hai Quran se Quran rasul-e rabb se
Karbala hai shuhada se shuhada Zaynab se

jis tarha nam-e Mohammad se hai nam-e Islam
ho nahin sakte juda Zaynab o Shabbir ke nam
sayyada ye hain vo hain qafela-e haqq ke imam

un se aghaz-e shahadat hai to in par etmam
maqsad-e zindagi-e Zaynab o Shabbr hai ek
pare do, tarz-e khat o mani-e tahrir hai ek

29. Ibid., 175.
30. Ibid., 175. The original is as follows:

sabr be chain hai Zaynab ki qiyadat ke lie
hain yeh itrat o Quran ki hifazat ke lie
yehi fanus hain ab sham-e imamat ke lie
yehi mamur hain tabligh-e risalat ke lie
tarz sar dene ka Zehra ke pisar se pucho
sabr ka hausla Zaynab ke jigar se pucho

31. Although Hosayn's only surviving son, Zayn al-Abedin, is alive, he cannot participate as vigorously as his aunt due to his illness. Tradition has it that when Ali's life was threatened, it was Zaynab who saved it by offering the forces of Yazid her own life instead.

CHAPTER 8

Gender and Moharram Rituals in an Isma'ili Sect of South Asian Muslims

REHANA GHADIALLY

The Muslim community of South Asia is diverse: Islam adapts to various cultures and environments while retaining those features that maintain its universality. Belief in one God, prayer, almsgiving, fasting, and pilgrimage to Mecca are common to all Muslims. Devotional rituals connected with Islam's early figures are aspects of religious life that display considerable diversity. A similar diversity is observed in life cycle rituals associated with birth, puberty, and death. Although research on popular Islam in South Asia is very scarce, Imtiaz Ahmad has discussed the diversity of observed Islam in India.[1] Some important beginnings have also been made by Western scholars. Peter Van Der Veer's "Playing or Praying: A Sufi Saint's Day in Surat," focuses on saint's day celebrations and the debates surrounding such occasions.[2] Vernon Schubel's book, *Religious Performance in Contemporary Islam: Shi'a Devotional Rituals in South Asia,* is devoted to Moharram public observances, the focus of this chapter, and includes a chapter on women's household rituals.[3] Gustav Thaiss has studied the changing character of Moharram rituals imported by Indian migrants to the Caribbean Islands in the nineteenth century.[4] Studies of Middle Eastern Muslim societies have tended to focus on the role of women in popular practices, while textual and establishment Islam is a male preserve. Much of this work is focused on the majority Sunni branch of Islam. An exception is Iran, where scholars have focused almost exclusively on the Twelver Shi'i sect, with virtually no attention to the sister Isma'ili branch. However, Iran is not the only locus of popular Shi'ism. This chapter aims to redress this situation by examining popular Shi'ism in South Asia, with special attention to sect and gender as categories of analysis.

I examine some of the ways in which Bohras, an Isma'ili sect of the Shi'i branch of South Asian Islam, demonstrate their love for the household of the Prophet in both public and private spheres, arguing that both men and women are active in Moharram rituals. The public nature of some of these observances makes for mixed-sex presence. However, the level of women's agency and participation diminishes with the publicness of each ritual: the more public the ritual is, the less involved women are, and, conversely, the more private the ritual, the more involved women are. Here I argue that although public rituals serve to maintain stereotyped gender identities, they also highlight the centrality of women for the survival of Islam both by keeping popular practices alive and by reiterating the support extended and suffering endured by early Islam's women. I also demonstrate the highly communal character of Moharram piety and its implications for sectarian identity.

Devotional allegiance to the Ahl al-Bayt is a strong Shiʿi practice and in theory its expression is expected of both men and women, but in practice, Bohra popular rituals are dominated by women. A variety of reasons are cited for men's underrepresentation. The time-consuming role of attending to business and supporting a family makes their participation marginal. The money men spend for ritual purposes is considered demonstration of this devotion and compensates for their underrepresentation. Men are visible in some popular practices, such as shrine visits and male *majales* (*daris*), but they participate most actively in the Moharram rituals. During the first ten days of this important month, men are expected to close shop, participate in these practices, and partake in the blessings (*barakat*).

The Bohra Sect

The Muslim community in South Asia is composed of the majority Sunni and the minority Shiʿi sects. Shiʿis are divided into two major groups: the larger Twelver and the smaller Ismaʿili sect. Bohras and Khojas are sister subsects of the Ismaʿili branch. Among the Bohras there are several divisions—Daudi, Sulaymani, Aliya, and Mahdibaghwalla, that arose as a result of debates about succession (*nass*) of the agent (*daʿi* or *sayyedna*) of the hidden Imam. The *daʿis* came to India in the eleventh century to spread the Ismaʿili faith. Today, *daʿis* are no longer engaged in outwardly directed propaganda work. This paper concentrates on the largest group, the Daudi Bohras, hereafter referred to as the Bohras (popularly known as the Boris). Although a professional class of Bohras does exist, they are primarily a trading community and are relatively prosperous vis-à-vis other Muslim sects in western India, with the possible exception of the sister Khoja sect. It is an endogamous Gujarati-speaking group, numbering a million and located predominantly in western India, Pakistan, and Sri Lanka. While Bohras are scattered all over the world, their largest concentration outside South Asia is in East Africa. Bohras are mostly urban based and most live in community enclaves (*mahallehs*) that are characterized by homes, shops, secular schools, religious schools (*madraseh*), mosques, community halls, and occasionally a cemetery with a shrine. The religious life of the sect is overseen by a well-organized cleric class, with the *da'i* or *sayyedna* at the apex and his local agents or *amels* at the grassroots. Between the two extremes are various religious officials sanctioned to perform different religious duties such as leading the congregation in prayer, giving religious counsel, overseeing the application of personal law, and so on. A few women of the cleric class receive religious training to provide counseling to the female members of the flock, but the formal religious establishment is exclusively male.

With World War II, the nationalist struggle, social progress among other communities, and reform initiatives within the Bohra sect, there have been changes in women's status and role. Higher education for women was approved, *purdah* (veil) rules were relaxed, and women's increased public presence was tolerated.[5] These sweeping changes, however, were not accompanied by the reform of the personal law, or *shari'eh*, granting men the right to unilateral divorce, polygamy with the high priest's approval, and greater inheritance.[6] Today, women's roles and their status are structurally determined by establishment ideology and tempered by class, education, and residential location. There is a gender-based division of labor, with women engaged in domestic chores and child care and men engaged in work outside the home and supporting their families.

The literacy rate among women approaches one hundred percent, and some college education or a college degree is now an accepted norm among the young. Increased educational aspirations have resulted in an increase in the age of marriage for girls. Almost fifty percent of women engage in some income-generating work, based on traditional skills of sewing and crocheting among the old and tutoring children among the young. A small percentage is employed in a limited range of professional pursuits, while another small number assist in the family business. Because much of this work is confined to the home, the income over which they have control is not high enough to challenge the economic power of the family men or the clergy class. Women enjoy considerable decision-making authority in the family. Women's public presence and mobility are also acknowledged, and increasingly more professions are gaining acceptance.[7]

A covering dress, called the *rida*—a revival of *purdah*, in the late seventies, in a modern guise—is mandatory for communal occasions. Unlike the traditional black one-piece garment, it is a colorful two-piece dress made of cotton or synthetic material, tacked with lace and baubles. As a result, the *rida* is perceived more as a community dress than a form of veiling.

The Texture of Observed Islam

The religious lives of the Bohra include seven fundamental duties. Affection for the Prophet Mohammad and his relations "is *walaya*, the first pillar of Islam." This is very real in the Bohra community, whose *kalama* (confession of faith) says, "There is no god but God and Mohammad is his Prophet and Mowlana Ali is the friend of God and the executor (*wasi*) of the Prophet." Besides affection, the six other duties that compose worship are prayers (*ebadat*), tax (*zakat*), fasting in the month of Ramadan (*rowzeh*), pilgrimage to Mecca (*hajj*), religious defense (jihad), and obedience to the Twenty-First Hidden Imam, Tayeb Abu al-Qasem Amir al-Momenin.[8]

For the Bohras, like other Shi'i sects, to be a Muslim is to offer allegiance to a person as well as to a message, and allegiance is due to those acknowledged to be the legitimate successors of the Prophet. Bohras believe that after his death the Prophet intended Ali, his son-in-law and cousin, to succeed him, and after Ali, authority would be designated to certain of those among his descendants through Fatemeh, who was the Prophet's daughter and Ali's wife, and the sole source of grandchildren for the Prophet. Abu Bakr, father-in-law and the successor to the Prophet, whose adherents came to be called the Sunnis, usurped the caliphate. For the Shi'is, Ali's role as imam is a matter of designation (*nass*) both by God and His Prophet, and this designation is both political and spiritual. The complex of faith for the Shi'is rests on a belief in God and His Prophet coupled with a belief in the doctrine of the divinely designated leadership (*emamat*). A consequence and characteristic of this belief is an emotional devotion to the cause and persons of the household of the Prophet.[9]

Devotion to the family of the Prophet constitutes the bedrock of Shi'i piety. A variety of rituals abound that center on the holy five (*panjatan pak*)—the Prophet, Ali, Fatemeh, Hasan, and Hosayn. The second in line are the imams, who inspire allegiance because of their personalities, knowledge, and virtuous actions. These exceptional people are held up as paradigms of behavior. Following the imams are the *dais,* or religious leaders of the missionary effort *(da'wa),* and other holy persons. Year-round expression of popular piety is the hallmark of the Bohra sect. One need only examine their calendar to find it marked with important days of birth and death anniversaries of the Prophet, his family, and other saints and holy persons. However, three months in the Islamic calendar see a heightening of popular religiosity. These are Ramadan, Rajab, and Moharram. The obligatory fasting *(rowzeh),* individual prayer at home or congregational prayer at the mosque or at temporarily erected enclosures in residential compounds, and special long prayers on important nights are the prime religious features of Ramadan. The women of the family spend time preparing a mini-feast for breaking the fast. All other religious activities dedicated to different Islamic figures and regional pilgrimages come to a standstill during this month. Rajab, popularly referred to as the month of Ali (Ali *no mahino),* is characterized by meetings of women's neighborhood groups devoted to Ali in mosques, halls, or homes to call out his name. Men do not gather to call out the name of Ali. Sweets are distributed at these meetings for blessing, and the end-of-the-month neighborhood circles hold a ritual meal in which both men and women participate. To accumulate religious merit *(savab),* some men, but more women, fast during this month.

Unlike Ramadan and Rajab, the month of Moharram mobilizes and energizes the entire community—men and women, rich and poor, young and old—on a scale unmatched at any other time of the year. Devotional allegiance to the Prophet and his family is seen most clearly and forcefully in the rituals commemorating the martyrdom of Hosayn at the Battle of Karbala. The origins of these practices can be traced to the *da'is* (leaders of the missionary effort) who came to India in the eleventh century from Yemen and Egypt to spread the Isma'ili faith. The Bohras were variously persecuted under the Sultanate of Delhi, later the Sultanate of Gujarat, and thereafter by some Mughal emperors. During these times, many practices were suppressed. Under the Mughal emperor Aurengzeb's rule (1658–1707), for example, religious practices and rituals, including pilgrimages to various shrines and mourning ceremonies for the martyrdom of Imam Hosayn, were banned. With Aurengzeb's death, the Bohras were again generally permitted to practice their faith freely and the lamentation assemblies held during the early days of Moharram were revived in the eighteenth century under the thirty-eighth *da'i*—Isma'il Badr al-Din.[10] This commemoration finds articulation today in numerous ways.

Remembrance and the Colors of Mourning

This section describes the four primary ritual forms and their main features. Moharram rituals extend for a total of forty days—the prescribed period of mourning. The first ten days are characterized by intense piety, with a tapering off for the remaining period. The Bohri *mahalleh* and the adjoining Muslim neighborhood become energized with the numerous comings and goings of people and intense bazaar activity. The forms of popular piety include the sermon (*w'aaz*), lamentation assemblies (*majales,* singular *majles*), ritual meal tray (*hajari*), and setting up of temporary water stalls (*sabils*). Barring the first day of this month, for the next nine days the *sayyedna* holds the sermons for the community at the main mosque in a selected city, which is announced in advance. Colombo, Nairobi, Karachi, Surat, and Bombay have been popular centers in the past. Bohras from all over India and the rest of the world make an effort, for a few if not all ten days, to reach the center and hear and see (*didar*) their religious leader. Special seating and feeding arrangements are made to accommodate the large numbers that travel to the *w'aaz* center. In towns with a substantial Bohra population, the *sayyedna*'s agents conduct sermons in mosques. The community hall, school, and the *madraseh* are thrown open for the faithful to come and listen to these sermons. The *sayyedna* sits on a high podium; seated below on the ground at some distance on three sides are the members of his family and *marasya* (Shi'ite dirge) readers. Behind them are the ordinary members of the community. In the mosque, women are seated on the floor above. They can see the men's section through wooden lattice-screens. Noon prayers and a communal meal follow the sermon. The *w'aaz* is one of few occasions for a pan-communal (*jama'at*) meeting, and the smaller sermons are similarly occasions for the local *jama'at* to come together. On cue from the high priest, the sermons are interlaced with mini-*majales* characterized by *marasya* reading by all-male parties. With the introduction of modern technology, major Bohra centers receive a live relay of the high priest's sermon for one day.

A second form of popular devotion and by far the most pervasive ritual of this forty-day period are the lamentation assemblies, or *majales*. The assemblies held at this time are referred to as Hosayn's *majales* (Hosayn *ni majales*) or *gham ni majales,* mourning assemblies, as opposed to celebratory assemblies (*khoshi ni majales*),[11] which are held all year round, except the forty days. While the form and structure of all *majales* are similar, some distinctions need to be mentioned. Celebratory gatherings held in honor of any Islamic figure are privately sponsored in the domestic space; they are vow centered and usually related to rites of puberty, betrothal, and marriage of girls. These are exclusively female gatherings addressing specifically female concerns. The *daris* is the only men's celebratory *majles* (actually mixed-sex), held usually in honor of *sayyedna* Hatem, the third *da'i* buried in Yemen, and it revolves around the vow of economic sustenance. In a certain sense, Moharram is observed year round since one *marasya* for Hosayn and the women of Karbala is recited and minimal hand-*matam* is done at all celebratory gatherings, but these primarily constitute happy events. Moharram *majales,* or lamentation assemblies, on the other hand, are exclusively devoted to the martyrdom of Hosayn, and they may be privately or group sponsored, held in the domestic or community space, and they are not vow related. These lamentation assemblies can be classified into two types—the men's *majales,* which in practice are mixed-sex, and the women's *majales,* which are exclusively female activities. In every ethnic enclave for every day of the first ten days, men's *majales* are held in halls or mosques. These are scheduled after supper and are sponsored by men's groups (*anjomans*) or *sabil* committees. The seating arrangement is sex segregated, and women's roles are more passive, since the cantors or *marasya*-reciters (*marasya padvawalla*) are men.

After the tenth day, men's *majales,* usually *sabil*-committee sponsored, take place on the important days such as the twelfth (*ziyarat*) and fortieth (*chehellom*) day after Hosayn's martyrdom. These are accompanied by a meal. Women's lamentation assemblies are not held in the first ten days, but are abundant after the tenth day. Traditionally, these gatherings were held in the home, but in recent years women have been encouraged by the religious establishment to have their gatherings in halls or mosques. In practice, it is often difficult to implement this edict. Whether a *majles* is held in the home or at the hall/mosque depends on a variety of factors. First, the size of the Bohra population in a place: a larger concentration provides greater freedom to sponsor gatherings in the home. Second, the size of the house: in bigger houses it is convenient to call a gathering. City-dwellers prefer to sponsor a *majles* in their homes, but in smaller towns where there is greater enclave living and conformity, women's *majales* are held in the mosque or a hall. These collectivities are held in the late afternoon and no men are present during the recitation. Women's assemblies in the home are followed by a meal, and a few close male relatives may be invited to partake in the blessed food. The hall- or mosque-based *majales* are sponsored singly or jointly by multiple families or by a local committee set up to collect cash for the purpose of a meal or sweet distributed for blessing (*salavat*). At women's *marasya* parties, reciters are invited by rotation to recite.

At domestic gatherings, the private sponsor may invite her favorite cantors, who are often booked in advance and may come year after year. The recitation lasts for just over an hour. Doors and windows are all thrown open, and homes are often decorated with bright lights, incense, flowers, and new curtains, giving the place a celebratory atmosphere. Two interpretations are given as to how one reconciles mourning with this celebratory touch. According to some, it is a celebration of Hosayn's sacrifice, his meeting with the Almighty, and Islam's survival, whereas a more common belief is that the Karbala figures are present at these gatherings and the sacred space needs to be pure and beautified.

A less common ritual is the *hajari,* or ritual meal tray. This is an exclusively female gathering scheduled on the seventh day (sixth night, to be precise) to commemorate the sacrifices of Abbas Alam Dar, the half brother of Imam Hosayn. This is the only all-women's ritual within the first ten days of this important month. For reasons that are not entirely clear, this practice has been discouraged by the establishment and is not observed in small towns. However, it continues to be popular among women in Mumbai, which has the largest concentration of Bohras. It is privately sponsored in the domestic space and guests usually include neighbors, close friends, and kin. There may or may not be a *majles* preceding the ritual meal tray. The distribution of water, a common Shiʻi practice, is related to the thirst of the martyrs of Karbala. For this purpose, temporary stalls (*sabils*) are erected in the Bohri *mahallehs* and are operative for ten days. These may be decorated with large mirrors and chandeliers, and on special nights are festooned with mini-lights and flowers, giving the enclave a festive atmosphere at night. Each *sabil* has its own all-male managing committee which is responsible for putting up and dismantling stalls. During these ten days, participants abstain from all forms of entertainment, such as watching television, going to the cinema, picnics, and so forth. Despite the overall mourning atmosphere, Moharram rituals bring together both sorrowful and festive features.

What are the main ingredients of these four rituals? The central feature of the *wʻaaz* is a monologue by the high priest. The *sayyedna*'s discourse and those of his various agents center on the history of Islam starting with Adam and Eve, the events at Karbala, the sacrifices of Hosayn, Abbas Alam Dar, and others at the battle, the illness of Hosayn's son Ali (Zayn al-Abidin), the suffering and loss of the women of the Ahl al-Bayt, and the injustices inflicted by the usurpers of the caliphate. Besides the religious discourse, the *sayyedna* and his representatives may touch on a variety of topics, such as cleanliness, personal hygiene, sound dietary habits, the correct treatment of children, gender relations, and so on. At no time are wider social and political issues addressed at these communal gatherings. *Marasya* recitation is part and parcel of the sermons. With a cue and encouragement from the high priest, the monologue is interspersed with *marasya* reading by male cantors accompanied by sobbing, hand-*matam*, and calling out "Ya Hosayn, Ya Hosayn," "Ya Ali Mowla, Ya Ali Mowla," in chorus by all present. The main ingredient of the *majales* is *marasya* recitation, which retells the stories of Hosayn and his companions, male and female, at Karbala. The purpose is to refresh one's memory, demonstrate allegiance, and evoke grief. Recitation is accompanied by sobbing and, for men, vigorous beating of the chest with both hands, and for women a more gentle beating with one hand, and calling out "Ya Hosayn, Ya Hosayn," "Ya Ali Mowla, Ya Ali Mowla." The day of Moharram, on which the *majles* is held, highlights the particular historical circumstances of the day. The men's *majales* have male cantors and are held in public halls, whereas women's *majales* have female cantors and are held in either domestic or public space. Some of the *marasyas* are well known to the women and they quietly join the cantors in recitation, feeling actively involved in the gathering. The gathering ends with a prayer (*du'a*) of supplication to the martyrs of Karbala to ease their difficulties and to heal their sorrows. A short prayer is said for the living *dai* for his health and long life and to invoke his blessing for the flock. The congregation then stands up and recites the *wazifo*, described as the equivalent of the community's anthem. It is a prayer of thanksgiving that marks the end of every *majles*. The most important ingredient of the *hajari*[12] is a ritual sweet, but other kinds of food are also included. While a blessing (*salavat*) may be said on any sweet, it is common on the seventh day to say a blessing on a sweet of colorful dough balls and bananas (*kani anea kela*). Traditionally, the banana has been associated with Abbas Alam Dar and symbolizes the standard of Hosayn, and the rest of the meal tray contains common food items found in a Middle Eastern meal. Nine women sit around a tray (*thal*) and help themselves to the blessed food, and then another nine sit till all the guests have partaken in the blessed sweets and food.

The main purpose of the temporary stalls (*sabils*) is to distribute water. Children often serve at these stalls, accepting donations in the form of petty cash, which are placed in a special box for that purpose (*niyaz*). On important nights, the stalls distribute different types of sherbet or milk shakes. These drinks are also sent to each *sabil* member's home for saying the blessing. The Bohra enclaves are a beehive of activity for ten days as men and women shop and move from sermons to *majales* and among homes, halls, and mosques for prayer. This activity reaches a climax on the seventh day as crowds stop to look at the richly decorated *sabils*. They help themselves to the drinks and ritual sweets offered at these stalls. The enclaves are full of vendors selling bananas, and sweetmeat shops are piled high with colorful sweet dough balls.

Shades of Mourning: Sectarian Rituals

It is not my purpose here to describe the rituals of sister Shiʿi sects, but simply to highlight major sectarian differences and similarities. Twelver Shiʿis observe a rich variety of mourning rituals. These include live *taʿziyeh* productions in major urban centers as well as videos narrating the history of Islam and depicting the Battle of Karbala. Cassette recorders blare out *marasyas* in enclaves and community halls. There is a nightly *majles* for ten days in their halls (*emamwadas*). The climax of these rituals is the *jolus*, or the procession on the tenth day, Ashura.[13] These rituals are dominated by men, but women dressed in black attend the night *majales*, sit on benches, and watch the videos showing Islam's past, drink water from the *sabils*, go to see the *taʿziyehs*, and observe the *jolus* from roads or from their windows. They also go to see the grave coverings (*zarihs*) and other icons put up in a room at their hall. Though women's participation is at the margins, all Moharram observances see a strong public presence of women and are strikingly mixed-sex in nature. Many Bohras, both men and women, used to go see the *taʿziyehs*, attend their nightly gatherings, and watch the procession. In recent years, however, the religious establishment has discouraged the community from participating in Twelver Shiʿi activities. The Khojas, another sister Shiʿi sect, is ritually highly insulated. They have no public observances during this month. Their single most important practice is the reciting of devotional poetry (*ginans*) which is attributed to their medieval Ismaʿili spiritual guides—the *dais* and the *pirs*. The *ginans* are recited in their prayer halls (*jamaʿat khanehs*) every day and on special occasions. Modern scholarship has ignored their popular practices; hence nothing definitive can be said of their observances.

Gender and Ritual

In this section, I highlight the gendered nature of the four rituals and their implications for gender identity. The *wʿaaz* has a small component of gender and gender relations. When gender relations are mentioned by the high priest, the focus is on traditional gender roles and the proper duties of husbands and wives. At one *w'aaz* I attended, the *sayyedna* spoke about the importance of not bothering men with the problems of the day as soon as they return home from work, but rather allowing them to rest and serving them tea. Men are urged to treat women with respect and affection. Fatemeh Zahra is projected as the ideal wife and mother; women who emulate her, those who are worthy wives and mothers, deserve respect and good treatment. At the priestly sermons, Hosayn and his male companions are lauded as models of self-sacrifice, and the implication is that similar sacrifices may be expected of men in future religious injustices. The suffering and supportive role of women at Karbala forms an important if not central motif of the discourse.

Whereas sermons cover more than just the narration of events at Karbala, lamentation assemblies focus entirely on Karbala. The men of Karbala are the centerpiece in men's *majales*. Islam's women at Karbala, their grief and loss, are secondary and lack the same salience. On the other hand, the women of Karbala are the heart of the *marasyas* read at women's gatherings, emphasizing their support, sorrow, loss, and strength. The women—Zaynab and Kolsum (Hosayn's sisters); Soghra, Kobra, and Sakineh (his daughters); and Banu (his wife)—involved in the tragedy are important players. The grief and suffering of Zaynab is the high point, with Sakineh's childlike nature and innocence forming another motif. One by one, the martyred Hosayn and his companions are carried to the tent of the suffering Zaynab, whose suffering and bravery at Karbala are emphasized as she cradles her dead sons and brother in her lap. Bravery and courage are not male qualities, but a resource given to women. Just as facing an enemy takes courage, so does seeing one's loved ones die. Sakineh's betrothal to Abdullah, the pulling out of her earrings by the enemies as the caravan moves to Misar, and her detention and eventual death are played out. Soghra was left behind in Medina because she was sick. One *marasya* focuses on her in which she watches the party (*kafileh*) depart for Karbala. Banu weeps as she cradles the dead body of her son Ali Asghar and cries out, "Whose cradle will I rock now? Though Fatemeh was not part of the Karbala *kafileh*, she is described as a mute and helpless witness to the fate of her son. Women members of the Ahl al-Bayt are emphasized in these dirges. The great and well-known women of Islam had all suffered, and suffering is part of life and a condition of keeping one's faith alive. The suffering Zaynab and other women experienced is universal and unique to women. Only women understand what it is to lose a brother, husband, or son. When the family is lost, the women's world is lost. The solidarity and support of the family, manifested in brother-sister, brother-brother, and father-children relations, is vital in trying times and is a vital motif of this discourse. Men were in the forefront, but women's support was critical to maintaining male morale and for the survival of Shiʿism. Their roles are perceived as being different from those of men, which does not necessarily imply that they are less crucial. By reciting these *marasyas,* participants reclaim what is important to them in Islam and, by appealing to the women of early Islamic history, they assert values central to their own self-image, those of sister, daughter, and mother.

The discourse of *hajari* centers on the sacrifices of Abbas Alam Dar and praise and appreciation of his personal qualities. Because of his youth and the compassion he showed in this battle, Abbas Alam Dar is perceived as approachable, generous, and softhearted. This ritual is an occasion to acknowledge the qualities women value in a male, an opportunity to make a vow (*mennat*), and petition for a boon from him. As one woman said, "He will give what you ask for." Because the *hajari* is held in the domestic space, it is a chance for women to bring bounty (*barakat*) to the home and accumulate religious merit (*savab*) for the entire family. The ritual meal tray and the women's *majales* emphasize the benefit to the family and home, as opposed to rituals that are public and communal in character. The *hajari* may also be seen as women's way of compensating for men's domination of *sabils,* especially on the seventh day of the martyrdom of Abbas Alam Dar, and an attempt to insert an all-women's ritual in the critical first ten days. In the putting up, management, and dismantling of the *sabils,* women have no role. They may become its members, make cash contributions for religious merit, partake in the water and sherbet, and participate in their sponsored assemblies. Moharram observances extend from the domestic through communal to public spaces and women's participation becomes more passive and marginal the more public a ritual becomes.

Meaning and Significance

What significance do these rituals have for the people, especially for the women? Here I use Vernon Schubel's definition of ritual as a performance involving an encounter with powerful symbols. This crucial month allows for reflection on the most powerful symbols of Shiʿi piety—the Ahl al-Bayt and the martyrs of Karbala. Meanings may be broadly classified into several categories, such as religious, social, educational, and functional. For both men and women, Moharram is a time to remember Karbala events, to grieve and mourn, thereby bringing about immediate spiritual benefit and catharsis. It is a time to learn about the tragedies in Islam's past and to demonstrate loyalty to Ali. For both men and women, it is a time of the year to accumulate religious merit and blessings (*barakat*). It is an occasion for the flock to call on (*do'a*) Hosayn to help and heal them, to ease their difficulties, and call them for pilgrimage to Karbala. In addition, it is an occasion for women, who are excluded from the formal religious establishment, to recognize their own role in Islamic piety. This role facilitates reflection on their condition and station in life and enables them to draw strength from the lives of Islam's women. As one woman said, "Listening to the *marasyas* gives me strength to fight my own battles with depression and a difficult marriage. Another said, "It gives me peace of mind." Karbala rituals confirm the importance of women in the history of Shi'i Islam. Women come away from these *majales* realizing that far from being outsiders living on the fringes of Islam, women have been at the center of the faith. The *majales* narratives teach women to follow in the footsteps of those other women who suffered for their beliefs. Men are the defenders of faith, and women are the supporters of men in the protection of the faith. Their role is indirect but just as decisive.

Moharram rituals are strongly communal in character. *W'aaz*, *hajari*, and *majales* offer acceptable ways of people getting together and all have social consequences. Men's *majales* and gathering around the *sabils* in the evenings are arenas for male bonding. For women, the opportunities to gather are considerably greater and longer. These practices, especially *hajari* and women's *majales*, allow women to engage in social exchanges that otherwise might be denied to them; they can create a women's subsociety and culture over which they have control, and they can autonomously address their various concerns. These practices also permit women access to the family's surplus income, because men would hesitate to refuse a demand to hold a ritual. Display of nice clothing and ornaments is discouraged. This is a time to demonstrate allegiance rather than status. Also at these gatherings, several social functions are accomplished; gifts (*hadyo*) brought from regional pilgrimage places or other kinds of travel are given to family and kin, invitations are extended for forthcoming religious gatherings and marriages, current news is exchanged, and so on. Women in their teens are socialized into the community's traditions and rituals. Many women hold these rituals because of interest (*shaukh*), faith (*iman*), and the need to continue with a family tradition.

Food is central to almost every ritual. Feeding family, friends, and neighbors has many meanings for the women. It is an expression of hospitality, an act of accumulating religious merit, and a sign of plenty and of being truly blessed. Offering food and eating around a tray is what binds people in a circle of friendship. Women, by having their own rituals from which men are excluded, counterbalance male hegemony over public and establishment religion. The *wʿaaz* is an educational vehicle both in Islam's history and in the practicalities of everyday living; the *majales* instructs the faithful in the verities of Islam.

No analysis of Moharram observances is complete without an analysis of their implications for gender and sectarian identity. Mourning rituals, as already mentioned, reinforce traditional gender roles and identity. Their role in maintaining sectarian identity is also important. Across sects, there are similarities in popular Islam, but also differences that set them apart. The month of mourning is an occasion for all Shiʿis to experience a shared history, to make a public statement about their allegiance, to remember, and to grieve. These emotions bind the pan-Shiʿi community. However, the manner of expressing this shared emotion sets them apart. Extreme and dramatic forms of expression such as flagellation with chains and knives (*zanjir ka matam*), walking on coals (*ag ka matam*), or mock funerals find little support among the Bohras. They are spectators in Twelver Shiʿis rituals, but their own practices are in-house, thereby creating and maintaining a sectarian identity. Popular observances among the Khojas are sparse and relegated to the privacy of their community prayer halls. The variety in observed sectarian rituals highlights the unity and diversity in observed Islam. The underlying unity suggests possibilities of a pan-Shiʿi identity, but this has been overshadowed by the need for a stronger sectarian identity.

Conclusions

Moharram rituals are part of a rich fabric of Bohra religious activities. It is a month of intensified piety, and due to its public nature, men dominate, though both genders participate. Although secondary, women are visible in all public and men's rituals, whereas men are excluded from female-dominated domestic observances. These rituals span from public-based to domestic-based, and women's agency increases as one moves from the public to the private sphere. Women's *majales* and the *hajari*, from which men are excluded, compensate for women's marginalization in other observances in the crucial first ten days. These exclusive gatherings allow

women to affirm their place in Shi'i piety and acknowledge their decisive role in Islam's history. They have also facilitated the development of
women's subsociety, a need apparently felt strongly among the women. The
need for women's subculture in a milieu characterized by mixed genders,
but also characterized by social distance between men and women, cannot be overstated. Based as they are in religious orthodoxy, these observances typecast women in traditional gender roles. Emancipatory potential
in patriarchal religion is problematic, and it may be that the women restrict their participation to popular practices in part to compensate for their
exclusion from the formal religious establishment.

The differences across sects in Moharram commemorations highlight
the continuing need to keep the social, cultural, and religious exclusive-
ness of each sect intact. The various sects are physically close, but this
does not translate into social closeness. Clearly, more scholarly attention to
Islam in South Asia is needed. Vernon Schubel alludes to women's *majales*
among Twelver Shi'i women, but the form and content these take during
this particular month is not known. Among the Khojas, knowledge about
what particular, if any, *ginans*, or devotional poems, are part of the mourning month would help complete the picture of this important event in the
Islamic calendar. Ritual and festival occasions spawn a thriving business
among the petty shopkeepers and hawkers in the enclave economy. These
are a source of economic sustenance to many a Bohra and other Muslims;
the relationship between ritual and riches would be worth exploring.

Notes

1. Imtiaz Ahmad, *Ritual and Religion among Muslims in India* (Delhi: Manohar,
1981).

2. Peter Van Der Veer, "Playing or Praying: A Sufi Saint's Day in Surat," *The
Journal of Asian Studies* 51:3 (1992), 545–564.

3. Vernon James Schubel, *Religious Performance in Contemporary Islam: Shi'a
Devotional Rituals in South Asia* (Columbia: University of South Carolina Press,
1993).

4. Gustav Thaiss, "Muharram Rituals or the Carnivalesque in Trinidad," *ISIM
Newsletter* (1999), 38.

5. Rehana Ghadially, "The Campaign for Women's Emancipation in an Isma'ili
Shii (Daudi Bohras) Sect of Indian Muslims, 1925–1945," *Dossier* 14/15 (1996a),
641–685.

6. Rehana Ghadially, "Women and Personal Law in an Isma'ili (Daudi Bohra)
Sect of Indian Muslims," *Islamic Culture* 1 (1996c), 27–51.

7. Rehana Ghadially, "On Their Own Initiative: Changing Lives of Bohra Muslim Women," *Manushi* 96 (1996b), 311–339.

8. J. Blank, *Mullahs on the Mainframe: Islam and Modernity among the Daudi Bohras* (Chicago: University of Chicago Press, 2001).

9. Schubel, *Religious Performance*.

10. F. Daftary, *The Isma'ilis: Their History and Doctrines* (Delhi: Munshiram Manoharlal Publications, 1990).

11. For details on celebratory rituals, see Rehana Ghadially, "Women's Religious Gatherings in a South Asian Muslim Sect," *Thamyris* 6:1 (1999), 43–63.

12. For a detailed account of the *hajari* ritual, see Rehana Ghadially, "Hajari (Ritual Meal Tray) for Abbas Alam Dar: Women's Household Rituals in a South Asian Muslim Sect," *The Muslim World* 93:2 (April 2003), 309–321.

13. For a detailed description of these observances, see Schubel, *Religious Performance*.

CHAPTER 9

Women of Karbala Moving to America
Shi'i Rituals in Iran, Pakistan, and California

MARY ELAINE HEGLAND

When Muslims come to America, what changes take place in religious beliefs, rituals, and practices? With so many people from Muslim societies migrating to the United States in recent decades, this question becomes all the more relevant. After September 11, 2001, even the most insular of Americans suddenly became aware of Islam and Muslims. Americans who are less familiar with Islam and Muslims have generally assumed Islam to be a monolithic religion consisting of beliefs uniformly held by all Muslims without regard to regional, generational, class, and cultural distinctions. Furthermore, many Americans see Islam and Muslims as existing "out there in the Middle East," far away from America. By looking at Shi'i Muslim women who have migrated from Iran, Pakistan, and India to Northern California, this chapter reminds us that Islam and Muslims are not just "out there" in the Middle East, North Africa, or Asia. They are also part of the United States. In fact, Muslims form the second largest religious group in the United States after Christians. Muslims and Islam are not "out there." On the contrary, they are "in here."

Comparing Shi'a women's rituals in an Iranian village, Peshawar, Pakistan, and among people of Iranian, Pakistani, and Indian backgrounds living in California's Santa Clara demonstrates that Islamic beliefs, the relative importance of Islam in people's lives, and levels of adherence differ, even within one Islamic tradition. The interpretations of Shi'i martyrdom stories, applications, and power and pervasiveness are modified through time, space, and political, cultural, economic, and social change. This comparison of Shi'i women's mourning ceremonies in three different countries confirms that Islamic belief and behavior systems are neither monolithic nor static. Muslim rituals, beliefs, worldviews, and practices vary greatly throughout the world. Consequently, Muslims cannot all be conceptualized as one uniform group.

In analyzing the level of participation in the religious rituals of Shiʿi women who have come to America, I examine the following conditions: (1) the trends in their society of origin, (2) their own personal situations before migrating, (3) the reasons and conditions of their emigration to the United States, and (4) their living situations in this country. Based on socio-cultural anthropological field research in the village of "Aliabad," Iran, in Peshawar, Pakistan, among Iranian Americans, and in a Santa Clara Valley mosque attended by people from Pakistan and India, in addition to study of other research publications, this chapter addresses the question of how Iranian and Pakistani/Indian Shiʿi women's ritual participation is transformed when people come from these countries to the United States. Through inter-viewing and participant observation with Shiʿi women in Iran, Pakistan, and the United States, I have attempted to understand personal meanings, benefits, and constraints of ritual involvement and affiliation with the mar-tyred saints of Karbala and the movements and communities they inspire. I aim to understand personally held viewpoints. At the same time, I am interested in how specific historical contexts influence people's interpre-tation of the Shiʿi martyrdom paradigm and how people wield this para-digm in society. Other Americans may also have a particular interest in how Shiʿi Islam and the beliefs and practices of immigrant Shiʿi Muslims are expressed within the American context.

The following questions will be addressed in this chapter: (1) How do women's needs and expectations of religious ritual change upon coming to the new environment? (2) To what degree do they continue to look to Shiʿi rituals to address their needs and problems? (3) Do they feel their rituals satisfy these personal expectations, or do they feel disappointed by these ritual practices and turn to other rituals or gatherings? (4) Do the patterns of women's participation in sex-integrated versus sex-segregated religious gatherings differ in the United States from the patterns of participation in their home countries, and if so, how? (5) Do men come to speak, preach, or lead women's rituals more or less than in home countries? (6) Do women take greater or lesser leadership roles in mixed gatherings and congrega-tions than in home countries? (7) In general, how do women's contributions to, and participation in, Iranian and Pakistani/Indian Shiʿi religious rituals differ in the Northern California setting? (8) If they have changed, what are the influences on and reasons for these modifications? Sociocultural an-thropological research in Iran between June 1978 and December 1979, in Peshawar, Pakistan, between August 1990 and January 1991 and between

July and September 1991, and in California's Santa Clara Valley from 1989 to the present, have provided material to entertain these questions about American Shi'i women's ritual participation.

Women and Shi'i Mourning Rituals in the Village of Aliabad, Iran

In 1978, when I was conducting fieldwork in Aliabad, a village outside of the southwestern Iranian city of Shiraz, women did not play prominent roles in Shi'i rituals. Several women held weekly *rowzehs*, or commemorative gatherings in which a male *rowzeh khan* or chanter recited stories about the martyrs of Karbala and led prayers for a few neighborhood women. The women listened and wept at the saddest parts in the stories, and then afterward shared tea and some conversation. Generally excluded from mosque attendance, women also faced restrictions during the Moharram commemorations of the martyrdom of Imam Hosayn and his compatriots. In the lunar month of Moharram, and especially during the days leading up to the tenth day of that month, which is the anniversary of the 680 AD martyrdom, and then the third day afterward, men paraded around the village dressed in black, chanting mourning couplets and practicing self-flagellation. Older or infirm men rhythmically gave themselves symbolic taps on the head. Family men generally beat themselves on the chest, while some of the younger men struck themselves on the back with a flail of chains, an innovation imported from the cities.

It was generally believed that women should ideally remain at home, though a few women and younger girls might edge along alleyway walls to watch, their veils wrapped carefully around themselves. Some watched from rooftops, making sure to stay far enough away from the edge to avoid notice. Women prepared food to distribute in connection with vows to the Karbala saints. Of course, the womenfolk of the family arranged and cooked for many of the commemorative meals held during the days of mourning. In 1978, however, people held such dinners far less frequently than in earlier days, before centralization of political power in the 1950s and 1960s.[1]

Before political centralization and pacification of the countryside, when local leaders competed for the position of village headman, lavish meals and nightly passion plays with actors hired from Shiraz demonstrated a headman or contender's wealth and power. Hosting Moharram feasts and performances helped attract and maintain political supporters. Gavam, a

powerful landlord who owned the land of Aliabad and lived in Shiraz, ratified the winner of local political competitions, conferring power and advantages upon the victor. The womenfolk of political leaders played crucial
roles in organizing and providing hospitality for the Moharram programs.
Outside women, especially neighbors and relatives, could attend these programs, sitting separately from the men. After political centralization, central and provincial political forces maintained their village representatives
in power. Large Moharram gatherings declined, and, with them came a
decline in the participation of women in listening and weeping at passion
plays as well as their behind-the-scenes but crucial roles in providing hospitality.

   During the 1978 and 1979 revolutionary period, religiously oriented political activity gained prominence. In urban areas, women, covered with
black veils, marched in separate groups from the men in political demonstrations, couched in Islamic religious terms, against the shah's government. Several village women participated in the ninth and tenth of Moharram marches in Shiraz. A few high school girls from Aliabad even returned
to march with the huge crowd of men who demonstrated in the village.
After these days, in the darkness after the electricity was turned off, a neighborhood group of women began holding nightly demonstrations in their
own dead-end alleyway. As time went by, the women and girls gained courage and ventured farther, finally walking the entire alleyway circle within
the village walls. Males joined them, with boys and teenagers coming out
first and men only later on.

   During the 1979 Moharram season, the local "peasant" faction celebrated their new political victory over the shah's government faction with
fluorescent commemorations. They did not allow supporters of the for-
merly powerful government representatives to participate in the men's self-
flagellation parade around the village. Again, several of the men from the
peasant faction hosted large commemorative feasts. Victorious supporters
of the newly reigning faction went all out for the parade on the third day
after the martyrdom anniversary. They hired horses and camels to carry
Shemr, Imam Hosayn's assassin, and black-robed men played the parts of
the captive womenfolk being taken to Damascus. During the December
1979 post-revolution mourning season, a few women and girls walked at
the rear of the men in some village mourning parades. Women played significant behind-the-scene roles organizing, cooking, and providing hospitality. However, village women did not convene their own segregated Moharram ritual gatherings.[2]

   Urban Iranian women enjoyed more opportunities to attend women's rituals. Although in joint male-female rituals they were expected to be out of sight or segregated and formed the smaller proportion of participants, they could attend home-based sex-segregated rituals for women. Often a woman preacher, or *rowzeh khan*, led these less formal women's rituals. Women enjoyed the socializing, as well as the spiritual and emotional solace, of listening to saints' stories, weeping, and praying, as anthropologist Anne Betteridge has documented for Shirazi women.[3] They could hope for assistance from the martyrs with mundane problems in exchange for their devotion. Refreshments and meals added to the attraction.

Women's participation in protest marches, often in memory of a person killed during the revolutionary struggle, added greatly to the numbers and impact. Peaceful marches, strikes, and printed, taped, and both formal and informal oral communication brought about the Iranian Revolution. The dramatic presence of masses of women covered in black chadors became a powerful symbol for this movement.[4] Ritual marches conflated the anti-shah movement with the Shi'i Karbala myth and paradigm, with its holy martyrs and captives, to create a powerful symbolic complex available to oppositional forces. The enormous protest marches of the ninth and tenth of Moharram in 1978 throughout Iran, with women composing some half of the participants, profoundly affected the Moharram ritual of the day and marked the turning point of the shift of power from the Pahlavi government to the revolutionary forces. The shah's government fell two months later, on February 11, 1979. Gradually, Shi'i religious figures monopolized political authority. Due to their leading roles in organizing and framing the revolution in a situation where secular opposition was outlawed, this takeover was relatively easy.[5]

Peshawar, Pakistani Shi'i Women, and Moharram Rituals

The Shi'is in Peshawar in 1990–1991 felt beleaguered by the Sunni population and discriminated against by the Sunni government of Pakistan.[6] Shi'is were angry about the unpunished 1988 assassination of the highest-ranking Pakistani ayatollah in Peshawar and by the frequent killings of Shi'is during Moharram rituals in Pakistan.[7] In addition to the violence and threats against their safety, Shi'is experienced discrimination in education and employment. Because of the political threat from the Sunni government and population in Peshawar, and the occurrence of much violence and killing during Moharram practices, Shi'is sensed the need for unity—the need to form an interest group. The conflict between Shi'is and the Sunni government and society resulted in diminishing expressions of the differences between the diverse Shi'i ethnic groups. Peshawar Shi'is from various ethnic groups strengthened their ties with each other, increasing communication and joining each other's rituals.

Peshawar Shi'i women built unity and ties among the various ethnic groups through their numerous mourning rituals. Male leaders promoted the ritual activities of their female family members. More active than males in Moharram rituals, women attended up to eight rituals a day at homes and *hosayniyyehs* (buildings dedicated to mourning rituals). Women usually led their own rituals, as preachers, *rowzeh khans,* mourning singers, couplet chanters, readers, and prayer leaders. These women demonstrated far more emotionally expressive and physically active mourning than I had witnessed in Iran. They chanted and sang together in loud voices, usually standing. Naturally, women did not strip the upper parts of their bodies, as did men. Although men beat their backs with flails of chain, drawing blood to flow down on to their loose white pants, women did not draw blood from themselves. Women nevertheless practiced vigorous self-flagellation. They flung either one or two arms up into the air, and then brought them rapidly back to strike themselves sharply on the chest with either one hand after the other or both at the same time, in time to the singing or chanting. During women's *majales* (mourning gatherings) at *hosayniyyeh*s, the sound of many palms hitting chests made reverberating, rhythmic throbs. Particularly when its handlers brought Zu al-Jenah—the white horse representing Imam Hosayn's bereft steed—into a women's ritual, the level of noise, emotion, and action heightened. Women broke out into more distraught weeping, chanting, and thumping of their heads. When they shifted to beating their heads, the sound, still very loud, changed from hollow to sharp. Women with particularly pressing problems ran after the horse, afraid of his hoofs yet determined to touch him or gain his attention with their frantic cries.

Some women developed a reputation as outstanding performers and were much in demand for *majales.* Shi'i women reached out to women of other ethnic groups, inviting them to their *majales* and reminding leaders to include songs and couplets in the different languages. Through their ritual participation, Shi'i women helped to bring Mohajerin (emigrants from India), Pushtun, and Qizelbash Shi'is into one large community and identity group.[8]

In this situation, women did not seem to challenge or question the gender constructions of their religion or their communities. Gender conflict was muted. To support their own interests, women appeared to feel that their best strategy was to stick to the "patriarchal bargain,"[9] providing labor and allegiance to their men and male-run communities in return for support and protection. Other opportunities were lacking. Women could not live on their own; they felt compelled to obey men and devote themselves to community, family, ethnic group, and religion. If they wanted satisfying lives and opportunities to develop excellence, they felt that they should look to family, community, and religion, rather than to personal autonomy. In the Peshawar situation, then, gender and ethnic differences were muted as Shi'i women cooperated to commemorate the martyrdom of Imam Hosayn and his group and support their co-religionists under siege from the surrounding Sunni population and government.

Women and Shi'i Rituals in California's Santa Clara Valley

Over time, or when people leave home areas to go to new environments, conditions necessarily change. The religious, spiritual, and social needs and opportunities of some women will evolve. Women may have new expectations of religious ritual, or they may find that religious ritual has little or no place in their lives. Depending on the extent to which women can modify ritual practices and gatherings to address their evolved spectrum of needs, they may continue to engage in these ritual practices, reduce their involvement, or seek out other associations or ritual gatherings.

Iranian Shi'i Women Questioning Religious Authority and Shi'i Rituals

Most Iranian women of Shi'i background in Northern California participate infrequently in Shi'i rituals. Iranian immigrants are of relatively upper socioeconomic class, well educated, and generally secular. Some American-educated women who came from religious families, such as *bazaris*, or clerics, may have sisters, mothers, grandmothers, or other female relatives who continued participating heavily in mourning rituals. Given the secularized middle- and upper-middle-class identity of the majority of Californian Iranian Americans, however, these women generally would not have been the most active in women's *sofreh*, *rowzeh*, and *majles* rituals, even in Iran.[10] The majority of Iranian women who have come to the United States are from secular, urban, middle-upper-class backgrounds. The rural women with whom I worked in Aliabad, or those with whom Anne Betteridge worked in Shiraz, who were religious and lower or middle class, would not commonly be found in the United States.

Iranians migrated to the United States both before and after the 1978–
1979 revolution. During the 1970s, Iranians formed the largest group of
foreign students in the United States. Many Iranian women were educated
in this country and are well integrated into American society. Women who
came to the United States from more secularized backgrounds with the aim
of pursuing their own educations and career development often traveled
here alone or received some support from a brother, sister, or other relative. These women might have become connected with the Confederation
of Iranian Students or other radical groups or women's organizations. Such
women devoted themselves to their education, career, and new connections
with other young Iranian students. In reaction to their new surroundings,
young Iranian women who came to the United States to pursue an education often went through a difficult phase of questioning their learned ideas
about self and social structure.

Many women have eventually emerged from this stage and, through
much struggle and a long process of effort and struggle for change, have
built up new structures of meaning and styles of life for themselves.[11] These
women are often not interested in maintaining the same type of ritual and
visiting circle social relations that are typical for women in their home
countries. Rather, they aim to develop more autonomous selves and to construct social circles comprised of other women in similar situations with
similar goals. These circles then become support groups for developing new
selves and gender roles, new types of relationships, and new ways of dealing with the world, rather than for maintaining "Islamic" lifestyles. Often
such women do not see themselves as primarily family members—wives
and mothers whose lives are dedicated to serving their families. Rather,
they want to see themselves as autonomous individuals, wishing to promote growth and development in themselves and in others. They often do
not wish to follow the expectations of others about what they should be
like and how they should live. Rather, these women wish to develop their
own independent values and expect a more egalitarian and mutually supportive relationship with a man. If a marriage fails to offer them such a
relationship, they are often willing to go through a divorce; many of them
have done just that.

These women, who have now been living in the United States for some
time, even up to thirty or more years, lead quite different lives from those
of their mothers. Often they are politically radical or leftist. They often are
atheist or agnostic, and often are committed to women's liberation. These
women participate very little, if at all, in Shi'i rituals. Originally, many
members of the large Confederation of Iranian Students went on to become

associated with other American and Iranian political, social, and cultural groups. An Iranian American friend provides an example of such a life history. "Azad" remembers herself as a pious and devout Muslim teenager. One of her sisters maintained her identity as a very religious woman. Azad, however, along with some fellow university students, turned to social criticism and Marxism. After earning a government fellowship, Azad came to the United States for graduate study. Here she became heavily involved in the Iranian student movement against the shah's regime. One year, she was elected to be the women's representative for the national leadership group. After the Iranian Revolution, however, critical of the new government's neglect of women's issues, she became disillusioned with male-dominated Iranian student groups. She devoted her efforts to women's groups and other groups and movements. Another friend related,

> Yes, I am from a religious family. Two of my uncles were theology professors at Tehran University. Two of my sisters-in-law wore a chador [veil] under the shah. Every year my father gave one of the biggest Moharram mourning ceremonies in my neighborhood. My brother supported a lot of theological figures in Iran. They were not necessarily Khomeini types, but they were religious. One of my nephews teaches theology at Tehran University. I was wearing a miniskirt and going to *sofrehs,* because they were in my house. There are a lot of families like this. Often, it is the mother and grandmother. My sisters-in-law are twenty years older than me, so they could be like that generation. My sister-in-law is very rigid in her ideas, but her own daughter—if you left it up to her, she probably wouldn't wear any skirt. . . . Until at least fourteen, I was very religious. I had fear of God. Then you read. . . . It's partly personality, partly exposure. Here, it is another generation. If you go a little back, it is different.

This friend, like Azad, had come from Iran on her own to attend university. She worked with the Confederation of Iranian Students, but later grew disillusioned with them because of their views and practices related to gender issues. Critical of Islamic strictures and many aspects of Iranian culture, she developed her own humanistic outlook. After earning her PhD, she went on to work with community groups fighting discrimination and hate crimes.

Iranian student groups met regularly on American campuses for intellectual and political discussions. Friends report a high intellectual level in these workshops, which served as forums for questioning their backgrounds in light of Western ideologies. Movement activists organized demonstrations against the shah and Shahbanu Farah during their visits to the United States.[12] For one large demonstration in Washington, D.C., in the early 1970s, a number of Iranian students from other states stayed at my home. When I participated in the large demonstration in front of the Kennedy Center where the shah appeared, my friends immediately gave me a face mask, which students used to hide their identities from the Iranian Secret Police. Although the Confederation of Iranian Students supported a revolution against the shah's government, members did not favor a Shi'i Muslim government. Students quickly turned against the Islamic Republic. Looking back, many of the women from CIS realized that gender issues had been stifled. Male leaders had judged that addressing separate concerns of women would be divisive. In any case, women's liberation stank of bourgeois attitudes, the men claimed. After the 1979 Iranian Revolution, these Iranian American women often joined feminist groups.[13]

Like Azad, Iranian American women of this generation in the Bay Area often have histories of CIS involvement. At present, they participate in Iranian feminist, welfare, cultural, professional, and political groups, in addition to working in demanding careers, tending to families and/or friends, and following personal interests. Extremely negative toward the Islamic Republic of Iran, they reject Shi'i rituals. Added to these secular Iranian women who came to the United States for education in the 1960s and 1970s are some Iranian women who came to the United States during and after the revolutionary period in order to escape Islamic Republic restrictions. For these highly secularized upper- and middle-class women, religion had little meaning, even when they were still in Iran. These women had experienced modernization in Iran, enjoyed lifestyles influenced by European or American culture, had access to higher education and various opportunities, and might have had interesting careers. These women did not have a place in their lives for women's Shi'i rituals while in Iran, and still do not now that they are in America.

Iranian Shi'i Women Maintaining Lower Ritual Participation

Another category of Iranian immigrants includes many of those who left Iran after the revolution. They work here, or if they have retired, live with or near their children. These Iranian immigrants brought with them cynicism and detachment developed in response to clerical rule in Iran. Although initially elated and victorious, many Iranians quickly lost the euphoria and emotional attachment they had felt toward the February 11, 1979, Revolution.[14] As early as the first few months after the revolution, some people in the village where I was conducting research in 1978 and 1979 were becoming cynical about the new regime. Although I remained in my village research site for only ten months after the revolution, I could discern the growing skepticism.[15]

Commonly, Iranians—whether living in Iran or abroad—develop their own religious interpretations and worldviews. Although individuals differ, Iranians generally hold mixed attitudes toward *mollas, akhunds,* and even higher-ranking clerics. Because the Iranian government calls itself Islamic, if people do not approve of the government, their rejection of the regime may also lead to an abandonment of Islam. In Iran, women used Islamic rituals—such as going to the cemetery to weep for the dead—as resistance: mourning for themselves and the country under the Islamic government, just as they had used mourning to oppose the shah's regime.

The majority of Iranians living in the United States see themselves as Muslims. They have faith in God and his prophets, or would at least identify themselves as Muslims. They revere the Prophet Mohammad and his family and the Twelve Imams, successors to Mohammad. They hold a quiet, personal belief in Islam; however, they are not always active with a Shi'i congregation, nor do they necessarily perform the daily prayers or fast during Ramadan. The majority of Iranian Americans do not regularly participate in ritual gatherings, although they have Muslim marriage ceremonies and attend Muslim funeral gatherings. Their negative attitude toward the Shi'i regime and how the clerics leading the country interpret the Shi'i faith increases their antipathy toward Shi'i religious figures and practices.

Even though the majority of Iranian Shi'i women in Northern California are relatively secularized, with a quiet, personal belief in God and Islam, women's ritual spaces hold meaning for many of them. For spiritual experience, personal solace, and social concerns and community, many Iranian women attend female-formed rituals at least occasionally. Especially those women experiencing grief, loss, or trouble find comfort in Shi'i *rowzehs,* Moharram rituals, and funeral rituals, whether mixed-gender or women-only. For quite a number of Iranian American women, spirituality is a significant—if relatively private—part of their lives. Some of these women seriously pursue personal religious development, perhaps trying a number of religious pathways. They subsequently may put together and modify beliefs and practices to build a satisfying spiritual and religious life. One deeply spiritual Iranian woman in Northern California experimented with several alternative religious groups before returning to Shi'i Islam, deciding at that point which aspects were meaningful for her as an individual. Then, after September 11, 2001, and the war in Afghanistan, disgusted with one and all God-centered religions, she attended a Unitarian congregation for a period at the invitation of an American friend. Finding it a good meditative practice, however, she continued sporadically performing *namaz*, the Muslim prayer routine, which is supposed to be performed five times per day.

Even relatively secularized Iranian American women who were educated in this country may attend the occasional *sofreh* or *rowzeh* for the sake of a mourning friend or a mother visiting from Iran, if nothing else.[16] Some participate in or even sponsor women's religious rituals for certain reasons, such as to seek important favors, pray for departed family members, or join rituals sponsored by friends or relatives. One friend, a lively social worker, made a religious vow that if she were able to find a new house and a new husband, she would host a *sofreh* for one of the Shi'i saints. Both wishes came to pass, and, with other invited friends and relatives, I attended her rituals with food offerings, ritualized prayers, and meditations about the saints. Less educated Iranian women immigrants, or older ones who have come to join children living and working in the United States, tend to participate relatively more often in women's public and private Shi'i rituals.

Iranian Women Modifying Religious Roles

Some Iranian women in the United States come from religious and traditional families and did not have access to the higher education, alternative ideas, or a privileged European- or American-influenced lifestyle which prompted other Iranian women into secularization and modernization. They came to the United States with husband and/or children after the revolution. Rather than emigrating to the United States for their own education or because they themselves did not want to live under the Islamic Republic's gender restrictions, they arrived in the United States accompanying family and for their benefit. However, if of middle age of more, these women had observed the shah's modernization programs and the improving standards of living due to the Iranian oil boom of the 1960s and 1970s. Most often, these women did not know English when they arrived, and they may not have had the opportunity to learn much English while living in the United States either. Some other Iranian women who do have more privileged backgrounds, interested in maintaining or developing spirituality, may also participate in gatherings. One cannot delineate strict boundaries between these categories of Iranian Shi'i women which I have constructed. Rather, it is a matter of degree. Also, over time, women may move in one direction or another regarding their religiosity, spirituality, and participation in rituals.

Some of these women participate in Shi'i congregations here. However, because of the form Iranian Shi'i congregations take in the American setting, some influences from American culture, and social organization before and after emigration, such women may participate in rituals in new ways and may take on new roles in religious activities. Iranian Shi'i women who do participate in Shi'i religious gatherings in California may attend mixed-gender rituals. Further, they can be active in speaking and taking leadership roles at mixed gatherings and congregations. Without explicitly articulating the desire to modify engendered Muslim beliefs and practices, Iranian women attending Shi'i gatherings in Northern California have enhanced their public religious roles. Some Iranian Shi'i women host women's *sofrehs* and *rowzehs* in their homes. Periodically, some Shi'i women have women's mosque or community center gatherings, and may also participate in mixed public Shi'i rituals.

Shi'i women who have moved to the United States have new religious opportunities. Women's participation in several Iranian Shi'i congregations in Northern California differs quite dramatically from women's religious activity in pre-revolutionary Iran. At the Pakistani/Indian Shi'i center in Northern California, a partition separates female from male worshippers. Women also sit separately from men in two Sunni mosques. In the three Iranian Shi'i congregations, however, women sit among the men. In the upstairs prayer space of one of these congregations, women arrange themselves behind the men for prayer, but there is no partition or curtain between them. Quite a few women, even in mixed gatherings, do not cover their heads. In the upstairs praying area of a congregation located in Oakland, women are expected to cover their heads. Young women stand near the entrance to the large room holding extra headscarves to offer women. Men and women remove their shoes before entering and store them in little cubicles next to the wall. In the downstairs area, where sermons, speeches, and programs are presented, men and women sit intermixed. Neither women nor men remove their shoes before entering this spacious area. In 1996, when the mosque was opened and I began attending, women wore head coverings in this downstairs hall. By late 2001, a minority of women still used a head covering. A scarf is not necessary here, young women at the entrance informed guests. Likewise, in the basement where meals are served, scarves are not required. In all three of these Iranian Shi'i congregations, women address mixed gatherings, using loudspeakers.

The female teacher of the associated Saturday Islamic school addressed the 1997 Oakland Eid al-Fetr mixed service—her voice booming out with the loudspeaker system—talking enthusiastically about the children's accomplishments, awarding prizes, and introducing the girls and boys who recited to the large audience. As the main attraction at the November 2001 celebration of the birth of the Hidden Imam,[17] young people acted out the story of his mother as she came to understand the impending birth. The tall teenager playing the part of the mother wore a cloth, leaving her face, an oval within the scarf edges, covered, but she spoke out her lines through an attached microphone. After the theatrical performance, when the young people went back to the stage for recognition, the tall teenager's face covering had been removed. This innovative focus on the mother of Imam-e Zaman, the Leader of the Ages, points to increased attention to women's roles, although it was still to the role of motherhood. I surmised that the Christmas story, along with Christian (especially Roman Catholic) veneration of the Virgin Mary influenced this dramatization.

In another Iranian Shi'i congregation, a female visitor from Iran, supporting the Islamic Republic's gender precepts and policies, spoke to a large mixed assembly. She wore a scarf, although most females in the audience did not, as she defended Islamic Republic policies and particularly the Shi'i policy of allowing men up to four wives and unlimited temporary wives (*sigheh* or *mot'eh*). A passionate debate followed as women and men in the audience attacked these views. Women also address mixed groups during this group's monthly Friday children's evening, as well as directing children's recitations. Organizers of the children's evening asked me to give a slide presentation about my Iranian village research at one of these gatherings. Although all the other women I saw there speaking to a mixed group wore a headscarf, I did not, and received only enthusiastic thanks. Women also lecture at the monthly Friday women's evening. The fact that neither of these spaces is actually a mosque may lessen restrictions on the role of women as speakers and make the women feel less constrained to cover their hair. In the upstairs praying area of one congregation, however, all women did cover their hair.

In a home where a relatively liberal mixed group meets to read and discuss the Qur'an, perform the evening prayer, and share a potluck dinner, few women cover their hair. In fact, they wear makeup and form-fitting Western clothing. Here, women are more active than men in leading Qur'anic discussion and reciting their own religious poetry. This home-based discussion group and the two South Bay Iranian Shi'i congregations are not led by a clergyman, but are organized by laypeople. In addition to meeting in a home or community center rather than in an actual mosque, the absence of a cleric socialized in Iranian religious environments undoubtedly loosens gender constraints. Almost all of the members of these three groups strongly disagree with the Islamic Republic's regime and the religious interpretations of its officials. These group members are sensitized to the ways in which the worldviews of Shi'is may differ, and from their perspective, how certain Shi'i religious authorities may be in error.

Iranian American women who are developing their own ideas about the place of religion in their lives generally believe that religion should be a private affair. No one should tell others how to live their religious lives or what they owe God, they feel. They have also developed new ideas about relationships, marriage, and family.

Women in a Pakistani/Indian Mosque
Maintaining Traditional Religious Roles

Women in the South Bay Pakistani/Indian Shi'i mosque where I attended Moharram rituals had experienced far less modernization, education, and exposure to alternative idea systems than Iranian women in the United States. They are less well off economically, and they and their husbands are more conservative socially and religiously compared with Iranian Americans. Many of these women even continue to wear Pakistani/Indian female dress of the *shalwar* (loose pants), *kamis* (long tunic), and *dupata* (shawl covering shoulders and chest and perhaps head). Women connected with the more fundamentalist Pakistani Shi'is are more likely to see themselves as closely tied to the family. It is difficult to remain single, to divorce, or if divorced, to avoid remarriage, and still retain good standing within such groups. Fundamentalists usually see a sexual division of labor in the family and in society, with women as the natural nurturers and caregivers for children, and men as natural workers outside of the shelter of the home to earn a livelihood and deal with the issues of the larger public world.[18] The public religious presence of Pakistani Shi'i women has not changed as much as that of the more liberalized Iranian American Shi'is, most of whom oppose the Islamic Republic's regime and have experienced modern, secular influences for some time.[19] The emigration history of Pakistani Shi'is to the United States is more recent than that of Iranians, and far fewer Pakistani Shi'is live in the Bay Area or in the United States in general than people of Iranian background.

As Shi'i Pakistani and Indian families came to the Bay Area in the last decade or two, women began to meet with each other. Women first began convening women's *majales* in their homes during the mourning season. Women's lamentation sessions during the mourning period increased over time. Finally, the growing Pakistani Shiʻi population founded a Shiʻi mosque in South San Jose. The congregation has already outgrown the small mosque and has raised funds to build a larger one. One ethnic group of Urdu speakers, both Pakistani and Indian, dominates at this San Jose Shiʻi mosque. Pakistani Shiʻi female Mohajerin, or migrants, and Indian Shiʻi women actually belong to the same ethnic and linguistic group. The families of Mohajerin women moved from India to Pakistan during the 1947 partition. Before 1947, any Shiʻi women immigrating to California from these two areas were citizens of the same country—India. They share culture, language, and kin ties. In their joint rituals, Pakistani and Indian women affirm their joint identity and ethnic group affiliation. Urdu speakers share Moharram rituals conducted in their own language. They do not wish to use English at the mosque or to create a Shiʻi congregation that includes other ethnic groups.

Peshawar Shiʻis, with the crucial cooperation of women, attempted to unite Shiʻis from Urdu-speaking Mohajerin, Pushtun, and Persian-speaking Qizelbash into one large sectarian community. Without the conflict with Sunnis and the attendant pressures of frequent killings and attacks on their religious spaces, South Bay Urdu-speaking Shiʻis, in sharp contrast, did not feel the pressing need to unite with Shiʻis from other ethnic and linguistic groups.

In California's South Bay area, Urdu-speaking Shiʻi women actively hold women's segregated Moharram mourning *majales* in homes and at the mosque. Women do not take on roles of reaching out to women from other groups to promote overall Shiʻi unity. They gather in smaller groups than the crowded Peshawar women's rituals in community *hosayniyyehs* and private homes and courtyards, or *emambarehs* (spaces dedicated to Imam Hosayn and his followers). Owners housed holy objects in their *emambarehs* and hosted Moharram rituals in these rooms or buildings. In the South Bay, women practiced chanting and self-flagellation less competitively and less rigorously than I had seen in Peshawar. When Pakistani and Indian Shiʻi women attend mixed mosque gatherings, they sit separately from men. During the summer 1993 Moharram season, I participated in many *majales* at the Pakistani Shiʻi religious center, where women gathered behind a high curtain and watched the *mowlana* delivering his sermon on two closed-circuit TVs.[20] When they wished to say something to another female, they were careful to murmur softly enough to avoid being heard by males on the other side of the curtain.

The Pakistani/Indian Shi'i congregation in the South Bay Area is rather fundamentalist. Women are not encouraged to participate visibly in mixed rituals. Neither are they encouraged to take on leadership roles or to be vocal or outspoken in mixed gatherings. I did not observe any such women's contributions in this Pakistani Shi'i congregation, in contrast to practices in the Iranian American home gathering, the two South Bay Iranian Shi'i congregations, and the Shi'i mosque in Oakland, where most members are Iranian.

The great majority of Bay Area Pakistani Shi'i women do not have an American education. Rather, they immigrated to the United States as married women to accompany their husbands, who most often found non-professional jobs. Iranians have had a longer history in the United States than Pakistani or Indian Shi'is. Upper-class Iranians came to study in the United States as early as the 1950s. From the 1960s onward, Iran became a relatively wealthy country due to the oil boom, enabling students to study abroad. During the revolutionary period, large numbers of relatively well-off Iranians left the country. Those who left earlier on often were especially successful in bringing their wealth with them. People of Iranian background living in the United States have enjoyed relatively higher salaries, and they tend to work in professional fields more often than other Americans. Pakistani and Indian Shi'is generally came to the United States to work. Those who attend the South Bay Shi'i mosque are much less well off financially and are less educated than Iranian Americans.

The situations of women naturally differ among these groups. Pakistani and Indian Shi'i women have relatively less autonomy and are less likely to seek divorce from an unhappy marriage. Rather than forming self-constructed and selected communities, these women remain connected to their original families and communities. Many Iranian women had already become relatively modernized and educated and were moving toward more autonomous selves when they came to the United States. And many Iranian women came by themselves for an education—itself an act of breaking away from the traditional cultural and social norms of Iran—and have developed relatively distinct gender ideas. This occurred more rarely among Shi'i women from Pakistan or India.

Pakistani and Indian Shi'i women attend the mosque, where they listen to sermons and lectures delivered by males and male clergy. More dependent on husbands and other male relatives, their gender views—at least those views that are verbalized—more or less replicate those of the men in the household. Pakistani/Indian Shi'i women, because they are relatively less likely to have been educated in this country, and they are generally not as affluent as Iranian Americans, have relatively fewer opportunities for independent public or social activities. Compared with Iranian immigrants, their home communities are not as Westernized or secularized, nor are they themselves. In Pakistan, in general, even among the middle and upper-middle classes, people have not become secularized to the same degree as their Iranian counterparts. Also, unlike their Iranian co-religionists, Shi'is from Pakistan and India are not fleeing what they consider to be a repressive Shi'i government. Rather, Shi'is in their home countries feel under siege by the majority Sunni populations and governments. Many Shi'is in their home countries of Pakistan and India feel strongly identified with their Shi'i co-religionists in the face of discrimination and even violence from the Sunni majority, and in India from non-Muslims. Inspired by the Shi'i revolution and then the Islamic Republic in Iran, Pakistani Shi'is were also responding to the growing fundamentalism of Pakistani Sunnis. During the 1990s and to the present, Sunni fundamentalists, funded in part by Saudi Arabia, have been attacking Shi'i mourning rituals and religious spaces. This sparked growing religiosity and fundamentalism on the part of Shi'is who, feeling the need for protection, pulled together and pursued solidarity with their fellow Shi'is.

Due to increasing emphasis on Shi'i gatherings and rituals, Shi'i preachers in Peshawar are gaining more access to women when women attend men's *majales,* sitting in areas segregated and hidden from males. Further, the more fundamentalist and radically sectarian Mohajerin female preachers were taking over leadership of even the Qizelbash and Pushtun women's rituals in Peshawar. For these reasons, Shi'i women immigrants from Pakistan and India, who maintain contact with their home communities, are less likely to question Islam or challenge their learned Shi'i rituals and interpretations. They are more likely to participate in segregated women's rituals than are Iranian women who have immigrated to the United States. Generally, these Pakistani/Indian women are not turning to secularism, agnosticism or atheism, Sufi practices, Christianity, or other religions, as are large numbers of Iranian emigrants.

What Will the Future Bring?

The great majority of Iranian immigrants either came to the United States as students and have become integrated into American society or left Iran because they were unhappy with the Islamic Republic's government. In general, Iranian Americans are more secularized than their Shi'i counterparts from South Asia. Either religion does not play a large role in their lives, or they hold Islamic beliefs as a more or less private matter. A few Iranian women in the Santa Clara valley have made a career preaching, educating, and reading the Qur'an and talking about the Karbala martyrs at segregated women's rituals. Many Iranian American women attend women's *rowzehs* or *majales* at least occasionally. Very few Iranian women, typically busy with education, career, and secular groups and interests, find time or inclination for frequent ritual attendance. Even during the month of Moharram, relatively few Iranian women maintain a strenuous ritual schedule. When they do attend religious rituals, they often participate in newer revised ritual forms that stress lectures and education in a mixed audience rather than mourning rituals.

Surely, Iranian American women will not return in droves to traditional forms of Shi'i ritual participation. In Iran, an Islamic government has been attempted. Now in power and responsible, the Shi'i government's flaws and human failings are apparent to many Iranian Shi'is. Shi'i Islam no longer ignites euphoric hope as a framework to protest injustice and exploitation, but rather is blamed by many for injustice, oppression, or corruption. Iranian Americans, many of whom are disgusted with what they perceive as the misuse of Shi'i Islam by the ruling clerics of Iran, feel little or no incentive to become more dedicated to Shi'i Islam and its rituals.

As Iranian American parents watch their children failing to learn Persian, forgetting Iranian courtesies, and losing interest in Islam and Iranian culture, many fear that their children are sloughing off their identity. Living in America leads Iranians, including the majority Shi'i, as well as the Sunni, Christian, Jewish, Bahai, and Zoroastrian minorities, to become more like other Americans. Educated, professional, and economically well off, younger Iranian Americans tend to aspire toward success in mainstream American society.

Iranians living in the United States have more reason than Muslims from other countries to feel negative and cynical about Shi'i clerics and state-promoted Shi'i Islam. During and after the 1979 Revolution, politically powerful Shi'i leaders and their lower-middle- and lower-class supporters and beneficiaries turned against the modernized and secularized educated or wealthy groups. Shi'i fundamentalists consider these people to be contaminated by the West and hold them up as enemies of Islam and Iran. Many supporters of the shah's regime and other dissidents of various political persuasions were executed, put under house arrest, or fired from their positions. Great numbers of Iranians left the country, some forced to flee secretly across borders. Iranians living in America usually feel extreme antipathy toward the Islamic Republic and may also extend their disdain to Shi'i Islamic beliefs and practices.

Other Muslims coming to American do not necessarily share these feelings. Among other nationalities, adherence to an "Islamic" lifestyle and participation in rituals in their adopted country may actually have increased. Economic conditions for the family may improve in the U.S. setting. More money may be available to be used toward religious activities, allowing women to sponsor religious gatherings, for example, which might have been a rarer experience for them at home. Yet another factor encouraging religious activity for women is the relative scarcity in this country of trained clergy and teachers of Islam. Women may fill the gap, taking over some responsibility for educating children, a responsibility that they did not have in their home countries.[21] With the fear of young people becoming influenced by American culture—dating and engaging in other non-Islamic practices, or perhaps even marrying a non-Muslim and leaving their religion—women may be called upon to organize youth activities. People may wish to develop a total community among the Muslim group in order to form a Muslim environment for the children where they may grow up with a supportive and family-like environment. This will provide them with an alternative to becoming enmeshed in American culture and social interaction with non-Muslim youth. In the secularized and largely Judeo-Christian U.S. environment, Muslims may become more conscious of their religious heritage and identity. In religious families, concern grows over maintaining this identity and providing children with the opportunities and environments where they will continue in Muslim practices and values rather than being seduced by the trappings of mainstream American culture. For some, religious practices and beliefs may be the main vehicle by which they can retain identity and a sense of community with their fellows from the home country.

In contrast to Shi'i tendencies in Peshawar, Pakistan, Shi'i Pakistanis in the Bay Area are not interested in uniting with other ethnic and language groups to form one large Shi'i community. Although clerics and leaders of the South Bay Shi'i mosque wished to conduct rituals and gatherings in English as a way of welcoming Shi'is from other backgrounds, the members have preferred to restrict their congregation to Urdu speakers. While leaders may wish to join the international Shi'i movement, the congregation has more local aims. In contrast to Shi'is in Pakistan and India, Bay Area Pakistani and Indian Shi'is do not feel besieged or pressured to unite with other Shi'is.

For women from the Middle East, mosque activities and the accompanying social interaction may replicate the intense social support and visiting which often exists with extended kin in their home societies. The time and energy which would have gone to seeing and assisting their relatives in their own country may be put to work in the United States by furthering the mosque-centered substitute family. Religious activities take on greater meaning and purpose as Muslims struggle to uphold Muslim identity and values. As Muslims attempt to provide their children with a Muslim community and keep them away from the corrupting influences of their American classmates, women's attention to mosque work becomes all the more acceptable and valued. Women associated with fundamentalist groups are often able to take a larger part in the activities of the mosque—to become leaders, teachers, and social directors. Through their involvement with the Islamic community, women may develop their own capabilities and expertise in dealing with the world outside of the home. They may even be able to find creative new paths to combining "Islamic" lifestyles and goals with American opportunities for career advancement, personal development, and increased autonomy.

Pakistani and Indian Shi'i women may follow some of these paths in their attempts to find ways to live in America as Muslims. However, as their daughters grow up, attend American schools, become educated, and set out on careers, some of them will likely begin to see alternatives to religiously framed worldviews. Eventually, the youth, like Iranian American young people born or raised in this country, will eschew their mother tongue and grow impatient with their parents' ways. The young people will want to live more like their American fellows. Some of the Pakistani and Indian Shi'i girls may come to realize the possibility of developing more self-autonomy and may become less enmeshed in their families or their religious and ethnic communities. More specifically, for our purposes, they may abandon their mothers' Shi'i rituals and interpretations.

It is no wonder that one of the main concerns of the *mowlana,* the Pakistani cleric, is the children. When lecturing at universities, he frequently talks about how to keep children from living an un-Islamic American life. Leaders try to keep young people within the Shi'i community. When I was conducting fieldwork at the Pakistani/Indian Shi'i mosque, the Sunday school had just graduated more than a hundred kids.

In the United States, there are usually more education and career opportunities and cultural acceptance of self-sufficient living for women than in the home countries of Muslim women. In addition, American society is relatively secularized. Muslims who come to the United States are affected by the secular nature of this country. The great majority of Muslims in America are not associated with a mosque. In spite of rekindled interest in Islam among some migrants, in general, religious activities and strict adherence to Islamic values have declined in accordance with the length of time spent in the United States. In an extensive research project among Muslims in America, Yvonne Haddad and Adair T. Lummis found that, over generations, views of Muslims about their religion became modified to stress aspects characteristic of all world religions, such as truth and justice, and in accordance with "American civil religion," rather than beliefs specific to Islam.[22]

Specifically among women, the influence of American values and social organization is difficult to avoid in the long run. Particularly when Muslim youth attend American schools, they share in the socialization process of other American students. The struggle to maintain them within the Islamic value system, community, and way of life is challenging. The realization of the significance to the future of Islam in this country combined with recognition of the difficulty of the challenge of keeping youth within the fold is a main reason for the growth of Muslim parochial schools in the United States

Among girls as well as boys, however, changes in worldview, as well as in behavior, are difficult to prevent, although they may be slowed down. It may be expected that the great majority of Muslims in the United States will experience secularization and internalizing of religious beliefs. More and more over time and through generations, on the whole, Muslims will likely see religion as a system of personal and private beliefs which each individual chooses for him- or herself. They will increasingly reject religion as a system of authority to which one must submit and will rather understand religion as available for the needs of the individual in his or her own specific life, to provide meaning, comfort, and guidance as each person sees fit.[23] Of course, we do not yet know what effects the large Christian fundamentalist movement in the United States will have on Muslims and their expression of Islam in the American environment.

As American women of Shiʿi Muslim background pursue education and careers and thus the possibility of self-sufficiency, they are less likely to be completely absorbed into the family unit and more likely to gain individuality and autonomy. One can expect such a course even for women of Pakistani/Indian Shiʿi background at some point. Such changes do not occur quickly. Even when one's belief system changes, behavioral changes do not automatically follow. Human beings are products of decades of socialization, and attitudes and behavioral patterns are difficult to change, even with determination and great effort. Muslim women in the United States, as well as American women who decide to take responsibility for themselves after having been raised to depend on men, usually must struggle through a long process of changing themselves. They may exercise greater decision making and self-reliance. Assuming more responsibility and autonomy and depending less on an authority structure to care for them and guide their behavior, they may begin to wonder about the need for a religious authority structure to provide beliefs and guidance for behavior.

Conclusion

Comparing emigrant Iranian and Pakistani/Indian Shiʻi women's participation in religious rituals in Northern California reveals differences in their religious participation. Contextualizing their American religious ritual participation in their home countries' religious politics, as well as their own education, economic status, and socioeconomic class helps to explain these differences.

Iranian women who came to the United States before the Iranian Revolution of 1978–1979 generally came from the educated, secularized upper-middle classes. Because of the oil boom and the Pahlavi government's determination to modernize Iran, teachers, bureaucrats, armed forces personnel, and businessmen expanded the middle and upper-middle classes. Families of people in such positions often declined in religiosity and took on more modern perspectives. Those young Iranian women from religious backgrounds generally changed during the process of their education. Young Iranian women who came to the United States to study aimed to pursue their own educations and careers. Iranian American Shiʻi women, with their secularized, modern middle- and upper-middle-class backgrounds, and with antipathy toward the Shiʻi religiosity enforced by Islamic Republic officials, have largely turned away from organized religion. Instead they retain a quiet, personal belief in Shiʻi Islam, find other outlets for religious beliefs and practices, or eschew religion altogether. Many may occasionally participate in women's segregated rituals for personal, spiritual, or social reasons. The minority of Iranian American women who are active in organized religion, whether in lay- or cleric-led congregations, increasingly see women with bare heads and women beginning to speak up in mixed religious gatherings.

Pakistani Shiʻi women, coming from a far less affluent and less secularized society, did not experience alienation from mainstream religious attitudes while still living in Pakistan. Even many upper-middle-class Shiʻis in Pakistan have not become agnostics or even believers in a quiet, personal type of religion, as was common in Iran. Further, these Shi'i Muslims feel oppressed by the majority Hindu government and population in India and the majority Sunni government and population in Pakistan. In Pakistan, the Sunni government and majority population have treated Shi'is with violence and harsh discrimination. Alarmed, Peshawar Shi'is of different ethnic groups united for mutual defense. Under such circumstances, women joined the effort of constructing joint identity and community. By no means did they feel alienated from their religious community. In response to political and communal tensions, conflicts, and even violence in South Asia, Shi'is minimized ethnic group differences and gender differences. People clung to their besieged religious community.

Rather than feeling cynicism about a Shi'i theocracy and bureaucracy, as Iranians do, Pakistani Shi'is are more committed to their religion, clerics, and dominant beliefs and rituals, which serve as a bulwark against the threatening societies surrounding them. Pakistani American Shi'i women live in more conservative and less educated and affluent families. A much smaller percentage of the women understand English compared with Iranian women. Less Westernized, secularized, and educated, Pakistani American Shi'i women are less integrated into American society. They have fewer opportunities for careers, socializing, and religiosity outside of their own families and language group. The smaller, more recent group of emigrant Pakistani and Indian Shi'i women have fewer reasons and opportunities to question their religious beliefs and practices and their gender teachings. As much as possible, they attend women's rituals. They do not experiment with other religious forms, nor do they sit intermixed with men in religious gatherings or take on public religious roles in front of men.

Research findings suggest a great difference between women who came to the United States from societies already well started in the direction of secularization and women who come, accompanying their husbands and families, from religiously oriented societies. Many Iranian women came to the United States in the 1970s from educated, relatively modernized, upper-middle-class families. They came to pursue their own education and personal development. A later group of women fled from the Islamic Republic's severe restrictions. Women coming from comparatively less well off and less educated families in Pakistan and India differ significantly. They are accompanying their husbands, who are here for education or work, often in semiskilled jobs. These women assumed they would be going on with their already established role in the family of homemaking. They aimed to support the work and development of husbands and children. Shi'i women in Pakistan and India had been more tightly intertwined with husbands and their families than Iranian women. Far more commonly than Iranian women, they lived in patrilineal extended family households. Such Muslim women from Pakistan and India had experienced far less modernization and secularization in their home countries. Compared with emigrant Iranians, Pakistanis are still living in a much more religious world. They feel pressured to protect Muslim identity, the rationale for establishing Pakistan, in opposition to Hindu India. Because of poverty in Pakistan, there is less urbanization, education, improvement in standard of living, exposure to alternative ideological systems, or increased opportunities. Rarely can women attain self-sufficiency. Younger people cannot easily gain autonomy from the older generation.

Although both immigrant groups, Iranian and Pakistani/Indian Shi'is, now live in the Bay Area, their backgrounds, their sect's situations in their own countries, and their current conditions result in different influences on their Shi'i ritual involvement. Religious practices become modified in different ways when transported to the American setting. The level and character of that transformation is influenced by conditions in immigrants' home countries, their related socioeconomic class membership in the United States, and their level of incorporation into American society.

Notes

    For research funding and support, I am grateful to the Social Science Research Council and the American Council of Learned Societies, SUNY Binghamton, the National Institute for the Humanities, the American Association of University Women's Educational Foundation, the Fulbright Commission, and Santa Clara University.

    1. In another southwestern Iranian village, women enjoyed even fewer opportunities for religious involvement than in Aliabad. See Erika Friedl, "Islam and Tribal Women in a Village in Iran," in *Unspoken Worlds: Women's Religious Lives*, ed. Nancy Auer Falk and Rita M. Gross, 125-133 (Belmont, Calif.: Wadsworth, 1989).

    2. For more about Aliabad village history and Shi'a ritual practices, see Mary Elaine Hegland, "Ritual and Revolution in Iran," in *Culture and Political Change*, ed. M. J. Aronoff, 75-100 (New Brunswick, N.J.: Transaction Books, 1983b); Mary Elaine Hegland, "Two Images of Husain: Accommodation and Revolution in an Iranian Village," in *Religion and Politics in Iran: Shi'ism from Quietism to Revolution*, ed. Nikki R. Keddie, 218-235 (New Haven, Conn.: Yale University Press, 1983c); Mary Elaine Hegland, "'Traditional' Iranian Women: How They Cope," *The Middle East Journal* 36 (1982b), 483-501; Mary Elaine Hegland, "Aliabad Women: Revolution as Religious Activity," in *Women and Revolution in Iran*, ed.

Guity Nashat, 171–194 (Boulder, Colo.: Westview Press, 1983a); Mary Elaine Hegland, "Political Roles of Iranian Village Women," *MERIP Reports* 138 (1986), 14–19, 46; Mary Elaine Hegland, "Women and the Iranian Revolution: A Village Case Study," *Dialectical Anthroplogy* 15 (1990), 183–192; Mary Elaine Hegland, "Political Roles of Aliabad Women: Public-Private Dichotomy Transcended," in *Women in Middle Eastern History: Shifting Boundaries in Sex and Gender*, ed. Nikki R. Keddie and Beth Baron, 215–230 (New Haven, Conn.: Yale University Press, 1991); Mary Elaine Hegland, "Gender and Religion in the Middle East and South Asia: Women's Voices Rising," in *Social History of Women and Gender in the Modern Middle East*, ed. Judith Tucker and Marlee Meriwether, 177–212 (Boulder, Colo.: Westview Press, 1999); and Mary Elaine Hegland, "Religious Ritual and Political Struggle in an Iranian Village," *MERIP Reports* 12:1 (1982a), 10–17, 23.

 3. See Anne Betteridge, "To Veil or Not to Veil: A Matter of Protest or Policy," in *Women and Revolution in Iran*, ed. Guity Nashat, 109–128 (Boulder, Colo.: Westview Press, 1983); Anne Betteridge, "Ziarat: Pilgrimage to the Shrines of Shiraz" (PhD diss., University of Chicago, 1985); Anne Betteridge, "The Controversial Vows of Urban Muslim Women in Iran," in *Unspoken Worlds: Women's Religious Lives*, ed. Nancy Auer Falk and Rita M. Gross, 102–111 (Belmont, Calif.: Wadsworth, 1989). Depending on size of settlement, class, ethnic group, and age level, Shiʿa women's ritual involvement varies greatly. In addition to publications by Anne Betteridge, see Friedl, "Islam and Tribal Women"; Erika Friedl, "The Dynamics of Women's Spheres of Action in Rural Iran," in *Women in Middle Eastern History: Shifting Boundaries in Sex and Gender*, ed. Nikki R. Keddie and Beth Baron, 195–214 (New Haven, Conn.: Yale University Press, 1991). See also the publications by Mary Elaine Hegland listed in note 2, above; Zahra Kamalkhani, "Women's Everyday Religious Discourse in Iran," in *Women in the Middle East: Perceptions, Realities, and Struggles for Liberation*, ed. H. Afshar, 85–95 (London: Macmillan, 1993); Zahra Kamalkhani, *Women's Islam: Religious Practice among Women in Today's Iran* (London: Kegan Paul International, 1997); Zahra Kamalkhani, "Reconstruction of Islamic Knowledge and Knowing: A Case of Islamic Practices among Women in Iran," in *Women and Islamization: Contemporary Dimensions of Discourse on Gender Relations*, ed. K. Ask and Marit Tjomsland, 177–193 (Oxford: Berg, 1998); and Azam Torab, "Piety as Gendered Agency: A Study of Jalaseh Ritual Discourse in an Urban Neighborhood in Iran," *Journal of the Royal Anthropological Institute* 2, 235–252; Azam Torab, "Neighbourhoods of Piety: Gender and Ritual in South Teheran" (PhD diss., University of London). Also see Elizabeth Warnock Fernea, *Guests of the Sheik: An Ethnography of an Iraqi Village* (New York: Anchor Books, 1965); Robert A. Fernea and Elizabeth Warnock Fernea, "Variation in Religious Observance among Islamic Women," in *Scholars, Saints, and Sufis in Muslim Religious Institutions in the Middle East since 1500*, ed. Nikki R. Keddie, 385–401 (Berkeley and Los Angeles: University of California Press, 1972); U. Sagaster, "Observations Made during the Month of Muharam, 1989, in Baltistan," in *Proceedings of the International Seminar on the Anthropology of Tibet and the Himalaya*, ed. C. Ramble and M. Brauen, 308–317 (Zurich: Ethnological Museum of the University of Zurich, 1993); and Vernon James Schubel, *Religious Performance in Contemporary Islam: Shiʿa Devotional Rituals in South Asia* (Columbia: University of South Carolina Press, 1993).

4. Several books document women's roles in the Iranian Revolution and its aftermath. See, for example, Mahnaz Afkhami and Erika Friedl, eds., *In the Eye of the Storm: Women in Post-Revolutionary Iran* (Syracuse: Syracuse University Press, 1994); Farah Azari, *Women of Iran: The Conflict with Fundamentalist Islam* (London: Attaca Press, 1983); Mandana Hendessi, *Armed Angels: Women in Iran*, Report No. 16 (London: Change, 1990); Haideh Moghissi, *Populism and Feminism in Iran: Women's Struggle in a Male-Defined Revolutionary Movement* (New York: St. Martin's Press, 1994); Haideh Moghissi, *Feminism and Islamic Fundamentalism: The Limits of Postmodern Analysis* (London: Zed Books, 1999); Guity Nashat, ed., *Women and Revolution in Iran* (Boulder, Colo.: Westview Press, 1983); Parvin Paidar, *Women and the Political Process in Twentieth-Century Iran* (Cambridge: Cambridge University Press, 1995); and Minou Reeves, *Female Warriors of Allah: Women and the Islamic Revolution* (New York: E. P. Dutton, 1989).

5. Shi'i women's rituals and participation in religious life have changed dramatically since the 1979 Iranian Revolution. See Hegland, "Gender and Religion"; Kamalkhani, "Women's Everyday Religious Discourse"; Kamalkhani, *Women's Islam;* Kamalkhani, "Reconstruction"; Torab, "Piety as Gendered Agency"; Azam Torab, "Politicization of Women's Religious Circles in Post-Revolutionary Iran," in *Women, Religion, and Culture in Iran,* ed. Sarah Ansari and Vanessa Martin, 143–168 (London: Curzon, 2002). However, recent manifestations of women's ritual and religious participation in Iran lie outside of the scope of this chapter.

6. For more discussion about Pakistani Shi'is, see Munir D. Ahmed, "The Shi'is of Pakistan," in *Shi'ism, Resistance, and Revolution,* ed. M. Kramer, 275–287 (Boulder, Colo.: Westview Press, 1987); Nikki R. Keddie, *The Shi'a of Pakistan: Reflections and Problems for Further Research* (Los Angeles: The G. E. von Grunebaum Center for Near Eastern Studies, University of California, 1993); S. V. R. Nasr, "Communalism and Fundamentalism: A Re-examination of the Origins of Islamic Fundamentalism," *Contention: Debates in Society, Culture, and Science* 4:2 (1995), 121–139; Vernon James Schubel, "The Muharram Majlis: The Role of a Ritual in the Preservation of Shi'a Identity," in *Muslim Families in North America,* ed. S. McIrvin Abu-Laban E. Waugh and R. Burckhardt Qureshi, 118–131 (Edmonton, Alberta: University of Alberta Press, 1991); Schubel, *Religious Performance;* and Vernon James Schubel, "Karbala as Sacred Space among North American Shi'a: 'Every Day Is Ashura, Everywhere Is Karbala,'" in *Making Muslim Space in North America and Europe,* ed. Barbara Daly Metcalf, 186–203 (Berkeley and Los Angeles: University of California Press, 1996).

7. Violence between Sunnis and Shi'is continued during the 1990s. For example, see J. F. Burns, "Attack on Mosque Kills 11 in Pakistan," *San Jose Mercury News,* March 11, 1995, A5, and Ahmed Rashid, "The Great Divide: Shias and Sunnis Battle It Out in Pakistan," *Far Eastern Economic Review* 158 (1995), 24.

8. For more discussion about Shi'i women and their rituals in Peshawar, Pakistan, see Mary Elaine Hegland, "Shi'a Women of NW Pakistan and Agency through Practice: Ritual, Resistance, Resilience," *PoLAR: Political and Legal Anthropology Review* 18:2 (1995), 1-14; Mary Elaine Hegland, "A Mixed Blessing—Majales: Shi'a Women's Rituals in NW Pakistan and the Politics of Religion, Ethnicity, and Gender," in *Mixed Blessings: Religious Fundamentalisms and Gender Cross-Culturally,* ed. Judy Brink and Joan Mencher, 179-196 (New York: Routledge, 1996);

Mary Elaine Hegland, "The Power Paradox in Muslim Women's Majales: Northwest Pakistani Mourning Rituals as Sites of Contestation over Religious Politics, Ethnicity, and Gender," *Signs* 23:2, 391–427; Mary Elaine Hegland, "Flagellation and Fundamentalism: (Trans)forming Meaning, Identity, and Gender through Pakistani Women's Rituals," *American Ethnologist* 25 (1998a), 240–266; and Hegland, "Gender and Religion."

9. See Deniz Kandiyoti, "Bargaining with Patriarchy," *Gender and Society* 2 (1988), 274–290.

10. According to Azam Torab, the rapid increase in women's and men's religious activities in the years leading up to the 1979 revolution took place largely in the more traditional, south Tehran areas, home to "small traders and retailers, skilled workers, artisans and lower income salaried employees." See Torab, "Politicization of Women's Religious Circles," 144.

11. For more information on and discussion of such processes among Iranian women in the United States, see Michele Brunet, "Self-Transformation among Iranian-American Women" (senior thesis, Santa Clara University, 1994), and Jennifer Fisk, "Iranian Women and the Creation of Self: The Path of Transformation" (senior thesis, Santa Clara University, 1994).

12. Afshin Matin-Asgari, *Iranian Student Opposition to the Shah* (Costa Mesa, Calif.: Mazda Publishers, 2002), and Ashraf Zahedi, *Challenging the Shah: Student Mobilization for Revolution* (forthcoming), have written about the Confederation of Iranian Students abroad.

13. Ashraf Zahedi analyzes gender issues related to the Confederation of Iranian Students abroad in Ashraf Zahedi, *Women of the Confederation: From Triumph to Despair* (forthcoming).

14. Not all Iranians, by any means, supported the revolutionary forces or considered Ayatollah Khomeini or other pro-Khomeini clerics as their religious leaders.

15. In March 1979, only some six weeks after the revolution, a young village kindergarten teacher misplaced her Nowruz (the Iranian New Year—March 21) bonus at a Shiraz religious establishment. Upon calling, she was told that yes, the little purse with the quoted amount of money had been found there. But when she went to pick it up, officials denied having it. No, nothing like that had turned up, they said. Certainly someone had stolen it. This "Islamic" government was corrupt, just like the last one, she commented bitterly to a few friends.

16. Also see N. Tohidi, "Iranian Women and Gender Relations," in *Irangeles: Iranians in Los Angeles*, ed. Ron Kelley, Jonathan Friedlander, and Anita Colby, 175–217 (Berkeley and Los Angeles: University of California Press, 1993).

17. The Twelfth (or Hidden) Imam, Shi'is believe, disappeared into occultation in 868 AD. Shi'is wait for his reappearance as Messiah, or Mahdi.

18. Not only Muslim, but also Christian and Jewish, fundamentalists generally take this stance. See, for example, Helen Hardacre, "The Impact of Fundamentalisms on Women, the Family, and Interpersonal Relations," in *Fundamentalisms and Society: Reclaiming the Sciences, the Family, and Education*, ed. Martin E. Marty and R. Scott Appleby, 129–150 (Chicago: University of Chicago Press, 1993).

19. For research about South Asians in America and their Muslim rituals, see Regula Burckhardt Qureshi, "Transcending Space: Recitation and Community among South Asian Muslims in Canada," in *Making Muslim Space in North America*

and Europe, ed. Barbara Daly Metcalf, 46–64 (Berkeley and Los Angeles: University of California Press, 1996); Schubel, "Muharram Majlis"; Schubel, "Karbala as Sacred Space"; Linda Walbridge, *Without Forgetting the Imam: Lebanese Shiʿism in America* (Detroit: Wayne State University Press, 1996b); Linda Walbridge, "Sex and the Single Shiʿite: Mutʿa Marriage in an American Lebanese Shiʿite Community," in *Family and Gender among American Muslims: Issues Facing Middle Eastern Immigrants and Their Descendants*, ed. Barbara Bilge and Barbara C. Aswad, 143–154 (Philadelphia: Temple University Press, 1996a); and Nilufer Ahmed, Gladis Kaufman, and Shamim Naim, "South Asian Families in the United States: Pakistani, Bangladeshi, and Indian Muslims," in *Family and Gender among American Muslims: Issues Facing Middle Eastern Immigrants and Their Descendants*, ed. Barbara Bilge and Barbara C. Aswad, 155–172 (Philadelphia: Temple University Press, 1996).

20. See also Qureshi, "Transcending Space"; Schubel, "Muharram Majlis"; Schubel, "Karbala as Sacred Space"; and Prnina Werbner, "'Sealing' the Koran: Offering and Sacrifice among Pakistani Labour Migrants," *Cultural Dynamics* 1:1 (1988), 77–97. Although finding that Muslim immigrants' mosque participation declined over time, Yvonne Yazbeck Haddad and Adair T. Lummis, *Islamic Values in the United States* (New York: Oxford University Press, 1987), document women's central religious roles both in informal, home-based rituals and in mosque organization.

21. Such educational involvement would not be available for women in their home countries. In one elementary Muslim parochial school, for example, the Islamic studies classes for all classes are taught by women who gained their knowledge about Islam from such resources as mosques, either in their home country or in the United States. Women are more often free of paid employment during the day and thus available for such service. There is also the feeling that women teachers are better able to deal with and reach the children, especially the younger ones.

22. See Haddad and Lummis, *Islamic Values in the United States*, 9, 166, and 155–172.

23. Such a process of change has also been occurring among American Catholics. A number of my students, in conducting research regarding attitudes and behavior of Catholics about such issues as divorce, birth control and abortion, and premarital sex, have found that many Catholics reject the authority structures and organization of the Church. Rather, they see Christianity as a personal and private belief system available to individuals. Published research has also indicated this trend.

CHAPTER 10

Women's Religious Rituals in Iraq

ELIZABETH WARNOCK FERNEA AND BASIMA Q. BEZIRGAN

The notion of a split between public and private worlds was a common paradigm in the mid–twentieth century that was used to describe the behavior of men and women in Middle Eastern society. The woman's world was supposedly the private world, the world of the family, a world not opened easily to strangers, a world where, it was granted, women might have had some domestic authority, or at least "influence." Man's world was the public world, the world of politics, the market place, more open to strangers and new ideas, the world where "real power," as well as per-haps even real "influence," was exerted in wider, less domestic, and, by inference, more important, domains.[1]

This was a convenient image, which, though less widely accepted today, was utilized to describe cultural activities, economic activities, social life, language, and even ritual. It was, however, an image that we in the West in-vented. Further, it did not tell us what happens when these two worlds came together or intersected. Obviously, as should have been apparent years ago, the public world was never totally segregated from the private world, and vice versa.

To illustrate this contention, we would like to look briefly but closely at a little-studied phenomenon in Middle Eastern society, that of suppos-edly exclusive female rituals. There are many such rituals and, regretfully, the literature supplies few descriptions. Why? Have we brought to this area our own ethnocentric notions of what was and what was not important for study? Surely women who have worked in the Middle East, Middle East-erners as well as Westerners, have always been aware of the wide range and variety of women's rituals. Have they not been considered "important" enough to be worthy of mention? Male informants may be at fault, for they, being hospitable people, have tended to tell the inquiring field-worker what he or she wants to be told, or will tell the field-worker what he, the male informant, wants to hear. Recently, there has been increased interest in the Middle Eastern woman's world, per se, but as woman's world only. Our feeling was that the closer one got to woman's world, and the more clearly one looked at what was actually happening there, the more one saw that it was not specifically or exclusively woman's world at all. It was man's and woman's and child's world together, the result of male-female interactions over time and space, an expression of situations and attitudes that indicate rather basic things about Middle Eastern society.

We have chosen to use rituals as examples because the ones we speak of here, from Iraqi society, are old, are related to religious activity and belief, and may indicate some cultural features—refined through the years— that deserve to be examined more carefully. Ritual has been described and written about in many interesting ways by Victor Turner, Van Gennep, and many others.[2] For our purposes, we define ritual as a formalizing of something, "an established or prescribed procedure for a religious or other rite."[3] Ritual therefore is viewed as a statement, a signification, in which something of importance can be given symbolic recognition, sometimes through reversing and inverting the ordinary order of things.

In the scope of a short paper, we cannot cover the great range of complex rituals involved in Muslim marriages, circumcisions, mourning ceremonies, naming ceremonies, and birth ceremonies, in which female and male and child worlds each play a part. We have chosen to focus on "women's rituals," based on vowing, fasting, and shared feasts of thanksgiving: the Feast of Zachariah, Sawm al-Banat, and Chay al-Abbas; the Ziyarat Salman Pak; one male ritual, the ta'ziyeh; and finally, a religious ritual, the Qurayeh, performed by both men and women, but separately (or so it seems), and in different ways.[4] We also cannot realistically cover the entire twentieth century, especially considering the difficulties inherent in conducting research in Iraq over the past two decades. Our analysis will, therefore, be restricted to the patterns of ritual performance observed in Iraq in the mid-twentieth century. While some of these patterns can still be observed today, the rituals have certainly evolved and changed, at least to some degree, since that time.

Women's Rituals

The Feast of Zachariah

The Feast of Zachariah was witnessed in 1957 in Daghara, southern Iraq (EWF). Held in late February that year, it was a shared feast following a one-day fast.[5] A woman made a vow. "If such and such is granted to me," she said, "I will fast for one day and then hold a feast on Zachariah's day." The women were generally married, though an unmarried woman who was older (late twenties or thirties, functioning as head of a household) could also make the vow. This wish was for something important, such as the return of a parent's, child's, or spouse's health, the conception of a son, or an improvement in the family's fortunes. Several women were celebrating the Feast of Zachariah and informants told us that many people celebrated this day every year, in thanks for past favors and particularly if their vows had been granted during the previous year. The principal of the village girls' school had celebrated the Feast of Zachariah every year for fifteen years in an effort to give thanks for her good fortune. Left alone with an aged mother and four younger sisters to support, she had been given the job as the single village schoolteacher; since that time, the school had grown, three teachers had been added to the staff, and she had been made principal. Each year she invited the teachers of the area to a splendid *futur*, the special breakfast which marks the end of the one-day fast. In a household where males lived, the father or elder brother usually purchased the food for the feast, but did not eat with the women celebrating the feast (BQB).

Sawm al-Banat

Sawm al-Banat, literally, "the girls' fast," usually took place near the time of Nowruz (the Iranian New Year's Day). It was for unmarried girls, usually those who had reached the age of puberty and above. A girl made a vow: "If such and such is granted to me, I vow to fast for one day." The request could be for something as simple as passing an examination in school, or for more difficult things such as an improvement in a parent or sibling's health or the hope that a marriage would be contracted with some particular cousin or admired youth. Her mother then sent the father out to buy the things required for the *futur*. The father was not, however, present at the time of the ceremony. The *futur* was prepared, plus a tray appropriate for the ritual, on which were placed lighted candles, powdered henna, dried *leban* (yogurt), a bar of a special soap from Aleppo, a loaf of bread, candies, nuts, and a copy of the Qur'an. The *futur* was a happy occasion. Friends, relatives, and neighbors (all female) were invited to the house of the girl who had made the vow, to share the goodies on the tray. Tea was served to all. While the tea was being drunk and the nuts and candies were being consumed by the women and their male and female children, another young girl made her vow. In this way, the circle of Sawm al-Banat celebrations went on and on, forming an occasion for gatherings of younger and older women who might otherwise have had few such opportunities for meeting.

Chay al-Abbas

Chay al-Abbas, literally "Abbas' tea," was the same sort of ritual but for married women. Occasionally, an unmarried woman who was older and who functioned as female head of a household could participate in Chay al-Abbas, as in the Feast of Zachariah. A woman made a vow that if such and such a wish was granted, she would prepare Chay al-Abbas. The wish could be for the birth of a child, the birth of a son, an improvement in a living child's health, improvement in a husband's business prospects, and so forth. When and if the wish was granted, the woman would tell her husband that she needed meat for Chay al-Abbas. The husband bought the meat and knew from this brief communication that such and such a day would be for Chay al-Abbas and therefore he should vacate the house for that day. No adult males participated, but male and female children were present. Invitations went out by word of mouth to all relatives, neighbors, and friends. Every woman dressed in her best clothing and wore all her finest jewelry, almost as though she were going to a wedding, for Chay al-Abbas was also a happy occasion. *Kubuz laham* (bread baked with meat in the dough) was served, but on this day it was called *kubuz al-abbas*. The bread was served to all guests, folded over fresh greens (chives and parsley). Tea followed. While the group was eating the *kubuz al-abbas*, another woman made a vow, thus forming a chain of vows as in Sawm al-Banat. If one did not have time for the ceremony itself, the bread and greens were still prepared and packets of the loaves and greens were sent to all relatives, neighbors, and friends. One hundred such loaves was not an unusual amount to be distributed for Chay al-Abbas.

Ziyarat Salman Pak

Ziyarat Salman Pak was the name given to the pilgrimage/picnic to the shrine of Salman Pak near the great arch of Ctesiphon, outside Baghdad. (Salman Pak was dedicated to Salman al-Farsi, one of the companions of the Prophet Mohammad.) This was also a springtime ritual during that year. Women who felt in need of the help of Salman Pak, women who were troubled or recently divorced or deserted, would make up a party consisting of themselves, their female relatives, and their children. They hired a bus, packed lunches, and set out for the shrine. Special songs were sung en route to the shrine, and if they passed a woman or women, the group on the bus sometimes shouted out:

Come with us, any woman who has been left by her husband.
Come with us, any woman in trouble.
Come with us to Salman Pak, for it is spring and we're going to enjoy ourselves.
We are a union together! (BQB)

After a ceremonial visit to the shrine, during which vows and prayers were often said, the women ate together on the grass nearby before returning home. Drumming and singing continued during the picnic. The only adult male involved in this particular ritual was the driver of the bus, unless one includes the historic figure to whom the visit was made.

In all four of these women's rituals, men were involved instrumentally, providing the meat for the Feast of Zachariah and for Chay al-Abbas, purchasing the treats for the *futur* of Sawm al-Banat, or driving the bus to Salman Pak. However, no adult males took part in the feasting and vow ritual, although children of both sexes were always present.

Similar ceremonies, focusing on vowing and communal fasting, were found among men in Shi'i Iraq, according to Robert Fernea, and in Shi'i Iran, according to Gustav Thaiss. Details of the ceremonies are few, though Fernea states that men tended to make such vows, but promised more private pledges, such as money for a Qur'anic school or money for charity, instead of communal social feasts, if their vow was fulfilled. Thaiss confirms this, and adds that "the making of vows is most common among women where the resultant gathering is known as *sofrehs haziat-i Abbas*."[6]

Ta'ziyeh

Ta'ziyeh literally means "expression of sympathy, mourning, and consolation." It was applied to a complex of ceremonies, processions, and morality plays that took place in Shi'i Muslim communities during the month of Moharram, to commemorate the death in battle on the fields of Karbala of the martyr Hosayn, grandson of the Prophet Mohammad. In this paper we do not speak of the passion play enacted by specialists who travel as troupes throughout parts of Iran (described by Peter Chelkowski).[7] We speak here of the local rituals that were celebrated annually by the male inhabitants of individual villages and towns throughout Shi'i areas of Iraq and Iran on Ashura, the tenth day of the month of Moharram.

Only men took part in the *ta'ziyeh*, or so it seemed. On Ashura, groups of men—one large group or several smaller groups—assembled together and then walked in procession from the village or town mosque to the tribal *modhif*, or guest house, or through the marketplace, crying aloud, ritually, with established chants and responses, expressing publicly their sorrow and mourning for Hosayn. Ritual chants were interspersed with the rhythmic beat of chains with which the men flagellated their own shoulders.

This was a public spectacle and everyone went to watch: women, children, and old men lined the streets of the village to see the local *ta'ziyeh* group. In towns and cities they gathered to watch a long procession of several groups. The climax of such local performances came during the annual pilgrimage to Karbala, forty days after Ashura, which was the day on which Hosayn was killed. At this time, hundreds of these groups of men from all parts of Shi'i Iraq and Iran traveled in procession together down the streets of Karbala; the streets were lined with male and female pilgrims and their children. They moved toward the same goal: the golden-domed tomb of Hosayn.

Only men marched, but women and children watched—and participated by adding their sobs and weeping to the atmosphere of ritual formalized mourning that permeated these performances. Often the men were either stripped to the waist for marching or wore sleeveless shirts that had been cut out at the shoulders to leave bare areas of skin. This is a point that should be stressed, for in everyday life in Shi'i Muslim society, men and women have traditionally covered their bodies almost totally; physical modesty has always been an admired virtue. In the *ta'ziyeh* this injunction was reversed for the men.

The *ta'ziyeh* was a formalized Shi'i religious ritual, but we would also suggest that it involved a demonstration of masculinity and some of the virtues associated with it in Muslim society: religious devotion, bravery, courage before pain, endurance, and so on. This was one time in the year when men paraded, often with bare upper bodies, before women, and not only the women of their family. Such a demonstration was not lost on the audience. While standing with women watching the *ta'ziyeh*, we heard comments that testified to the women's awareness of the men's appearance and behavior in such a situation of duress: "Look at Hasan. Is he all right?" "See Hadhi, he never flinches." "Ali has something wrong with his chest. Don't marry your daughter to him."

If such rituals provided an opportunity for male performance before a female public, it was perhaps appropriate that many, though not all, men were dedicated to participation in the *ta'ziyeh* by their mothers, through

Table 10.1. Male and Female Behaviors in Tunisian *maraboutic* Ceremonies

Male Behavior	Female Behavior
Silence	Noise
Obscurity	Clarity
Closed milieu	Open milieu
Gravity	Joy

another ceremony of vowing. Thus, the men participated in the *ta'ziyeh* to fulfill their mothers' promises that a greatly desired male offspring, or one who has lived through a crisis of illness, would perform such religious service as a measure of thanksgiving.

The Qurayeh

Sophie Ferchiou, in a most illuminating article in *L'Homme,* was, to our knowledge, one of the first observers to systematically compare male and female participation in the same ritual.[8] In Ferchiou's case, these were Tunisian *maraboutic* ceremonies. She points out how men's and women's behavior differed in the celebration of the rituals of the *zaweeya* cults, and she sets up contrasting pairs of underlying qualities which dominated each celebration (see table 10.1).

Ferchiou suggests that these qualities—attributes of accepted behavior—could generally be reversed in everyday life, outside the ritual context. The same reversal of qualities can be seen in the case of the Qurayeh, or religious reading, which customarily took place in southern Iraq every evening during the first ten days of Moharram, and usually every evening during the month of Ramadan. Table 10.2 briefly summarizes the differences.

The Qurayeh differed from the Tunisian situation somewhat. Men did not attend female Qurayehs, but women could attend male Qurayehs as observers, provided they sat outside the area where the males had congregated. On such occasions, according to male relations, women were encouraged to further their religious and intellectual education (BQB). However, in the Tunisian ceremonies, men were not allowed in female rituals and women did not generally attend the male rituals.

The Qurayeh, then, like the *maraboutic* ritual, provided contrasting ritual expressions of appropriate male and female behavior in what might be regarded as the same ceremonies. In public places in Iraq, for example, women were supposed to appear grave and quiet, to do whatever must be

Table 10.2. Male and Female Behaviors in the Qurayeh in Southern Iraq

Men's Qurayeh	Women's Qurayeh
Held usually in public closed places, such as market areas, the *mudheef,* or tribal guesthouse, the mosque; also could be held in private homes	Held only in private homes, usually in the courtyards, an open place
Neat attire, but no special clothes; men participated by listening to the sermon and joining in the prayers occasionally, but without moving from a seated position; generally, a passive attitude	Special "dress-up" clothes were preferred, such as the *hashmi;* women actively participated, weeping, responding enthusiastically, moving in a circle, tearing at their clothes, beating their chests; generally, an active attitude
Individual meditation, silence	Group involvement, noise
Grave and serious social occasion with little visiting before or after	Grave social occasion, but with much visiting before and after

done quickly, return home, and stay in their own houses. The Qurayeh provided the reversed situation for women. Men in public were involved in group activity, were not expected to be quiet and grave, nor to cease socializing when their business was done. The Qurayeh provided a reversed situation for them as well.

If we look at all these rituals, what do we observe? Women's rituals involved men as instrumental forces. The men helped the women prepare for the rituals (bringing meat for Chay al-Abbas and the Feast of Zachariah, purchasing the treats for Sawm al-Banat, driving the bus for the Ziyarat Salman Pak). However, the performance of the ritual itself was left to females alone. This worked in reverse for male rituals. Women could prepare the house for the Qurayeh, as well as cook food and prepare tea to serve at the end of the *taʿziyeh* or the Qurayeh. They also left the form of the ritual itself for the males alone, though they could *observe* these rituals, as in the Qurayeh and the *taʿziyeh.* Further, women were involved as promoters of the *taʿziyeh* (promising their sons to the service), and they also could involve men in their rituals as persons to be aided through fasting and vowing ceremonies. Did men's rituals also involve women as persons to be aided? Evidence for this was lacking at the time when these observations were made.

What are we suggesting? That though the private/public split, that passing paradigm, may have seemed to apply rather neatly to ritual, this was only superficially so. Actually, men and women were inextricably twined in various symbolic and instrumental ways throughout such rituals. Females were involved in male rituals in some way, and men were involved in female rituals in some way, if only instrumentally. Of course, as children, both males and females were involved in female rituals particularly. When the rituals were finished, husbands and wives and brothers and sisters, as well as fathers and daughters and mothers and sons, discussed who was present and what had taken place during the course of the occasion. That was the way the circle went, as informants said.

Further, on the basis of these examples, we see that the old notion of a private/public split did not hold well when we actually examined women's social lives. In Muslim society of the 1940s and 1950s in southern Iraq, women were not to mingle with others outside the family; this was preferred behavior, ideal behavior. But what happened in practice? Women had set up situations where they did meet each other, just as the church socials in the early years of the United States and the self-help ceremonies of pioneer days created situations where women could gather together. Iraqi women ritualized their social life so that they, in fact, met with many women outside the family on numerous occasions throughout the year and in socially sanctioned situations as well: they met for religious guidance, but also for solidarity, personal interaction, business purposes, and the all-important reason of choosing marriage partners for their children. Our few examples were but a fraction of the total number of situations per year in which such activity took place. These forms of women's social life were found in all classes of society, and variants of the rituals we have described were developing as Iraqi society was beginning to change. In the 1950s, for example, the Ottoman institution of the *kabool*, or weekly "at-home tea party," had replaced, among middle-class women of the southern provincial towns, some of the vowing ceremonies. Among other women the *kabool* merely supplemented the vowing ceremonies.

Vowing ceremonies, when found among men, did not tend to involve them as much in socializing. Men's economically productive lives have tended to place them in public, social situations on a daily basis. (Hence, perhaps, the meditative quiet Qurayeh and the lack of ritualized social gatherings among men paralleling the female occasions such as the Feast of Zachariah and Chay al-Abbas.) Women's economically productive lives, centered in the home, did not tend to place them in contact with other women. The rituals we have described provided socially sanctioned bases for gatherings as well as for religious improvement (hence the noisy, emotionally participatory women's Qurayeh). As women's economically productive lives have tended to decline, as in some of the oil-rich states like Kuwait, ritual and visiting have come to dominate their lives.[9] We need to examine the areas in which men and women have operated together. In ritual, we suggest, such areas may be formalized and thus more easily set up for examination and further study. If we are to begin to understand the process of male-female interaction in any part of Middle Eastern society, we need to look closely not only at what men and women have done separately and together, but also at what areas have been really segregated (without children, for example). Our paper is an exploratory effort to indicate some of the untapped resources that may be analyzed to this end.

Notes

1. For the most nuanced discussion of this paradigm, see Cynthia Nelson, "Public and Private Politics: Women in the Middle Eastern World," *American Ethnologist* 1:3 (1974), 551–563.

2. Victor Turner, *The Ritual Process: Structure and Anti-Structure* (Chicago: Aldine, 1969), and Arnold Van Gennep, *Rites de Passage,* trans. Monika B. Vizedom and Gabrielle L. Caffee (Chicago: University of Chicago Press, 1960).

3. *Random House Dictionary of the English Language* (New York: Random House, 1987).

4. These occasions are recorded as remembered and witnessed in Baghdad and witnessed and recorded in Baghdad and Diwaniyeh during childhood and young adulthood (BQB). Occasions were also witnessed and recorded in southern Iraq during 1956–1958 (EWF).

5. The story of the prophet Zachariah, father of John the Baptist, appears in the Qur'an, 3:37–41, 9:1–15, and 30:89–90. It is also found in the New Testament, Luke 1:5–25. The gist of the account is approximately the same. Zachariah officiates as a priest in the temple of the Lord. An angel appears to him, announcing that a son will be born to him and his wife, Elizabeth, who is barren. Zachariah is troubled because he believes he is too old. The angel reassures him, and, as a sign of the truth of the prophecy, Zachariah is struck dumb for three days. Informants from Daghara had transformed Zakariah into a woman, Zekariiyah, who was described as very old, poor, and in the desert without food. She fasted all day and in the evening found a well, from which she drank water, and some barley, from which to make bread. The barley was changed into wheat, which made much better bread (EWF).

6. Personal communication, Robert A. Fernea (EWF), n.d.; Gustav Thaiss, "Religious Symbolism and Social Change: The Drama of Husain," in *Scholars, Saints, and Sufis: Muslim Religious Institutions since 1500,* ed. Nikki R. Keddie, 349–366 (Berkeley and Los Angeles: University of California Press, 1972a).

7. Peter J. Chelkowski, "Ta'ziyeh: Indigenous Avant-Garde Theatre of Iran," in *Ta'ziyeh: Ritual and Drama in Iran*, ed. Peter J. Chelkowski (New York: New York University Press, 1979a).

8. Sophie Ferchiou, "Survivantes mystiques et culte de possession dans le maraboutisme Tunisien," *L'Homme* 12 (1972), 47–69.

9. Personal communication, Afaf Meleis (EWF), n.d.

CHAPTER 11

From Mourning to Activism
Sayyedeh Zaynab, Lebanese Shiʿi Women, and the Transformation of Ashura

LARA Z. DEEB

Like Shiʿi Muslims around the world, Lebanese Shiʿis commemorate the martyrdom of Imam Hosayn, grandson of the Prophet Mohammad, each year during the first ten days of the Islamic month of Moharram. Lebanese metonymically refer to the entire ten-day period as Ashura—technically the term for the tenth of the month, the day on which the battle actually took place. Commemorating Ashura in Lebanon involves holding and attending both private and public *majales,* or mourning gatherings in which the history of the martyrdom is retold, and tenth-day *masirat,* or lamentation processions, during which men often perform *latam,* a ritual-ized striking of one's body in grief. In observation of the standard mourn-ing period, some continue attending *majales,* with less regularity, for forty days after the tenth.

Historically, both the structure and the meaning of Ashura and these lamentation events have been fluid, incorporating different elements in dif-ferent locales and reflecting the changing political and social status of Shiʿi Muslims in Lebanon. However, a particularly dramatic transformation has been taking place over the past two decades, mirroring shifts in the Leban-ese Shiʿi Islamic movement,[1] particularly the growing popularity of the Shiʿi political party Hezbollah. This change is characterized by many Lebanese Shiʿis as a shift from what they label a "traditional" Ashura to what I am calling an "authenticated" one.

There are a wide range of Ashura meanings and practices—indeed a con-tinuum of Ashura commemorations—that are not reducible into two static and absolute categories, but I have found it useful to follow the contrast set up by my interlocutors in order to trace these recent changes. Participants in both types of commemorations labeled Ashura as it was commemorated for much of the twentieth century (and continues to be commemorated) as "traditional" (*taqlidi*). Those who instead participated in what I call "authenticated" Ashura often opposed their commemorations to these "traditional" ones, using temporal and value-laden oppositions ("now" versus "before," "developed" or "cultured" versus "backward") in order to underscore the distinction.[2] Advocates of "authenticated" Ashura generally used the adjective *haqiqi* to describe their commemorations and interpretations, a term for which the range of meaning includes "true," "real," "genuine," and "authentic." I have chosen to use the latter term in translation because it captures both the truth claims being made and the emphasis on accuracy of method included in those claims.

One important element in this shift in Ashura commemorations involves the reinterpretation of the behavior of Sayyedeh Zaynab at Karbala, a reinterpretation bearing consequences for the participation of Lebanese Shiʿi women in their community. Inherent in the details of this transformation, both generally and with regard to Zaynab, lies a paradox—that Ashura has been made modern through attempts to reauthenticate it, or make it more authentic than tradition.

In what follows, I will first provide the particular context for this change in Lebanon, followed by a description of the transformation and its inherent paradox. I then focus more closely on a comparison of two women's *majales,* moving to a discussion of the specific changes in the depictions of Zaynab's behavior at Karbala and how she represents an ideal standard for emulation by women in the community. Finally, I conclude by touching briefly upon women's self-conscious engagement with the authentication of Ashura and their utilization of these newly emergent social ideals.

A short side note is necessary before I continue: in Lebanon, as in many places, religion and identity are often conflated. Obviously, not all Lebanese Shiʿis commemorate Ashura, just as not all Lebanese Shiʿis embrace "Shiʿi" as part of their identity. However, since the 1970s, identification with, and support of, Shiʿi-specific political parties and movements has grown exponentially in the country. This is due to multiple factors, including a charismatic leadership, the perceived failures of the Lebanese Left in resisting the Israeli occupation, successes of the Islamic Resistance, a general polarization of sectarian identities during the civil war, and the continued consolidation of those identities by postwar politics. This paper is based primarily, though not exclusively, on field research conducted from October 1999 through July 2001 in a particular Lebanese Shiʿi community located in a Hezbollah-dominated area of the southern suburbs of Beirut. This is a community in which people are religiously active—praying, fasting, and tithing regularly—and where many explicitly embrace either "Shi'i" or "Muslim" as a part of their identity.

Catalysts for Change in the Lebanese Context

So-called "traditional" Ashura commemorations have occurred in rural Lebanon and in what are today the southern suburbs of Beirut since the beginning of the twentieth century. However, the urban visibility of Ashura grew in tandem with the urbanizing Shi'i population in the 1960s. These commemorations were viewed by many nonparticipants[3] as a frightening display of the "backward" (*motakhallef*) traditions of Shi'i Muslims and were cited as one of the points of difference marking the Shi'is as less modern and developed than other communities in Lebanon. For Lebanese Shi'is, this stigma followed a history marked by political and economic marginalization: in a nation-state in which sectarian political-economic power translated to selective access to modernization for particular areas of the country, Shi'i Muslims resided primarily in the least developed rural regions and did not have access to infrastructure and institutional developments occurring in the rest of Lebanon.[4]

Aside from being stigmatized as "backward" and not modern, until the mid-1980s, "traditional" Ashura was not strongly opposed within the Lebanese Shi'i community. The initial signs of reform of the Ashura paradigm came in 1974 with the first inclusive mobilization of the Shi'is as a confessional group. In March of that year, Sayyid Musa al-Sadr founded the "Movement of the Deprived"[5] (*harakat al-mahrumin*). Since Sayyid Musa's "disappearance" in 1978,[6] his legacy has been claimed by both of the Lebanese Shi'i political parties, Harakat Amal and Hezbollah.[7] Norton notes that "under Imam Musa's considerable influence, religious commemorations became vehicles for building communal solidarity and political consciousness."[8] However, while Sayyid Musa was the first to link contemporary Shi'i political mobilization in Lebanon with Ashura, transformation of the ritual with regard to both practice and meaning did not take root for another decade. Around that time a combination of factors, including the Islamic Revolution in Iran (1978), the Lebanese civil war (1976–1990), the Israeli invasions (1978 and 1982) and continued occupation (until 2000), and the formation of Hezbollah, led to the emergence of opposition within the Shi'i community to "traditional" commemorations.

This opposition reflected trends in Iran, where reformist and Islamist intellectuals had contributed to the emergence of a new Ashura discourse that linked it to an alternative and revolutionary Shiʿism, in contrast to a politically quietist one.[9] Indeed, many Lebanese Shiʿis point to the 1979 Islamic Revolution as the pivotal catalyst for mobilization and religious reform within their community. Furthermore, the transformation of Ashura in Lebanon took place in a context of war and occupation. While the horrific consequences of the Lebanese civil war[10] were felt throughout the country, it was the predominantly Shiʿi regions of the south and the Bekaa that bore the brunt of the two Israeli invasions and the Israeli occupation that continued until the summer of 2000.[11] Finally, the growing popularity and widening scope of Hezbollah[12] in the late 1980s and early 1990s provided a structure within which the transformed version of Ashura could thrive.

Ritual Reconfiguration: From "Traditional" to "Authenticated" Ashura

The shift from "traditional" to "authenticated" Ashura is especially apparent with regard to three areas: the *masirat*, the *majales,* and, most crucially, the meaning of the events of Moharram.

Masirat

The most obvious change in the *masirat* has occurred in the style of *latam* that men and boys perform following the *majles* (sing. of *majales*) on the tenth of Moharram. The traditional style of *latam*—best exemplified by the Ashura *masirat* in the southern Lebanese town of Nabatieh[13]—involves the shedding of one's own blood. Those performing *latam* form small groups and march quickly, almost at a jog, as they invoke the names of Ali and Hosayn and hit the small wounds that have been cut at their hairlines, so that blood flows down their faces and stains their white shirts (representing shrouds) or bare chests a bright red.[14] Women generally do not participate in these *masirat*,[15] though they make up at least half of the crowd that lines the street and leans over balconies and from nearby rooftops to watch.[16]

As the revolutionary Shiʿi Islamic movement in Lebanon took shape and grew in popularity, the shedding of blood during *latam* was criticized as un-Islamic because it involves purposely injuring oneself. Again following the lead of Iran,[17] Lebanese Shiʿi clerics issued fatwas condemning the practice, and Hezbollah banned it outright in the mid-1990s. In Lebanon, this was accompanied by calls for those who feel the need to shed their blood during Ashura to do so for the community good, by instead donating blood to local blood banks.[18] In addition to condemning *latam* involving blood, the mobilizing Lebanese Shi'i movement, in typical fashion, called upon women to participate actively and publicly in Ashura commemorations, as well as in the community more generally.[19]

A sharp contrast to "traditional" *masirat* and *latam* is presented by Hezbollah's "authenticated" *masirat* in the southern suburbs of Beirut. These *masirat* exhibit military order, with large groups of men and boys performing *latam* organized by age and dressed uniformly as scouts or entirely in black. They march in three neat rows behind a microphone-bearing leader, who initiates *nadbat*, lamentation songs or elegies, and chants and ensures that the groups perform *latam* in perfect unison so that it provides a percussive accompaniment. Crucially, the style of *latam* performed does not involve blood;[20] instead, those performing it begin by swinging both arms downward, then up, then out away from their bodies, and finally in to strike their chests loudly with their hands.[21]

Another significant difference is that women are no longer relegated to an observational role. The Hezbollah *masirat* include women and girls, dressed in full *'abayeh*,[22] who are organized by age, like the men. The women's groups form the second half of the *masira* (sing. of *masirat*), and, while they do not perform *latam*, each group is led in chants, or *nadbat*, by a leader. Often, one group of young women will walk chained together, with their faces covered, representing the women in the Imam's party who were taken captive by Yazid's army. Both the active participation of women in the *masirat*, as well as the new style of *latam*, are viewed by many Lebanese Shi'is as both "more developed" (*mutatawwur*) and more authentic historically—perhaps a response to those stereotypes that link traditional Ashura to being less modern than the rest of Lebanon.

Majales

During a *majles*, a recitor (*qari'*)[23] narrates a part of the events of the first ten days of Moharram in a lamentation style reminiscent of a liturgy, detailing graphically the suffering and martyrdom of Imam Hosayn and those with him. Some recitors include a sermon that explains lessons to be learned from Karbala and the meanings of the events. The effect on the audience parallels these shifts in tone, with the lamentation liturgy evoking intense crying that quiets to a pensive concentration during the sermon sections.

While all *majales* include the lamentative narration of the *masa'eb*, the tragic events of Karbala (lit. calamities or misfortunes), recitors characterized as traditional will include as much detail of suffering as possible in this narration, in order to elicit maximum levels of emotion from the audience. Many add poetic embellishment and dialogue among Imam Hosayn, his sister Sayyedeh Zaynab, and others who were with them. The ultimate goal for these recitors is to move people to cry as much as possible for the martyred Imam and his family and companions. Shaykh Abbas,[24] at the office of Sayyid Mohammad Hosayn Fadlallah, undoubtably the most prominent Lebanese Shi'i *marja' al-taqlid*, explained that this resulted from the lack of proper training:

Our problem is that many recitors do not go to school to learn to recite, they just learn at home. Especially in the villages, anyone with a good voice can decide, "I want to become a recitor." There is no organization to change this, or to forbid such incorrect recitations. The recitors do not have to be trained in a theological seminary [*hawza*] and this is the big problem. There are some who are very traditional [*taqlidi*] and backward [*motakhallef*] and others who are cultured [*muthaqqaf*].[25] The backward ones read only to make people cry, but the cultured ones teach lessons in their recitations.[26]

As alluded to by the shaykh, *majales* considered authenticated are characterized by longer sermons and a more restrained narration of the events of Karbala. Eliciting an emotional response is still a goal, but a secondary one. These *majales* are intended to teach religious, social, and political lessons; to instruct the audience about the "true" meanings of Karbala and to link the history of the past to the present. Those who recite *majales* and strive for authenticity are concerned with the historical accuracy of their narrations and avoid including unfounded exaggerations that they see as being "merely" to heighten emotions and make people cry. Again, links can be seen between being authentic and being modern—namely in the promotion of "scientific" and textually based, and therefore "accurate," histories over exaggerations, which are viewed as "myth."

The perspective of a woman who has attended *majales* over the past three decades is provided by Hajjeh[27] Dalal:

They are reciting the same story about Hosayn; this person who reads the *majles* recites the same basic story as another person who is reciting. But the lecture differs among people. It depends on the audience and the lecturer and the topic he is explaining and his own relationship to Ashura. But they are better than before. They are better because they are being tied into our daily lives, this linking of the past to the present and the future, this is better. Before we used to just go and listen to the story of Hosayn, it was rare that you found a lecture. Now, we are not just going to cry for Imam Hosayn, we are going to learn from his school. The lecture is important, it is clarifying why it is that you are crying, and why Imam Hosayn was martyred. It is not just the crying for Imam Hosayn, it is about learning the lessons from the school of Imam Hosayn.[28]

Meaning

As can be inferred from these descriptions of traditional *majales* and *latam*, the emotions surrounding Ashura commemorated in this way center on both grief and regret. Tears shed for the martyrs of Karbala are tears that are *mustahabb*, or religiously commendable. It is believed that both evoking these tears and shedding them are acts that bring *'ajr*[29] (divine reward) and that may increase one's chances of entering heaven.[30] Blood spilled in memory of the events of Karbala is similarly an embodied demonstration of grief and an empathetic expression of solidarity with the Imam's pain and sorrow. Yet it can also be an expression of regret or remorse.[31] Some of those who perform the traditional style of *latam* explain that this demonstrates their regret for not being at Karbala with the Imam—a reference to those Shi'is who originally called upon the Imam to come and lead their revolution, but who then failed to arrive at Karbala in time to either protect the Imam or stand and die with him. In the context of pre-1970s Lebanon, when Shi'i Muslims were the least politically organized group in the country, all these meanings can be seen as related to the Lebanese Shi'i community's general political quietism. The emphasis during Ashura was on individual religious experiences of mourning and regret, embodied through tears and blood. While at first glance the association of blood and quietism may seem contradictory, in this instance the shedding of blood is directed at the self, rather than outward, implying a personal expression of grief, an internal struggle with regret, and the potential for individual salvation, rather than collective political or social action.

Yet from the perspective of the emergent alternative Shi'ism that espoused the authentication of Ashura, the blood and tears of these commemorations are considered to be both un-Islamic and passive:

Too much crying leads to personalities who cry—the Shi'is will become equated with crying, the Shi'is will take on crying as a cultural trait, and this is not a good thing, it is wrong. Emotions are necessary, but they should be understood as a way of arriving at learning the lesson of Hosayn. The heart should be used to reach the head, not as an endpoint in and of itself.[32]

Accompanying the discouragement of traditional *latam* and the histori-cal authentication of the *majales* was a redirection of the message of Ashura outward, shifting the meaning from one of personal mourning, regret, and salvation to a revolutionary lesson. This is not to say that notions of *'ajr* and personal salvation have been stripped from Ashura, but rather that the pri-mary emphasis and tone of the commemorations have undergone a shift. In-deed, those who advocate authenticated Ashura insist that *'ajr* comes from attending or holding *majales* and remembering Hosayn, Zaynab, and those who were with them, but *not* from the act of crying itself.

In the context of war and deprivation, where the Lebanese Shi'i commu-nity needed to mobilize militarily and socially, the message of revolution in the events of Moharram was highlighted.[33] This was done by emphasiz-ing the importance of historical accuracy and evidence in order to remove the myths and unearth the authentic historical record—one which demon-strated that the battle and martyrdom of the Imam took place in a context of revolution. As with the *masirat* and the *majales,* the paralleling of authen-tic and modern appears here as well. The notion of "revolution" is distinctly modern,[34] yet those who advocate authenticated Ashura find revolutionary meaning in the historical record; a reinterpretation of the events of Karbala couched as the unearthing of "true" history.

Hajjeh Fatemeh, who is considered an exemplary recitor of authenti-cated *majales*, explained this revolutionary lesson of Karbala to me as fol-lows: "In every era there is an oppressor and an oppressed . . ."[35] The role of Ashura was to remind people that

> there is a Yazid and a Hosayn in every time, in every nation, in every government, and people should always have the spirit of revolution against oppression, because time repeats itself, history repeats itself, in every age there is injustice. Revolution allows people to fight the oppression and we need these humanitarian principles.[36]

Two Women's *Majales*

The following juxtaposition of two women's *majales* will provide a more nuanced depiction of the differences appearing in Ashura commemorations in Lebanon. The basic structure of these two *majales* is essentially the same: in both, the recitor opens the *majles* with a quiet group recitation of *surat al-fatiha*, the opening verses of the Qur'an. Along with the salutations that may follow, this serves to highlight the sacred context of the *majles* and to bring participants into the mind-set of spiritual contemplation. The recitor may then insert a *nadba*, or elegy, though these are more commonly left to the end of a *majles*. The lamentative narration of a portion of the events of Karbala, the *masa'eb*, follows, with a sermon of varying length inserted in the middle. At the close of the lamentation, the recitor will usually lead the singing of at least one *nadba*, with women singing along when they know the words, while striking their chests or thighs in slow time. Especially if held in a private home, the *majles* may be dedicated to particular members of the hostess' family. Finally, *majales* often conclude with everyone standing and facing the direction of Hosayn's tomb in order to recite in unison *ziyarat al-Hosayn*, a supplicatory prayer directed toward the Imam. Hospitality is always immediately apparent following a *majles*, especially when it has been held at someone's home. Coffee and sweets are routinely offered, though some women go so far as to prepare a light lunch for their guests.

A "Traditional" Women's *Majles*

7 Moharram 2001 CE/ 1422 AH.[37] As we walked to the *hosayniyyeh*, Um Hasan and the others expressed nervousness that Hajjeh Fatemeh would not be reading this evening; she did not read yesterday because her voice had given out from the pressures of the week. Their worries were alleviated upon our arrival though, as other women there assured us that one day's rest was enough for Hajjeh Fatemeh, who, if at all possible, would not allow anything to interfere with her Ashura recitations. At the entrance, Aziza and I draped scarves over our heads "out of respect for the *hosayniyyeh*," but as soon as we were seated, she told me we could remove them because only women were present. Including the two of us, there were only about ten non-*mohajjebeh* (nonveiled) women there. Most participants wore their headscarves over loose dresses or the coat-dresses typical of *shar'i* (Islamically mandated) dress, though a few were in full *'abayeh*, including Hajjeh Fatemeh. The room was large enough to hold at least a hundred people, with a small kitchen and bathroom off to one side. Benches lined the walls and rows of plastic chairs filled the room. There was a podium at one end with a large airbrushed painting of a Karbala scene behind it. The podium was draped in black, and black cloth banners hung along the walls with sayings printed on them, including "al-

salamo ʿalaykom ya sayyed al-shohada'" (peace be upon you, Sayyid of the martyrs). When the room was full, Hajjeh Fatemeh walked to the podium, turned on the microphone, and began. Her voice was shaky and rough, but it seemed to clear as her recitation progressed. After opening with a quiet group recitation of *surat al-fatiha*, she greeted all who were at Karbala, saying, "al-salamo ʿalaykom ya Hosayn, al-salamo ʿalaykom ya . . . ," including *ʿali ibn al-Hosayn* (Ali, son of Hosayn), *awlad al-Hosayn* (the children of Hosayn), *ashab al-Hosayn* (the friends of Hosayn), *ʿAbbas, akhu al-Hosayn* (Abbas, brother of Hosayn), and finally, with special emphasis and emotion flooding her voice, *Zaynab, ukht al-Hosayn* (Zaynab, sister of Hosayn). She then led a short *nadba*, segueing from it into her lamentative narration of the *masa'eb*.

The focus this evening was on Abbas, Hosayn and Zaynab's brother and Zaynab's "supporter." The instant Hajjeh Fatemeh's voice broke into lamentation, sobs arose throughout the room. After about ten minutes, Hajjeh Fatemeh paused, took a few deep breaths, and then gave a short lecture, only about ten minutes in length, linking the characteristics of a good Muslim to the character of Abbas. She then returned to the lamentation, and, this time in the Iraqi dialect, described Abbas' death in vivid detail. She described the thirst of the children, their cries, and the way Abbas decided to try to get water for them. How, on his first attempt, he was wounded on his return from the Euphrates and the water spilled. How, despite his wounds, he made a second attempt to reach the river, but was caught and killed, his hands cut off, leaving bloody stumps. How his lifeless handless body returned to the camp draped over his horse, and how, upon seeing this, Zaynab cried out, "What were you doing leaving us like that? How can you leave us, you who are responsible for us?" And most of all, how Zaynab cried and mourned.

This was the longest lamentation I have heard so far. Again, as soon as the lamentation began, the women listening began to weep loudly. A few young girls, perhaps eight or nine years old, were sitting around the foot of the podium, two of them crying intensely. The levels of emotion in the room were overwhelming, sobs filled the air, some women cried out at moments, screaming, or speaking under their breath as they wept. This was particularly true of the older women, though this entire audience was older than the ones in homes tend to be. Even Aziza, who usually sat calmly and cried silently to herself at *majales*, had pulled her knees up to her chest and wrapped herself around them, her body shaking as she wept.

Hajjeh Fatemeh, too, was overtaken with emotion, throwing her head back as she lamented, tears streaming down her face, her voice rising and breaking as she cried out the words, sometimes screaming into the microphone "ya Zaynab" or "ya Hosayn." At one point she stopped articulating altogether, buried her head in her arms on the podium, and just wept like that for about five minutes, while the rest of the women in the room continued crying. Eventually, Um Zein stood and took Hajjeh Fatemeh some water, and she slowly lifted her head and resumed her lamentation where she had left off.

When the lamentation ended, everyone dried their eyes and slowly began singing two *nadbat* (pl. of *nadba*), mostly in unison. Everyone seemed to know the words, especially to the choruses: *ramz al-ʿataʾ, ruh al-shohadaʾ, li-man bakayt huwa al-Hosayn fi Karbalaʾ* (the symbol of giving, the spirit of the martyrs, he for whom I cried was Hosayn at Karbala), and *dammi mu ʾaghla min dammak ya Hosayn, jismi mu ʾaghla min jismak ya Hosayn* (my blood is not more precious than your blood oh Hosayn, my body is not more precious than your body oh Hosayn). As they sang, the women struck the left side of their chests with their right hands, providing a slow percussive accompaniment to the *nadbat*. One of the little girls had moved her shirt to one side and was hitting her chest so hard she left a red welt. The women sitting near me noticed this favorably, one of them saying it was obvious how moved the little girl was and how much she understood. At the conclusion of the *nadba*, several young women stood and brought coffee and sweets.

An "Authenticated" Women's *Majles*

11 Moharram 2001 CE/1422 AH. When we arrived, the door to the apartment was open, but as there were no men in sight, several women began removing their headscarves as they entered. Um Ali was rushing around greeting people and trying to seat everyone comfortably. Chairs were set up in the formal living room in three concentric circles, spilling out into the hallway and onto the adjacent balcony on the other side of the room. My friend and I found two empty chairs and squeezed in. There were around forty women present, ranging in age from very old to young brides with babies. A few mothers who had brought young children sat in the hallway so that they could keep half an eye on their kids, who were playing in a back room. Only four of us were not *mohajjabeh*. Everyone was dressed almost entirely in black, with only a few patches of white or gray here and there: a pattern on a scarf, embroidery trimming an ʿabayeh, or perhaps a white shirt showing under a black blazer.

About fifteen minutes after we arrived, one of Um Ali's daughters walked around the room distributing tissues to everyone present. On that cue, Layla, the young woman in a full 'abayeh who was reciting at this majles, picked up her microphone and began in a clear voice, leading everyone in a quiet recitation of surat al-fatiha, then salli 'ala Mohammad wa ali Mohammad thrice.[38] She then spoke a few sentences about the importance of Ashura, segueing directly into her recitation. Her tone grew more and more lamentative as she began to detail the masa'eb, but she remained clear relative to some of the other recitors I have heard and used only Lebanese dialect. As soon as her voice made the shift from normal speech to lamentation, several of the older women in the room began to weep loudly. Others buried their faces in their tissues; a few, mostly younger women, just lowered their heads, tears streaming silently from their eyes. In her lamentation, Layla detailed the masa'eb of the sabaya (the young women), and Zaynab in particular, after the Battle of Karbala. She described how they coped with the deaths, the trauma the women experienced as the men were all killed, and the way the survivors were paraded through the desert as prisoners being taken to Yazid, even though they were Ahl al-Bayt (members of the Prophet's family).

At this point, after ten or fifteen minutes, Layla rather abruptly broke her lamentation and returned to her normal speaking voice. The sobs in the room stopped with her, and everyone straightened their backs, lifted their heads, and wiped their tears. Layla then launched into a relatively long lecture about the corruption of Yazid and his followers, the intensity of the loss suffered by Zaynab and the sabaya, and the strength that Zaynab then demonstrated in standing up to Yazid and confronting him with his crimes. She then presented an explication of the saying of the Prophet, "Hosayn minni wa 'ana min Hosayn" (Hosayn is from/of me and I am from/of Hosayn). She explained that this meant that anyone who is a friend of Hosayn, who loves Hosayn, is in turn loved by the Prophet and loved by God. Likewise, anyone who stands against Hosayn stands against the Prophet and God.

Layla's voice then began to shake again and she returned to her lamentat. The women listening immediately resumed their weeping, as Layla detailed the approach and entrance of Zaynab and the sabaya into the prison of Yazid's palace. At one point, another prisoner hears that the new arrivals are from Medina and inquires, "How are Ahl al-Bayt?" Zaynab has to respond that they are all dead, but continues in a strong voice, "I, I am of the house of the Prophet, I am of Ahl al-Bayt, I am Zaynab, granddaughter of the Prophet Mohammad, sister of Imam Hosayn, I am Zaynab, ana

Zaynab!" This affirmation brought the sobs in the room to a crescendo, after which Layla quietly ended her recitation. Faces were dried and tissues thrown away as Layla blessed the house where we had gathered, dedicating the *majles* to the souls of the household's dead. She then asked the women to recite *surat al-fatiha* three times, once for the dead of the household, once for the martyrs of Karbala, and once for the martyrs of the Islamic Resistance who had died fighting the Israeli occupation of south Lebanon.

Then she instructed us to stand and face the direction of Hosayn's tomb, in order to recite *ziyarat al-Hosayn* in unison. Following this recitation, she introduced a *nadba,* calling upon the women to strike their chests in solidarity and grief, and reciting the chorus of the *nadba* twice so they would be able to learn it and sing along. During her introduction, Um Ali and her daughters stood and left the room. Layla then sang the verses, allowing the women to sing the chorus on their own in between, with everyone lightly tapping their chests (right hand to heart generally) or thighs in slow rhythm. That marked the end of the *majles,* and Um Ali's daughters were waiting at the doorway of the living room with trays of coffee and sweets. Most of the women sat and socialized for fifteen minutes or so before beginning to leave. As always, women commented quietly on the voice of the reader. This time several older women noted that Layla didn't have "the most moving voice" as compared to other readers; the response to this by one of the women's daughters was "yes, but she was very clear."

Juxtaposition

The first discernible difference between these *majales* concerns the participants' ages. The participants at the traditional *majles* were mostly older women, while the authenticated *majles* was attended by women ranging widely in age. In general, privately held *majales* tend to have a wider age spectrum because women invite members of their extended families, as well as friends, colleagues, and neighbors, but the responses of participants often vary by age, with older women more prone to intense displays of emotionality. In part this reflects differing attitudes toward Ashura; traditional *majales* usually attract an older audience, while authenticated *majales* appeal to younger and more educated women. Yet several women also noted that they felt more comfortable "letting loose" in larger public *majales* because household *majales* had a more formal air to them. Public *majales* vary widely as well: in contrast to the participants at the public *majles* at the *hosayniyyeh* described here, attendance at the public *majles* sponsored nightly by Hezbollah in the southern suburbs of Beirut tends to consist of younger women. Some of the younger women I spoke with questioned older women's tears. Nada, a young woman who attends one or two *majales* a day during Ashura, noted,

> Some of these women just go to cry, but they don't know why they are crying or why they are supposed to be crying. It's just tradition and habit. They go from *majles* to *majles* all day long crying. The recitor begins, you begin to cry, this is how it is for them. And worse, some of them are crying about ones they have lost, not the Imam Hosayn.[39]

When I asked her what the correct way of participating in a *majles* would be, she explained, "You are supposed to think about what the recitor is saying, and understand it, and then it will affect you and you will cry because of what you are learning, for the right reasons, because you understand the true tragedy of it."[40]

The age difference between the recitors is significant as well, with older recitors more likely to present *majales* located toward the traditional end of the spectrum. In addition to placing less emphasis on the didactic aspects of the events of Karbala, older recitors are less likely to have trained in a theological seminary than are younger ones. While Hajjeh Fatemeh has trained in the local women's seminary, she began her training after she had already been leading *majales* for over a decade. She initially began reciting as a way to express the deep extent of her love for Ahl al-Bayt, who often came to her in dreams. Layla, on the other hand, came to lead *majales* through her studies at the seminary. She also reads to express her love for Ahl al-Bayt, but emphasizes the importance of teaching others in her community their history and learning lessons from their example.

Another distinction in these two *majales* is linked to a common tension in vocal expression in the performances of many recitors between clarity (*wuduh*) and tenderness/compassion (*hanan*). Recitors who are considered traditional are generally praised for their ability to move people with the tone and quality of their voices, sacrificing clarity for emotionality. For this reason, traditional recitors sometimes shift into the Iraqi dialect during their lamentations. Listeners may not understand every word, but the manner of recitation and the beauty of symbolism is often moving in itself. As one woman explained, many, especially older, recitors had been trained in Najaf, in Iraq, and brought the dialect with them, but others choose to draw on the Iraqi dialect because "it is known that Iraqi is the dialect of compassion and longing," and the Iraqi tradition of Karbala poetry is considered richer than the Lebanese. In contrast, recitors who are concerned that their audiences understand every word of the recitation and its lessons are apt to use only the Lebanese dialect to ensure comprehensibility.

In both these *majales*, indeed, in all *majales*, powerful levels of emotion are generated and maintained, yet, again, the extent and intensity of emotion varies. Women often take emotional cues from the recitor, though the locale matters as well, and ultimately, the differences are individual ones. In general, however, participants in authenticated *majales* are inclined to more tempered expressions of grief and sorrow. Differences in intensity of emotional expression are reflected in the relative lengths of time that recitors spend on the lamentation as compared with the sermon, and in the affect of the recitor herself. Every recitor I saw was clearly engaged emotionally in her recitation, reliving the events of Karbala with Ahl al-Bayt, yet older recitors—whether because of their longer experience with *majales* or because of differences in their approaches to Ashura—often seemed to enter a trancelike state in which their grief emanated from them to wrap itself around the other participants. The narrations of the *masa'eb* themselves differ somewhat as well; each recitor chooses the poetry she will include in her lamentation, and traditional recitors often narrate bloodier descriptions of the deaths, prolonged dialogue among Hosayn, Zaynab, and others who were with them, and what authenticated recitors often call "exaggerations." As noted above, ultimately it is the order in which the two goals of *majales* are prioritized that differs; one emphasizing mourning for Ahl al-Bayt and its soteriological effects, and the other focusing on lessons to be learned from their example and applied to life today.

Sayyedeh Zaynab: From Mourner to Revolutionary Role Model

By far the most striking difference in content between these *majales*—and what is for many women the most essential aspect of the revolutionary lesson that emerged from this transformation—lies in the reinterpretation of the behavior of Sayyedeh Zaynab[41] during and following the events of Karbala:

Before they would present Sayyedeh Zaynab as crying, screaming, wailing, but, no, Zaynab set the stage . . . for revolution against tyranny. She didn't mourn Hosayn but thought how to save the rest and how to keep his message going. She was imprisoned, and yet she stood up with all confidence and spoke her point of view instead of feeling defeated. This changed our lives, we are now ashamed to feel weak, or to feel sorrow. Whenever we are faced with a problem, we remember the words, and feel shamed if we complain. No, we instead feel strong and deal with it and move on.[42]

Traditional narrations often portrayed Zaynab as buried in grief, pulling at her hair and shedding copious tears over the dead and dying. Representations that had depicted her as a plaintive mourner were transformed to renderings that accentuated her courage, strength, and resilience. Recitors of authenticated *majales*, along with their audiences, criticized these portrayals of Sayyedeh Zaynab for their exaggerated emphasis on her tears:

Before, if you were listening at a *majles,* they would describe Sayyedeh Zaynab as crying a lot and grieving and tearing her clothing. Now, the shaykhs, of course the experienced ones who know, said that this is something incorrect, and isn't mentioned at all. In fact, it's the opposite, she was in control of herself and patient, and she wasn't affected emotionally in this way.[43]

Some readers will add talk for Sayyedeh Zaynab, things she would not have said, I do not like it when they portray her as crying. Sayyedeh Zaynab was strong, she stood up in the face of the oppressor, she was not weak, she told him that she was the victor, she considered herself the victor by the blood of Imam Hosayn. She is the victor in meaning. Sayyedeh Zaynab proves that we did not lose.[44]

In particular, three new characteristics emerge in the reformulation of Sayyedeh Zaynab's behavior at Karbala: her strength of mind, her compassion and dedication to others, and her courage to speak out publicly. Consistent with their expected role as mothers of martyrs, Lebanese Shi'i women in this community frequently pointed to Zaynab's strength of mind and ability to endure the loss of all the men in her family. Numerous mothers who had lost sons in the Islamic Resistance and sisters who had lost brothers explained that they coped with their grief by emulating the equanimity of Sayyedeh Zaynab as she watched her male relatives die. They often compared their losses to hers, and, in so doing, expressed feeling that they had lost little in comparison: "We didn't lose everyone, like Sayyedeh Zaynab did. We have to say, if she could go on, why can't we? And we at least have role models; there is acknowledgment in society for the mothers of martyrs; the Sayyedeh had none of that."[45]

The other two qualities seen in Zaynab's example that were emulated by women highlight her ability to act despite her grief and the turmoil of her surroundings. Women often compared their contributions to society with hers, observing that they had given relatively little, and citing her as one of the most salient models encouraging their active engagement with the welfare of their community. In the context of the southern suburbs of Beirut, this translates to hundreds of women participating visibly in the community by volunteering their time and energy to work in Islamic social service organizations (*jam'iyyat*). One woman who is active in a *jam'iyya* explained it thus:

> Sayyedeh Zaynab, after the martyrdom of Imam Hosayn, she brought up his children, all the orphans . . . she stood by their side, and lessened their pain, even though Imam Hosayn was her brother, when he was martyred, that was her brother who died, and the children of her brothers were martyred, and *her* children were martyred. . . . She was able to handle all the suffering that she experienced, and all the problems and pain, and at the same time she could help others. She has taught us that no matter what we experience . . . it will never be as much as what she dealt with. Because of this she is the model for our community work.[46]

Finally, more than either of her other ideal attributes, Sayyedeh Zaynab's outspokenness positions her as the "heroine of the heroes" for many Lebanese Shi'i women. They emphasize that she confronted Yazid during her imprisonment and spoke eloquently, accusing him publicly of his crimes, and that she played an indispensable role in spreading the message of Karbala and revolution after the Imam's martyrdom. As Salwa noted:

> What would have happened if Imam Hosayn went to Karbala and was martyred and Sayyedeh Zaynab wasn't there? Because the story always begins after the martyrdom. So Zaynab, she went and witnessed, and she was the one who carried the truth of Karbala with her. She stood before Yazid and spoke to him, and she showed the world the events that occurred when Imam Hosayn was martyred. So it was she who carried the message of revolution to others. It was she who made possible Ashura. This is the role of women.[47]

In keeping with Zaynab's role in carrying the message of revolution to others, Lebanese Shi'i women contribute to the authentication of Ashura through their participation in *majales* and *masirat* and through their constant informal conversations about Ashura narratives and events. Whether over coffee in a neighbor's kitchen or en route to or from a *majles* with a cousin or friend, women often debated the historical accuracy of details of the events of Karbala.[48] For example, sitting on the balcony one afternoon, Aziza and her neighbor discussed at length whether it could be corroborated that—as the recitor of a *majles* the day before had depicted—Imam Hosayn had indeed given his young daughter Ruqayya a cup before his death, telling her that it would turn black inside if he were killed. Some of these conversations were sparked by a listener's skepticism toward a specific recitor, others triggered by discord between the version of an episode recited in a *majles* just attended and the version broadcast over the radio in the car on the way home.

On another occasion, while walking home from a *majles* at a nearby mosque, Nahla questioned the shaykh who had recited, wondering, "Is it really possible that Imam Hosayn put his tongue on his son's and felt that it was dry like wood? I don't think I've ever heard any evidence for that, and I am not convinced that it is accurate. I am going to ask my uncle Hasan."[49] Nahla did later relay her doubts to her uncle, who she felt was more knowledgeable regarding religious matters than she, and he confirmed her suspicions, assuring her that he was unaware of any evidence for that particular detail. Had his response not persuaded her—as occurred on other occasions—she would have telephoned the office of her *marjaᶜ al-taqlid* in pursuit of the most "authentic" rendition of the events possible. In these instances, women are not only participating actively in the commemoration of authenticated Ashura, but in the authentication process itself.

In many ways, these authenticated discourses about Sayyedeh Zaynab set a standard of behavior to which many Lebanese Shiᶜi women aspire today. Authenticated Ashura and Zaynab's role during and following Karbala have become one of the most significant narrative frameworks that women draw upon in their daily lives. As articulated emphatically by Hajjeh Um Ali:

> Now, whenever I am faced with some problem, I ask myself, am I going to act like Zaynab or not? Do you understand what this means? If someone knocks at my door am I going to help him or not? Am I going to feel with others or not, am I going to give even more of myself or not, am I going to have the courage to face oppression or not? Do you understand how important this is?[50]

Closing Considerations

Within this transformation of Ashura practices and meanings in Lebanon, and the juxtaposition within the community of what is "traditional" with what is "authenticated," lies a paradox—seen in the conflation of what is modern with what is authentic. The condemnation of drawing one's own blood during *latam*, the importance placed upon historical and textual accuracy over myth, the emphasis on revolutionary meaning over soteriological aims, and the active incorporation of women into both ritual and public community life are all aspects of the transformation that are cited as modern by members of this community or that draw upon distinctly modern concepts. Paradoxically, it is through these modern concepts and practices that advocates of authenticated Ashura strive to assert authenticity itself. To its advocates, authenticated Ashura is both more modern and more authentic than tradition.

Most interesting, especially with regard to the participation of women, is that this process is in part self-conscious. Women express a keen awareness that "the West" is looking at them *as women* in particular, scrutinizing how they are "treated" and what their societal roles are. One member of the Hezbollah Women's Committee observed, in a tone both amused and curious, that "all these Westerners come to interview us because they are looking to see if Islam is modern, and 'how the women are treated' or 'what the women do' has become the sign of which cultures are modern." [51] Another woman, a volunteer at two local *jam'iyyat*, one of them affiliated with Hezbollah and the other independent, iterated:

> We Muslims in general are accused of being reactionary, going backward, we are accused of concealing women, that women must be only housewives, that the *jihad* of women is nothing. But if we go and research in the history of Islam, what do we find? That Sayyedeh Zaynab, peace be upon her, the daughter of Amir al-Mu'minin [Imam Ali, lit. Prince of Believers], whose father and brothers walked around her so that no one would see even her shadow, this Zaynab, she went to Karbala with Imam Hosayn. He knew that he was going to be martyred, and Zaynab went with him. And it was Zaynab who was considered the spreader of Karbala's message. A woman! So why are we accused like this? [52]

The incorporation of women into Ashura as active participants in the *masirat*, and the reformulation of Zaynab as the ideal role model for women to emerge from the Ashura narrative, have occurred in part self-consciously and represent an active engagement with discourses and arguments about Islam, gender, and modernness that extend beyond Shiʿism and Lebanon. At the same time, within their community, women are utilizing the salient example of Sayyedeh Zaynab as an outspoken, strong, and compassionate activist to push the boundaries of what is acceptable and expected for pious Lebanese Shiʿi women.[53]

The unprecedented public participation of women in community service through numerous *jamʿiyyat* provides an excellent example of the effects of the transformed Karbala paradigm on women's lives.[54] While discussing the importance of their community work—whether explaining their own reasons for volunteering, encouraging new recruits, or bemoaning what they perceived as the insufficiency of charity or volunteerism—activist women frequently drew upon Zaynab's model. In doing so, they posited themselves simultaneously as good moral Muslim women *and* active and necessary participants in the public welfare of their community.

Notes

The field research in Beirut on which this paper is based was done from October 1999 through July 2001 and was made possible by a Social Science Research Council International Dissertation Research Fellowship, a National Science Foundation Dissertation Research Fellowship, a grant from Emory University's Internationalization Fund, and a PEO International Scholar Award. A portion of this paper was presented at the 2001 annual meeting of the American Anthropology Association. I am grateful to that panel and audience as well as to Donald L. Donham and Mary Elaine Hegland for their valuable feedback. Finally, my greatest gratitude is reserved for the many women and men in Lebanon who shared such an important part of their lives with me and who continue to do so.

1. Here I use the phrase "Lebanese Shiʿi Islamic movement" loosely to refer to what began with the "Movement of the Deprived" (*harakat al-mahrumin*), founded in 1974 by Sayyed Musa al-Sadr. This was taken up in different forms after his disappearance by the political parties Harakat Amal and Hezbollah, as well as by his sister, Sayyedeh Rabab al-Sadr, and Sayyed Mohammad Hosayn Fadlallah, among others. For more on the history of this movement, as well as the history of the Shiʿa in Lebanon, see Fouad Ajami, *The Vanished Imam: Musa al-Sadr and the Shiʿa of Lebanon* (Ithaca, N.Y.: Cornell University Press, 1986); Majed Halawi, *A Lebanon Defied: Musa al-Sadr and the Shiʿa Community* (Boulder, Colo.: Westview Press, 1992); and Augustus Richard Norton, *Amal and the Shiʿa: Struggle for the Soul of Lebanon* (Austin: University of Texas Press, 1987).

2. Shiʿis who argued for the authentication of Ashura described this process as the establishment of *al-maʿna al-haqiqi* or *al-fahm al-haqiqi* (the true/correct/authentic meaning or understanding) of Ashura through reexamining and reprioritiz-

ing historical texts. Indeed, people pointed to scholarly attempts to ascertain the most accurate history of the events surrounding the Imam's martyrdom in an effort to combat what they viewed as a misguided mythologization of Ashura.

3. It is difficult to ascertain who participated in these traditional Ashura commemorations. Nonparticipants include non-Shiʿi Lebanese, though political leaders would sometimes attend a commemoration held at the home of a prominent Shiʿi elite. Nonparticipants also include Shiʿi Lebanese who did not commemorate Ashura. I hesitate to call them "nonreligious Shiʿa" because that would require a longer discussion of the multiple valences of being *mutadayyin*, "religious."

4. The institutionalization of sectarianism in the Lebanese political system was accompanied by a more subtle process through which the category of sect became increasingly important to the groups themselves. As noted by Suad Joseph, "The Politicization of Religious Sects in Borj Hammoud, Lebanon" (PhD diss., Columbia University, 1975), a sectarian political leadership supported the establishment of sectarian social institutions (e.g., schools, hospitals) rather than public secular ones, so that sect became a means of accessing resources. Shiʿa underrepresentation in the government led to poverty as government funds were routed into other sectarian communities. Differential population growth added to their underrepresentation so that by the late 1960s, class differentiation in Lebanon fell largely along sectarian lines. See Helena Cobban, *The Making of Modern Lebanon* (London: Hutchinson, 1985), and Nazih Richani, *Dilemmas of Democracy and Political Parties in Sectarian Societies: The Case of the Progressive Socialist Party of Lebanon, 1949-1996* (New York: St. Martin's Press, 1998). While there were elites from every sect, the majority of Shiʿis fell into the lower classes. For more on the history of Shiʿi Muslims in Lebanon, see Ajami, *The Vanished Imam*; Cobban, *The Making of Modern Lebanon*; Halawi, *A Lebanon Defied*; Michael Hudson, *The Precarious Republic: Political Modernization in Lebanon* (New York: Random House, 1968); and Norton, *Amal and the Shiʿa*.

5. For details regarding Sayyid Musa and the Movement of the Deprived, as well as the linking of Ashura to this social movement, see Ajami, *The Vanished Imam*; Michel M. Mazzaoui, "Shiʿism and Ashura in South Lebanon," in *Taʿziyeh: Ritual and Drama in Iran*, ed. Peter J. Chelkowski, 228-237 (New York: New York University Press, 1979); and Norton, *Amal and the Shiʿa*.

6. Sayyed Musa disappeared while on a visit to Libya in 1978. While many accept the likelihood that he was assassinated at that time, there are still those in Lebanon who carefully speak of him only in the present tense, in the belief that he will return. This is viewed by others in the community as an unorthodox conflation of his disappearance with that of Imam al-Mahdi, the Twelfth Imam, who is to return on Judgment Day.

7. Amal began in 1975 as a militia extension of the Movement of the Deprived; the latter name was eventually dropped and "Harakat Amal" was used to refer to a larger political organization (Norton, *Amal and the Shiʿa*). Hezbollah was founded in 1982 by a group that broke away from Harakat Amal and the Amal-dominated Lebanese National Resistance, citing their overly secular nature and their ineffective efforts at resisting the Israeli occupation. However, Hezbollah did not make its first public statement or announce the establishment of the Islamic Resistance (*al-muqawama al-islamiyya*) until 1985.

8. Ibid., 41. The linking of the Battle of Karbala to politics has a long history. Mayel Baktash, "Taʿziyeh and Its Philosophy," in *Taʿziyeh: Ritual and Drama in Iran,* ed. Peter J. Chelkowski, 95–120 (New York: New York University Press, 1979), notes that the first public community commemorations of Karbala—sponsored by Sultan Muʿizz al-Dawla in 963 CE/352 AH, just two years after he declared his opposition to the existing caliphate—were "allegorical affairs, redolent of revolution" (96).

9. Kamran Aghaie, "The Karbala Narrative in Shiʿi Political Discourse in Modern Iran in the 1960s–1970s," *The Journal of Islamic Studies* 12:2 (2001), 151–176; Mary Elaine Hegland, "Two Images of Husain: Accommodation and Revolution in an Iranian Village," in *Religion and Politics in Iran: Shiʿism from Quietism to Revolution,* ed. Nikki R. Keddie, 218–235 (New Haven, Conn.: Yale University Press, 1983c); Mary Elaine Hegland, "Islamic Revival or Political and Cultural Revolution? An Iranian Case Study," in *Religious Resurgence: Contemporary Cases in Islam, Christianity, and Judaism,* ed. R. Antoun and M. E. Hegland, 194–219 (Syracuse, N.Y.: Syracuse University Press, 1987); and Nikki R. Keddie, *Iran and the Muslim World: Resistance and Revolution* (New York: New York University Press, 1995).

10. For a comprehensive journalist's overview of the events of the Lebanese civil war, see Robert Fisk, *Pity the Nation: The Abduction of Lebanon* (New York: Simon and Schuster, 1990).

11. Throughout the occupation, Shiʿi villages in the south and the Bekaa suffered regular bombardment. Additionally, most of the participants (and martyrs) in the military resistance to the Israeli occupation were Shiʿi Muslims, organized primarily through Hezbollah's Islamic Resistance, but also, though to a much lesser extent, through Harakat Amal and other Lebanese parties. In effect, war did not end for this community in 1990, as it did for much of Lebanon, but continued until May 2000.

12. Since its establishment in 1982, Hezbollah has grown from a loosely structured military resistance movement into an organized and legitimate political party, with members in the Lebanese parliament, numerous local elected officials, a newspaper, radio and television stations, and numerous varied social organizations, in addition to the Islamic Resistance. For more on the party's development and political philosophy and goals, see Amal Saad-Ghorayeb, *Hizbu'llah: Politics and Religion* (London: Pluto Press, 2002).

13. When Ashura was primarily a rural folk tradition for Shiʿi Muslims in Lebanon, it was centered in Nabatieh, and today, people still pour into the town during Ashura, to participate in *majales* and the traditional mourning procession and to watch what has become a spectacle. For another description of Ashura in Nabatieh, see Augustus Richard Norton and Ali Safa, "Ashura in Nabatiyye," *Middle East Insight* 15 (2000), 21–28.

14. It is this scene that has contributed to the sensationalization and exoticization of Ashura in Nabatieh, and the flood of reporters and tourists that fills the town each year. The opening sentence of the Lebanese English-language newspaper *The Daily Star*'s article on Ashura in Nabatieh provides an apt example of this sensationalism: "The Shiites of Nabatieh commemorated the 10th day of Ashura in traditionally gruesome fashion Wednesday, with thousands of chanting, blood-soaked mourners thronging the town square" (Nicholas Blanford, "One

Way or the Other, Ashura Brings Blood," *The Daily Star* (Beirut), April 5, 2001, http://www.dailystar.com.lb/05_04_01/art2.htm).

15. During Ashura in Nabatieh in 2000, I did see six women who had participated in *latam*. My hosts in Nabatieh seemed as surprised as I was to see this, but they later explained that these women had probably shed their blood in fulfillment of vows made earlier in the year.

16. Given the strict gender segregation seen in many Shi'i communities with regard to religious ritual, it is worth making the small point here that the less strict gendering of Lebanese society is reflected in Lebanese Shi'i ritual. On gender segregation, see Hegland, "Two Images of Husain"; Mary Elaine Hegland, "Flagellation and Fundamentalism: (Trans)forming Meaning, Identity, and Gender through Pakistani Women's Rituals," *American Ethnologist* 25 (1998a), 240–266; Mary Elaine Hegland, "The Power Paradox in Muslim Women's Majales: Northwest Pakistani Mourning Rituals as Sites of Contestation over Religious Politics, Ethnicity, and Gender," *Signs* 23:2 (1998b), 391–427; Elizabeth Warnock Fernea, *Guests of the Sheik: An Ethnography of an Iraqi Village* (New York: Anchor Books, 1965); Robert A. Fernea and Elizabeth Warnock Fernea, "Variation in Religious Observance among Islamic Women," in *Scholars, Saints, and Sufis in Muslim Religious Institutions in the Middle East since 1500*, ed. Nikki R. Keddie, 385–401 (Berkeley and Los Angeles: University of California Press, 1972); Azam Torab, "Piety as Gendered Agency: A Study of Jalaseh Ritual Discourse in an Urban Neighborhood in Iran," *Journal of the Royal Anthropological Institute* 2 (1996), 235–252; and David Pinault, *Horse of Karbala: Muslim Devotional Life in India* (New York: Palgrave, 2001). While *majales* are gender-segregated—with women's and men's *majales* held separately or with women seated in a separate section of the building or room (e.g., in the Hezbollah public *majales*, women fill the rear half of the tent, while men sit in the front half)—men and women mix relatively freely outside while watching *masirat*. Interestingly, this may be particularly true of traditional Ashura, as several older informants expressed looking forward to Ashura in Nabatieh each year during their youth because of the "carnavalesque" atmosphere and the freedom they had to walk around the town looking at members of the opposite sex.

17. Ayatollah Khomeini frowned upon the practice before his death in 1989, and Ayatollah Khamenei officially condemned shedding blood during Moharram rituals in a 1994 fatwa, citing not only self-injury but also the negative image of Islam that these rituals project both within and outside the Islamic community. See Houchang E. Chehabi, "Ardabil Becomes a Province: Center-Periphery Relations in Iran," *International Journal of Middle Eastern Studies* 29 (1997), 235–253, and Pinault, *Horse of Karbala*.

18. Indeed, the Islamic Health Committee's offices in the southern suburbs report receiving so many blood donations during Ashura that they have a large surplus each year immediately after the commemoration; over the past five years, donations during this time have increased exponentially. According to Blanford, "One Way or the Other," in Nabatieh itself, Hezbollah has set up a blood donation center on the tenth of Moharram since 1998, attracting over five hundred donors in 2000. The call for people to go to blood banks instead of shedding their own blood is also seen in Pinault's discussion in *Horse of Karbala* of local criticism to self-flagellation during Moharram in India.

19. The classic examples of women's mobilization as part of larger national or religious revolutionary or resistance movements are Iran and Algeria. See also Julie Peteet, *Gender in Crisis: Women and the Palestinian Resistance Movement* (New York: Columbia University Press, 1996), on women and the Palestinian national resistance, and Hegland, "Power Paradox," on women in the Pakistani Shiʻi Islamist movement.

20. Several people who view self-bleeding as un-Islamic only use the standard Arabic term *latam* to refer to the authenticated form of the practice to further distinguish between styles that do and do not involve the shedding of blood. They then refer to the style involving blood only by the colloquial phrase "hitting *haydar*." Also, in spoken Arabic, authenticated *latam* is often simply described by the verb *nadab*, to mourn or lament, with context indicating the specific act that is referred to (e.g., striking oneself versus singing an elegy).

21. This specific style of *latam* is a hybrid of faster-paced Iranian and slower-paced Iraqi styles, and seems to have become the dominant style of *latam* for Hezbollah as well as followers of Sayyid Fadlallah within the past six or seven years.

22. ʻ*Abayeh* is the colloquial Arabic word for the Iranian-style long loose black cloak women wear over their hair and clothing, leaving only the face and hands visible. In Lebanon, wearing an ʻ*abayeh* often signifies either membership in or strong identification with Hezbollah or relation through blood or marriage to a prominent religious figure (though not all Hezbollah women wear the ʻ*abayeh*; some opt for the generally more common "*sharʻi* dress" instead, which consists of a long coat-dress worn with a scarf [*hijab*] carefully pinned to show only the face). It is far more rare to see a Lebanese Shiʻi woman wearing a face veil (*fish*), and women who do are sometimes criticized by others in the community for behaving as though they are as "important" as the women of the Prophet's family.

23. A *qariʼ* is a "recitor" (especially of religious texts) or a "reader." Most recitors of Ashura *majales* carry and refer to a text, often a notebook or their own notes, but they seem to move fluidly between reading and recitation.

24. With the exception of prominent religious and political figures, such as Sayyid Mohammad Hosayn Fadlallah, or unless otherwise noted, all names have been changed and identities disguised.

25. Advocates of authenticated Ashura commonly use the opposition "backward" (*motakhallef*) versus "cultured" (*muthaqqaf*) to structure contrasts between traditional and authenticated commemorations and understandings.

26. Interview with "Shaykh Abbas," June 18, 2001.

27. *Hajjeh* is a term of respect used to address women who have completed the *hajj*, the female counterpart to "Hajj." However, it is sometimes used as a generic term of respectful address for all older women.

28. Interview with "Hajjeh Dalal," September 11, 2000.

29. As used in common parlance in this community *ʼajr* denotes divine recompense—afterlife credits one can accumulate through good deeds, among them mourning Hosayn, that will be added up on Judgment Day.

30. See Pinault, *Horse of Karbala*, and David Pinault, *The Shiʻites, Ritual, and Popular Piety in a Muslim Community* (New York: St. Martin's Press, 1992b), for detailed discussion of the intercessionary importance of mourning the events of Karbala in Shiʻism; Aghaie, "Karbala Narrative," also discusses the soteriological importance of Karbala in the traditional Moharram narrative paradigm.

31. Forms of *latam* that draw blood, including flagellation, are often seen as embodiments of grief leading to intercession, or as the demonstration of solidarity with the Imam. Vernon James Schubel, "The Muharram Majles: The Role of a Ritual in the Preservation of Shiʿa Identity," in *Muslim Families in North America,* ed. S. McIrvin Abu-Laban E. Waugh and R. Burckhardt Qureshi (Edmonton: University of Alberta Press, 1991), expresses this clearly: "This is part of the reason behind such acts as flagellation and firewalking—a desire to demonstrate physically the willingness to suffer the kinds of wounds that would have been incurred at Karbala" (122). I would add "regret" to these meanings—regret stemming from an identification with Shiʿi Muslims from Kufa who did not stand with Hosayn, but also encompassing a generalized remorse for all the times in one's life that one did not live up to Hosayn's example.

32. Conversation with a reformist shaykh, June 21, 2001.

33. Again, the success of the Islamic Revolution in Iran and what Hegland, "Two Images of Husain," calls the " 'Imam Husain as Example' framework" fueled this reinterpretation within the Lebanese context. Lebanese Shiʿa supporters and members of Hezbollah persist in using the term "revolutionary" to discuss their goals as well as those of Imam Hosayn at Karbala—this despite Hezbollah's official withdrawal of the goal of staging a revolution to establish an Islamic state in Lebanon during the 1992 election campaigns. The revolutionary or political meanings and uses of the Karbala paradigm in various contexts have also been discussed by Aghaie, "Karbala Narrative"; Mary-Jo Delvecchio Good and Byron J. Good, "Ritual, the State, and the Transformation of Emotional Discourse in Iranian Society," *Culture, Medicine and Psychiatry* 12 (1988), 43–63; Hegland, "Two Images of Husain"; Keddie, *Iran and the Muslim World;* Roy Mottahedeh, *The Mantle of the Prophet* (New York: Simon and Schuser, 1985); and Gustav Thaiss, "Religious Symbolism and Social Change: The Drama of Husain," in *Scholars, Saints, and Sufis: Muslim Religious Institutions since 1500,* ed. Nikki R. Keddie, 349–366 (Berkeley and Los Angeles: University of California Press, 1972a), among others.

34. In his explication of the concept of "revolution," Donald L. Donham, *Marxist Modern: An Ethnographic History of the Ethiopian Revolution* (Berkeley and Los Angeles: University of California Press, 1999), reminds us that while the notion seems to be a natural part of the world, the concept of revolution as "an attempt rationally to design a new political order" did not emerge until after 1789 (1). No doubt the linking of Islam and revolution—originally in Iran—owes much to Ali Shariʿati and other Islamic intellectuals who were much influenced by Marxism and the political left.

35. Interview with "Hajjeh Fatemeh," March 21, 2001.

36. Ibid.

37. This description of a *majles,* as well as the one that follows, is taken from my field notes.

38. *"Salli ʿala Mohammad wa ali Mohammad"*—a phrase that is an element of prayer—is here used as a salutation that assists in the shift to a sacred framework. It is commonly invoked at intervals during sermons or speeches given by religious/political leaders as well.

39. Conversation with "Nada" after a *majles,* March 30, 2001.

40. Ibid.

41. The importance of Fatemeh as a role model for women—with her ideal char-

acteristics being piety and unfaltering support of her husband and sons—has been noted, as well as the shift from Fatemeh to Zaynab as the ideal for women that accompanied the Islamic Revolution and the revolutionizing of Shiʿism more generally. See Nikki R. Keddie, "Women in Iran since 1979," *Social Research* 67 (2000), 405–438, and Pinault, *Horse of Karbala*. Interestingly, Fatemeh was only occasionally mentioned in the *majales* I attended over 2000 and 2001 in Lebanon, and rarely mentioned by women as their primary role model. Instead, women almost always mentioned Zaynab.

42. Interview with "Hajjeh Um Hadi," February 15, 2001.

43. Conversation with "Hajjeh Rula," a recitor, after a *majles*, April 10, 2000.

44. Interview with "Suha," June 14, 2001.

45. Group interview at the Martyrs' Association, January 30, 2001.

46. Interview with "Hajjeh Dalal," September 11, 2000.

47. Group interview at the Martyrs' Association.

48. While some of these conversations no doubt were prompted by the necessity of assuring that the anthropologist present recorded the "correct" version of the Imam's martyrdom, as indeed I was urged to do, heated conversations during which I was not present were frequently related to me after the fact, and on several occasions I joined such discussions already in progress.

49. Conversation with "Nahla," March 12, 2000.

50. Interview with "Hajjeh Um Hadi."

51. Comment made at an open discussion held by the Hezbollah Women's Committee on women and community service in Lebanon, February 24, 2000.

52. Group interview at the Emdad Association, February 24, 2000.

53. For discussion of how women use ritual settings and activities to open new social and cultural spaces for themselves, see Hegland, "Power Paradox," an elegant work on Peshawar women's utilization of participation in Moharram rituals for self-expression and empowerment, and Torab, "Piety as Gendered Agency," an analysis of how Iranian women use prayer meetings to transform gender constructs. For discussions of the limits and expectations of gendered activism, see Sondra Hale, *Gender Politics in Sudan: Islamism, Socialism, and the State* (Boulder, Colo.: Westview Press, 1996), and Peteet, *Gender in Crisis*.

54. This is not to say that both women's participation in the community and the example set by Sayyedeh Zaynab do not remain clearly bounded, in keeping with beliefs about the essential nature of women as nurturing. Yet, when clarifying the different natures of the sexes, Lebanese Shiʿi women always emphasized that different did not mean differently valued. They actively espoused gender equity (ʿadala) as opposed to gender equality (*masawa*), with the former term embracing difference and the latter entailing "sameness." In doing so, they promoted feminist interpretations of Islam that emphasized what Leila Ahmad, *Women and Gender in Islam: Historical Roots of a Modern Debate* (New Haven, Conn.: Yale University Press, 1992), calls the "ethical egalitarianism" of Islam. See also Annabelle Böttcher, "Im Schatten des Ayatollahs: Schiitische Feministische in Libanon am Anfang" (In the Shadow of the Ayatollah: Shii Feminist Theology in Lebanon and the Beginning), *Neue Zuericher Zeitung*, March 7, 2001, 5.

Bibliography

Abadi, Ayub Naqvi. 1999. *Tarjuman-e Karbala: Zaynab Bint e-Ali*. Karachi: Aliya Publications.

Abadi, Jalil Azadi Ahmad. 1996. *Gol-ha-e ghargh dar khun*. Tehran: Chapkhaneh-e Golbarg.

Abu Lughod, Lila. 1986. *Veiled Sentiments*. Cairo: American University Press.

Afkhami, Mahnaz, and Erika Friedl, Eds. 1994. *In the Eye of the Storm: Women in Post-Revolutionary Iran*. Syracuse: Syracuse University Press.

Aghaie, Kamran Scot. 1994. "Reinventing Karbala: Revisionist interpretations of the 'Karbala Paradigm.'" *Jusur: The UCLA Journal of Middle Eastern Studies* 10: 1–30.

———. 2001. "The Karbala Narrative in Shiʻi Political Discourse in Modern Iran in the 1960s–1970s." *The Journal of Islamic Studies* 12(2): 151–176.

———. 2004. *The Martyrs of Karbala: Shiʻi Symbols and Rituals in Modern Iran*. Seattle: University of Washington Press.

———. Forthcoming. "Religious Rituals, Social Identities, and Political Relationships under Qajar Rule: 1850s–1930s." In *Religion and Society in Qajar Iran,* ed. Robert Gleave. London: Routledge/Curzon Press.

Ahmad, Imtiaz. 1978. *Caste and Social Stratifiction among Muslims in India*. New Delhi: Manohar.

———. 1981. *Ritual and Religion among Muslims in India*. Delhi: Manohar.

Ahmad, Leila. 1992. *Women and Gender in Islam: Historical Roots of a Modern Debate*. New Haven, Conn.: Yale University Press.

Ahmad, Sayyed Al-e. 1983. "Salam-e akhar." In *Suz-e Karbala*, ed. Sayyed Hasan Abbas Zaydi, 350. Karachi: Ahmad Book Depot.

Ahmed, Munir D. 1987. "The Shi'is of Pakistan." In *Shi'ism, Resistance, and Revolution,* ed. M. Kramer, 275–287. Boulder, Colo.: Westview Press.

Ahmed, Nilufer., Gladis Kaufman, and Shamim Naim. 1996. "South Asian Families in the United States: Pakistani, Bangladeshi, and Indian Muslims." In *Family and Gender among American Muslims: Issues Facing Middle Eastern Immigrants and Their Descendants,* ed. Barbara Bilge and Barbara C. Aswad, 155–172. Philadelphia: Temple University Press.

Ajami, Fouad. 1986. *The Vanished Imam: Musa al-Sadr and the Shi'a of Lebanon.* Ithaca, N.Y.: Cornell University Press.

Akhtar, Sayyid Vahid. 1996. "Karbala, an Enduring Paradigm of Islamic Revivalism." *al-Tawhid* 13: 113–125.

Akhtar, Vahid. 1991. *Karbala ta Karbala.* Aligarh: Vahid Akhtar.

Ali, Meer Hasan. 1973 (1832). *Observations on the Mussalmans of India.* Karachi: Civil and Military Press.

Ali, S. A. 1975. *A Short History of the Saracens.* Karachi: National Book Foundation.

———. n.d. *Mujahida-ye Karbala.* Lucknow, India: Sarfaraz Qaumi Press.

Allen, Terry. 1988. *Five Essays on Islamic Art.* Manchester, U.K.: Solipsist Press.

al-Naqvi, Sayyed Ali Naqi. 1974. *A Historical Review of the Institution of Azadari for Imam Husain.* Karachi: Peer Mahomed Ebrahim Trust.

al-Shafe'i, Sayyed Mohammad. 1373 AH. *Payramun-e Hamaseh-e Ashura.* Tehran: Markaz-e Chap va Nashr-e Sazman-e Tablighat-e Eslami.

Amanat, Abbas. 1997. *Pivot of the Universe: Nasir al-Din Shah Qajar and the Iranian Monarchy, 1831–1896.* Berkeley and Los Angeles: University of California Press.

Ameed, S. M. 1974. *The Importance of Weeping and Wailing.* Karachi: Peer Mahomed Ebrahim Trust.

Ameeni, Ibrahimi. 1405 AH. *Fatemeh Zahra: Islam ki Misali Khatoon,* trans. Akhtar Abbas. Lahore: Shafaq Publishers.

Anasori, Jaber, ed. 1992. *Shabih khani, kohan olgu-ye nemayeshha-ye Irani.* Tehran: Chapkhaneh-e Ramin.

Anis, Mir. n.d. *Marsiyeh dar hal-e sani-ye Zahra hazrat Zaynab Kobra.* Hyderabad: Aijaz Printing Press.

Ansari, M. 1991. "Iranians in America: Continuity and Change." In *Rethinking Today's Minorities,* ed. V. N. Parrillo, 119–142. New York: Greenwood Press.

Arberry, A. J. 1964. *The Quran Interpreted.* Oxford: Oxford University Press.

Arif, Iftikhar. 1983. *Mehr-e do nm.* Karachi: Danyal.

Arnold, Matthew. 1871. "A Persian Passion Play." *Cornhill Magazine* (December): 676.

Ayati, Mohammad Ebrahim. 1996. *Barresi-e tarikh-e Ashura*. 9th ed. Tehran: Nashr-e Sadduq.

Ayoub, Mahmoud. 1978. *Redemptive Suffering in Islam: A Study of the Devotional Aspects of "Ashura" in Twelver Shi'ism*. New York: Mouton.

Azari, Farah. 1983. *Women of Iran: The Conflict with Fundamentalist Islam*. London: Attaca Press.

Aziz, A. 1978. *Abu Bakr: The Caliph*. Karachi: Ghazanfar Academy.

Bahrampour, T. 1999. *To See and See Again: A Life in Iran and America*. Berkeley and Los Angeles: University of California Press.

Baktash, Mayel. 1979. "Ta'ziyeh and Its Philosophy." In *Ta'ziyeh: Ritual and Drama in Iran*, ed. Peter J. Chelkowski, 95–120. New York: New York University Press.

Bamdad, B. o.-M. 1977. *From Darkness into Light: Women's Emancipation in Iran*. New York: Exposition Press.

Bauman, Richard. 1977. *Verbal Art as Performance*. Austin: University of Texas Press.

Beach, W., and P. Japp Beach. 1983. "Storyfying as Time-Travelling: The Knowledgeable Use of Temporally-Structured Discourse." In *Communication Yearbook 7*, ed. R. Bostrom. New Brunswick, N.J.: Transaction Books-ICA.

Beeman, W. O. 1982. "A Full Arena: The Development and Meaning of Popular Performance Traditions in Iran." In *Modern Iran: The Dialectics of Continuity and Change*, ed. Michael E. Bonine and Nikki R. Keddie, 361–382. Albany: State University of New York Press.

Beiza'i, Bahram. 2000. *A Study of Iranian Theatre*. Tehran: Roshangaran and Women's Studies Publishing.

Benjamin, Walter. 1968. "Theses on the Philosophy of History." In *Illuminations*, ed. Hannah Arendt, 253–264. New York: Schocken Books.

———. 1992. "What Is Epic Theatre?" In *Understanding Brecht*, 1–23. London: Verso.

Betteridge, Anne. 1983. "To Veil or Not to Veil: A Matter of Protest or Policy." In *Women and Revolution in Iran*, ed. Guity Nashat, 109–128. Boulder, Colo.: Westview Press.

———. 1985. "Ziarat: Pilgrimage to the Shrines of Shiraz." PhD diss., University of Chicago.

———. 1989. "The Controversial Vows of Urban Muslim Women in Iran." In *Unspoken Worlds: Women's Religious Lives*, ed. Nancy Auer Falk and Rita M. Gross, 102–111. Belmont, Calif.: Wadsworth.

Biddis, M. 1970. "Introduction." In *Gobineau: Selected Political Writings*, ed. M. Biddis. London: Jonathan Cape.

Black, Max. 1962. *Models and Metaphors: Studies in Language and Philosophy*. Ithaca, N.Y.: Cornell University Press.

Blank, J. 2001. *Mullahs on the Mainframe: Islam and Modernity among the Daudi Bohras*. Chicago: University of Chicago Press.

Bogdanov, L. 1923. "Muharram in Persia: Some Notes on Its Mysteries and Ceremonies." *Visva-Bharati Quarterly* 1: 118–127.

Bouttaiux-Ndiaye, Anne-Marie. 1994. *Senegal behind Glass: Images of Religious and Daily Life*. Munich: Prestel.

Bozorgmehr, M. 1997. "Internal Ethnicity: Iranians in Los Angeles." *Sociological Perspectives* 40(3): 387–408.

Bozorgmehr, M., and G. Sabagh. 1988. "High Status Immigrants: A Statistical Profile of Iranians in the United States." *Iranian Studies* 21: 5–36.

———. 1989. "Survey Research among Middle Eastern Immigrant Groups in the United States: Iranians in Los Angeles." *Middle East Studies Association Bulletin* 23: 23–34.

Bozorgmehr, Mehdi, Georges Sabagh, and Claudia Der-Martirosian. 1993. "Beyond Nationality: Religio-Ethnic Diversity." In *Irangeles: Iranian Life and Culture in Los Angeles,* ed. Ron Kelley, Jonathan Friedlander, and Anita Colby. Berkeley and Los Angeles: University of California Press.

Bravmann, René A. 1980. *Tribal Art in West Africa*. Cambridge: Cambridge University Press.

Browne, Edward. G., ed. 1893. *Tarikh-e Jadid or New History of Mirza Ali Muhammad the Bab*. Cambridge: Cambridge University Press.

———. 1926. *A Year amongst the Persians, 1887–1888*. Cambridge: Cambridge University Press.

Brunet, Michelle. 1994. "Self-Transformation among Iranian-American Women." Senior thesis, Santa Clara University.

Calmard, Jean. 1975. "Le culte de l'Imam Husayn: Etudes sur la commémoration du Drame de Karbala dans l'Iran pré-safavide." PhD diss., University of Paris III.

———. 1979. "Le Patronage des Ta'ziyeh: Elements pour une Etude Globale." In *Ta'ziyeh: Ritual and Drama in Iran,* ed. Peter J. Chelkowski, 121–130. New York: New York University Press.

———. 1996. "Shi'i Rituals and Power: The Consolidation of Safavid Shi'ism: Folklore and Popular Religion." In *Safavid Persia,* ed. Charles Melville, 139–190. London: I. B. Tauris.

Cardoza, R. 1990. "The Ordeal of Moharram: Shiites in India Mourn Their Savior." *Natural History* 99: 50–57.

Centlivres, Pierre, and Micheline Centlivres-Demont. 1997. *Imageries populaires en Islam*. Geneva: Georg Editeur.

Chehabi, Houchang E. 1997. "Ardabil Becomes a Province: Center-Periphery Relations in Iran." *International Journal of Middle Eastern Studies* 29: 235–253.

Chelkowski, Peter J. 1971. "Dramatic and Literary Aspects of Taʿziyeh-Khani—Iranian Passion Play." In *Review of National Literatures: Iran*, ed. Javad Haidari, 2: 121–138. New York. St. John's University Press.

———. 1979a. "Taʿziyeh: Indigenous Avant-Garde Theatre of Iran." In *Taʿziyeh: Ritual and Drama in Iran*, ed. Peter J. Chelkowski. New York: New York University Press.

———, ed. 1979b. *Taʿziyeh: Ritual and Drama in Iran*. New York: New York University Press.

———. 1980. "Iran: Mourning Becomes Revolution." *Asia* 3: 30–37, 44, 45.

———. 1985. "Shia Muslim Processional Performances." *The Drama Review* 29(3): 18–30.

———. 1986. "Popular Shiʿi Mourning Rituals." *al-Serat* 12, 209–226.

———. 1988. "When Time Is No Time, and Space Is No Space: The Passion Plays of Husayn." In *Taʿziyah: Ritual and Popular Beliefs in Iran*, ed. Milla Riggio, 13–23. Hartford, Conn.: Trinity College, Hartford Seminary.

———. 1989. "Narrative Painting and Painting Recitation in Qajar Iran." In *Muqarnas: An Annual on Islamic Art and Architecture*, ed. Oleg Grabar, 98–111. Leiden: E. J. Brill.

———. 1993. "Rawda-Khwani." In *The Encyclopedia of Islam*, ed. E. van Donzel C. E. Bosworth, W. P. Heinrichs, and G. Lecomte. Vol. 8. Leiden: E. J. Brill.

———. 1995. "Taʿziyeh." In *The Oxford Encyclopedia of the Modern Islamic World*, ed. John L. Esposito et al., 4: 200–202. New York: Oxford University Press.

Chelkowski, Peter J., and Frank J. Korom. 1993. "Moharram in Trinidad: A Festive Mourning." *The India Magazine of Her People and Culture* 13(2): 54–63.

Clarke, Lynda. 1986. "Some Examples of Elegy on Imam Husayn." *al-Serat* 12: 13–28.

Cobban, Helena. 1985. *The Making of Modern Lebanon*. London: Hutchinson.

Cole, Juan R. I. 1988. *The Roots of North Indian Shi'ism in Iran and Iraq: Religion and State in Awadh, 1722–1859*. Berkeley and Los Angeles: University of California Press.

———. 1993. "I Am All the Prophets: The Poetics of Pluralism in Baha'i Texts." *Poetics Today* 14(3).

Collins, Charles Dillard. 1988. *The Iconography and Ritual of Siva at Elephanta*. Albany: State University of New York Press.

Cook, M. 2000. *The Koran*. Oxford: Oxford University Press.

Daftary, F. 1990. *The Isma'ilis: Their History and Doctrines*. Delhi: Munshiram Manoharlal Publications.

Dallalfar, A. 1994. "Iranian Women as Immigrant Entrepreneurs." *Gender and Society* 8: 541–561.

———. 1996. "The Iranian Ethnic Economy in Los Angeles: Gender and Entrepreneurship." In *Family and Gender among American Muslims: Issues Facing Middle Eastern Immigrants and Their Descendants*, ed. Barbara Bilge and Barbara C. Aswad, 107–128. Philadelphia: Temple University Press.

Dana'i, Morteza, ed. 1996. *Naghmeh-ha-e Karbala*. Vol. 2. Tehran: Entesharat-e Sa'id Novin.

Daneshvar, S. 1991. *A Persian Requiem*. London: Peter Halban.

Das, N. 1992. *The Architecture of Imambaras*. Lucknow, India: Lucknow Mahotsava Patrika Samiti.

de Gobineau, M. le Comte. 1900. *Religions et les philosophies dans l'Asie Centrale*. Paris: Ernest Leroux.

———. 1970. "Essays on the Inequality of Races." In *Gobineau: Selected Political Writings*, ed. Michael Biddis. London: Jonathan Cape.

De Warzee, Dorothy. 1913. *Peeps into Persia*. London: Hurst and Blackett Ltd.

Donham, Donald L. 1999. *Marxist Modern: An Ethnographic History of the Ethiopian Revolution*. Berkeley and Los Angeles: University of California Press.

D'Souza, A. 1993. "Love of the Prophet's Family: The Role of Marathin in the Devotional Life of Hyderabad Shi'ahs." *Bulletin of the Henry Martyn Institute of Islamic Studies* (Hyderabad, India) 12(3–4): 31–47.

Elahi (Butehkar), Hasan. 1996. *Zaynab-e Kobra*. Tehran: Moassaseh-e Farhangi-e Afarineh.

Elgood, Heather. 1999. *Hinduism and the Religious Arts*. London: Cassell.

El Guindi, Fadwa. 1999. *Veil: Modesty, Privacy and Resistance*. Oxford: Berg.

Elwell-Sutton, L. P. 1980. "The Persian 'Passion Play.'" In *Folklore Studies in the Twentieth Century*, ed. V. J. Newall. Totowa, N.J.: Rowman and Littlefield.

Ende, W. 1978. "The Flagellations of Muharram and the Shiʿite 'Ulama.'" *Der Islam* 55: 19–36.

Eqbal, Zahra. 1979. "Elegy in the Qajar Period." In *Taʿziyeh: Ritual and Drama*, ed. Peter J. Chelkowski, 193–209. New York: New York University Press.

Eshtehardi, Mohammad Mohammadi. 1997. *Sugnameh-e al-e Mohammad*. Qom, Iran: Entesharat-e Naser-e Qom.

Farman Farmaian, S., with D. Munker. 1992. *Daughter of Persia: A Woman's Journey from Her Father's Harem through the Islamic Revolution*. New York: Crown.

Farrokhzad, F. 1985. *A Re-birth*. Costa Mesa, Calif.: Mazda Publishers.

Fazel, M. 1998. "The Politics of Passions: Growing Up Shia." *Iranian Studies* 32(3–4).

Ferchiou, Sophie. 1972. "Survivantes mystiques et culte de possession dans le maraboutisme Tunisien." *L'Homme* 12: 47–69.

Fernea, Elizabeth Warnock. 1965. *Guests of the Sheik: An Ethnography of an Iraqi Village*. New York: Anchor Books.

Fernea, Elizabeth Warnock, and Basima Q. Bezirgan, eds. 1977. *Middle Eastern Muslim Women Speak*. Austin: University of Texas Press.

Fernea, Robert A., and Elizabeth Warnock Fernea. 1972. "Variation in Religious Observance among Islamic Women." In *Scholars, Saints, and Sufis in Muslim Religious Institutions in the Middle East since 1500*, ed. Nikki R. Keddie, 385–401. Berkeley and Los Angeles: University of California Press.

Fisher, Robert E. 1993. *Buddhist Art and Architecture*. London: Thames and Hudson.

Fisk, Jennifer. 1994. "Iranian Women and the Creation of Self: The Path of Transformation." Senior thesis, Santa Clara University.

Fisk, Robert. 1990. *Pity the Nation: The Abduction of Lebanon*. New York: Simon and Schuster.

Flaskerud, Ingvild. 2000. "Tazia: Shia islamske pasjonspill over et martyrium." *Historie: Populærhistorisk magasin* 1, 50–57.

Freedberg, David. 1989. *The Power of Images*. Chicago: University of Chicago Press.

Friedl, Erika. 1989. "Islam and Tribal Women in a Village in Iran." In *Unspoken Worlds: Women's Religious Lives*, ed. Nancy Auer Falk and Rita M. Gross, 125–133. Belmont, Calif.: Wadsworth.

———. 1991. "The Dynamics of Women's Spheres of Action in Rural Iran."

In *Women in Middle Eastern History: Shifting Boundaries in Sex and Gender*, ed. Nikki R. Keddie and Beth Baron, 195–214. New Haven, Conn.: Yale University Press.

Frishman, Martin, and Hasan-Uddin Khan. 1994. *The Mosque: History, Architectural Development, and Regional Diversity.* London: Thames and Hudson.

Ghadially, Rehana. 1996a. "The Campaign for Women's Emancipation in an Isma'ili Shii (Daudi Bohra) Sect of Indian Muslims, 1925–1945." *Dossier* 14/15: 641–685.

———. 1996b. "On Their Own Initiative: Changing Lives of Bohra Muslim Women." *Manushi* 96: 311–339.

———. 1996c. "Women and Personal Law in an Isma'ili (Daudi Bohra) Sect of Indian Muslims." *Islamic Culture* 1: 27–51.

———. 1999. "Women's Religious Gatherings in a South Asian Muslim Sect." *Thamyris* 6(1): 43–63.

———. 2003. "Hajari (Ritual Meal Tray) for Abbas Alam Dar: Women's Household Rituals in a South Asian Muslim Sect." *The Muslim World* 93(2): 309–321.

Gholami, Mohammad, ed. 1996. *Montakhab al-masa'eb, hazrat-e emam Hosayn alayhi al-salam va yaran-e 'u.* 2 vols. Qum: Moassaseh-e Entesharat-e 'Allameh.

Goffman, Erving. 1972. "The Neglected Situation." In *Language and Social Context,* ed. Pier Paola Giglioli, 61–66. New York: Penguin Books.

———. 1974. *Frame Analysis.* New York: Harper and Row.

Good, Mary-Jo Delvecchio, and Byron J. Good. 1988. "Ritual, the State, and the Transformation of Emotional Discourse in Iranian Society." *Culture, Medicine and Psychiatry* 12: 43–63.

Grabar, Oleg. 1987. *The Formation of Islamic Art.* New Haven, Conn.: Yale University Press.

Guppy, S. 1988. *The Blindfold Horse: Memories of a Persian Childhood.* Boston: Beacon Press.

Haddad, Wadi. 1988. "Islam: A Brief Overview." In *Ta'ziyah: Ritual and Popular Beliefs in Iran,* ed. Milla Riggio, 1–8. Hartford, Conn.: Trinity College, Hartford Seminary.

Haddad, Yvonne Yazbeck, and Adair T. Lummis. 1987. *Islamic Values in the United States.* New York: Oxford University Press.

Haidari, S. A. J. n.d. *Goldasteh-e morad.* Bombay: Haidari Kutub Khana.

Halawi, Majed. 1992. *A Lebanon Defied: Musa al-Sadr and the Shi'a Community.* Boulder, Colo.: Westview Press.

Hale, Sondra. 1996. *Gender Politics in Sudan: Islamism, Socialism, and the State*. Boulder, Colo.: Westview Press.

Hanassab, S. 1993. "Caught between Two Cultures: Young Iranian Women in Los Angeles." In *Irangeles: Iranians in Los Angeles*, ed. Ron Kelley, Jonathan Friedlander, and Anita Colby, 223-229. Berkeley and Los Angeles: University of California Press.

Hardacre, Helen. 1993. "The Impact of Fundamentalisms on Women, the Family, and Interpersonal Relations." In *Fundamentalisms and Society: Reclaiming the Sciences, the Family, and Education*, ed. Martin E. Marty and R. Scott Appleby, 129-150. Chicago: University of Chicago Press.

Hasnain, N. 1988. *Shias and Shia Islam in India: A Study in Society and Culture*. New Delhi: Harnam Publications.

Haydari, Sayyed Anis Jahan. n.d. *Guldasteh-e morad*. Bombay: Kaidari Khutub Khana.

Hedin, Sven. 1910. *Overland in to India*. London: Macmillan.

Hegland, Mary Elaine. 1982a. "Religious Ritual and Political Struggle in an Iranian Village." *MERIP Reports* 12(1): 10-17, 23.

———. 1982b. "'Traditional' Iranian Women: How They Cope." *The Middle East Journal* 36: 483-501.

———. 1983a. "Aliabad Women: Revolution as Religious Activity." In *Women and Revolution in Iran*, ed. Guity Nashat, 171-194. Boulder, Colo.: Westview Press.

———. 1983b. "Ritual and Revolution in Iran." In *Culture and Political Change*, ed. M. J. Aronoff, 75-100. New Brunswick, N.J.: Transaction Books.

———. 1983c. "Two Images of Husain: Accommodation and Revolution in an Iranian Village." In *Religion and Politics in Iran: Shiʿism from Quietism to Revolution*, ed. Nikki R. Keddie, 218-235. New Haven, Conn.: Yale University Press.

———. 1986. "Political Roles of Iranian Village Women." *MERIP Reports* 138: 14-19, 46.

———. 1987. "Islamic Revival or Political and Cultural Revolution? An Iranian Case Study." In *Religious Resurgence: Contemporary Cases in Islam, Christianity, and Judaism*, ed. R. Antoun and Mary E. Hegland, 194-219. Syracuse, N.Y.: Syracuse University Press.

———. 1990. "Women and the Iranian Revolution: A Village Case Study." *Dialectical Anthropology* 15: 183-192.

———. 1991. "Political Roles of Aliabad Women: Public-Private Dichotomy Transcended." In *Women in Middle Eastern History: Shifting Bound-

aries in Sex and Gender, ed. Nikki R. Keddie and Beth Baron, 215-230. New Haven, Conn.: Yale University Press.

―――. 1995. "Shiʿa Women of NW Pakistan and Agency through Practice: Ritual, Resistance, Resilience." *PoLAR: Political and Legal Anthropology Review* 18(2): 1-14.

―――. 1996. "A Mixed Blessing—Majales: Shiʿa Women's Rituals in NW Pakistan and the Politics of Religion, Ethnicity, and Gender." In *Mixed Blessings: Religious Fundamentalisms and Gender Cross-Culturally,* ed. Judy Brink and Joan Mencher, 179-196. New York: Routledge.

―――. 1998a. "Flagellation and Fundamentalism: (Trans)forming Meaning, Identity, and Gender through Pakistani Women's Rituals." *American Ethnologist* 25: 240-266.

―――. 1998b. "The Power Paradox in Muslim Women's Majales: Northwest Pakistani Mourning Rituals as Sites of Contestation over Religious Politics, Ethnicity, and Gender." *Signs* 23(2): 391-427.

―――. 1999. "Gender and Religion in the Middle East and South Asia: Women's Voices Rising." In *Social History of Women and Gender in the Modern Middle East,* ed. Judith Tucker and Marlee Meriwether, 177-212. Boulder, Colo.: Westview Press.

Hegland, Mary E., and Ashraf Zahedi. 1998. "Payvand and IFWC: Maintaining Iranian Identity in California's Bay Area." *DANESH Bulletin* 3(1): 12-17.

Hejazi, Sayyed Ali Reza. 1995. "Imam Husain ibn Ali (A) in the Mirror of Poetry." In *Imam Khomeini and the Culture of Ashura.* Abstracts of papers presented at the International Congress on Imam Khomeini and the Culture of Ashura. Tehran: The Institute for Compilation and Publication of the Works of Imam Khomeini, International Affairs Department.

Hendessi, Mandana. 1990. *Armed Angels: Women in Iran.* Report No. 16. London: Change.

Higgins, P. J. 1997a. "Adolescent Ethnic Identities: Iranians in the United States." *DANESH Bulletin* 1(2): 10-14.

―――. 1997b. "Intergenerational Stress: Parents and Adolescents in Iranian Immigrant Families." In *Beyond Boundaries: Selected Papers on Refugees and Immigrants,* ed. Ruth Krulfeld and D. Baxter. Arlington, Va.: American Anthropological Association.

Hillenbrand, Robert. 1994. *Islamic Architecture: Form, Function, and Meaning.* Edinburgh: Edinburgh University Press.

Hjarpe, J. 1982. "The Taʿzia Ecstasy as Political Expression." In *Reli-*

gious Ecstasy, ed. N. G. Holm. Stockholm: Almqvist and Wiksell International.

Hjortshoj, K. 1987. "Shiʿi Identity and the Significance of Muharram in Lucknow, India." In *Shiʿism, Resistance, and Revolution*, ed. M. Kramer, 289–309. Boulder, Colo.: Westview Press.

Homayuni, Sadeq. 1989. *Taʿziyeh dar Iran*. Shiraz, Iran: Entesharat-e Navid.

———. 1999. "Zan dar taʿziyeh-ha-e Irani." *Faslnameh-e Honar* 40.

Hudson, Michael. 1968. *The Precarious Republic: Political Modernization in Lebanon*. New York: Random House.

Husted, W. R. 1993. "Karbala Made Immediate: The Martyr as Model in Imami Shiʿism." *The Muslim World* 83(3–4): 263–278.

Hymes, Dell. 1972. "Toward Ethnographies of Communication." In *Language and Social Context*, ed. Pier Paolo Giglioli, 21–44. New York: Penguin Books.

———. 1974. *Foundations in Sociolinguistics: An Ethnographic Approach*. Philadelphia: University of Pennsylvania Press.

Ibn Manzur, Mohammad Ibn Mokarram. 1988. *Lisan al-Arab*. 18 vols. Beirut: Dar Ihyaʾ al-Turath al-ʿArabi.

Ipsirolu, M. S. 1971. *Das Bild im Islam: Ein Verbot und seine Folge*. Wien and München: Verlag Anton Schroll.

Jafri, S. H. M. 1979. *The Origins and Early Development of Shiʿa Islam*. London: Libraire du Liban.

Jayawardena, C. 1968. "Ideology and Conflict in Lower Class Communities." *Comparative Studies in Society and History* 10(4): 413–446.

Jensen, Robin Margaret. 2000. *Understanding Early Christian Art*. London: Routledge.

Joseph, Suad. 1975. "The Politicization of Religious Sects in Borj Hammoud, Lebanon." PhD diss., Columbia University.

Kamalkhani, Z. 1993. "Women's Everyday Religious Discourse in Iran." In *Women in the Middle East: Perceptions, Realities, and Struggles for Liberation*, ed. H. Afshar, 85–95. London: Macmillan.

———. 1997. *Women's Islam: Religious Practice among Women in Today's Iran*. London: Kegan Paul International.

———. 1998. "Reconstruction of Islamic Knowledge and Knowing: A Case of Islamic Practices among Women in Iran." In *Women and Islamization: Contemporary Dimensions of Discourse on Gender Relations*, ed. Karin Ask and Marit Tjomsland, 177–193. Oxford: Berg.

Kandiyoti, Deniz. 1988. "Bargaining with Patriarchy." *Gender and Society* 2: 274–290.

Karimi, S. 1996. *Asheghan-e Karbala*. Tehran: Nashr-e Mehrzad.

Kashani, H. M. J. 1910. *Ketab-e Noqtat al-Kaf*. Leiden: E. J. Brill.

Kashefi, M. H. Va'ez. 1962. *Rowzat al-shohada*. Tehran: Chapkhaneh-e Khavar.

Kathir, Ibn. 1358 AH. *al-Bidaya wa al-nihaya*. Cairo: Matba'a al-Sa'ada.

Keddie, Nikki R. 1993. *The Shi'a of Pakistan: Reflections and Problems for Further Research*. Los Angeles: The G. E. von Grunebaum Center for Near Eastern Studies, University of California.

———. 1995. *Iran and the Muslim World: Resistance and Revolution*. New York: New York University Press.

———. 2000. "Women in Iran since 1979." *Social Research* 67: 405–438.

Khansari, Molla Aqa. n.d. *Kolsum naneh*. Tehran: Entesharat-e Morvarid.

Khorrami, P. M. K., and M. M. Khorrami, eds. 1999. *A World Between: Poems, Short Stories, and Essays by Iranian-Americans*. New York: George Braziller.

Kippenberg, H. G. 1984. "How Dualistic Beliefs Are Performed by Shi'is: The Stages of Kerbala." In *Struggles of Gods*, ed. H. G. Kippenberg, 125–142. Berlin: Mouton.

Kohlberg, E. 1988. "Imam and Community in the Pre-Ghayba Period." In *Authority and Political Culture in Shi'ism*, ed. S. A. Arjomand, 25–53. Albany: State University of New York Press.

Kordi, G. 1992. *An Iranian Odyssey*. London: Serpent's Tail.

Korom, Frank J. 1994a. "Memory, Innovation, and Emergent Ethnicity: The Creolization of an Indo-Trinidadian Performance." *Diaspora* 3(2): 135–155.

———. 1994b. "The Transformation of Language to Rhythm: The Hosay Drum of Trinidad." *The World of Music* 3: 68–85.

———. 2003. *Hosay Trinidad: Muharram Performances in an Indo-Caribbean Diaspora*. Philadelphia: University of Pennsylvania Press.

Korom, Frank J., and Peter J. Chelkowski. 1994. "Community Process and the Performance of Muharram Observances in Trinidad." *The Drama Review* 38(2): 150–175.

Lammens, H. 2001. "Fatima." *Concise Encyclopedia of Islam*, ed. H. A. R. Gibb and J. H. Kramers, 101–102. Boston: Brill.

Lindell, D. T. 1974. "Muharram in Hyderabad." *al-Basheer* 3: 14–29.

Loeffler, R. 1988. *Islam in Practice: Religious Beliefs in a Persian Village*. Albany: State University of New York Press.

Lord, Albert B. 1960. *The Singer of Tales*. Cambridge: Harvard University Press.

Lutz, Catherine, and Lila Abu-Lughod, eds. 1990. *Language and the Politics of Emotion*. Cambridge: Cambridge University Press.

Maatouk, Frederic. 1974. *La representation de la mort de l'imam Hussein a Nabatieh*. Beirut: Université libanaise, Institut des sciences sociales, Centre de recherches.

Mahani, Najmeh Khalili. 2003. "Bahram Baizai, Iranian Cinema, Art Cinema. *Offscreen*. Available: http://www.horschamp.qc.ca/new_off screen/bazai,html

Mahdi, A. A. 1997. "The Second Generation Iranians: Questions and Concerns." *DANESH Bulletin* 1(2): 3–10.

Mahdjoub, M.-D. F. 1988. "The Evolution of Popular Eulogy of the Imams among the Shia." In *Authority and Political Culture in Shi'ism*, ed. S. A. Arjomand, 54–79. Albany: State University of New York Press.

Majlesi, Allameh. 1996. *Tarikh-e chahardah ma'sum*. Tehran and Qom: Entesharat-e Sorur.

Matin-Asgari, Afshin. 2002. *Iranian Student Opposition to the Shah*. Costa Mesa, Calif.: Mazda Publishers.

Mazzaoui, Michel M. 1979. "Shi'ism and Ashura in South Lebanon." In *Ta'ziyeh: Ritual and Drama in Iran*, ed. Peter J. Chelkowski, 228–237. New York: New York University Press.

Metcalf, Barbara Daly. 1996. *Making Muslim Space*. Berkeley and Los Angeles: University of California Press.

Milani, F. 1992. *Veils and Words: The Emerging Voices of Iranian Women Writers*. Syracuse, N.Y.: Syracuse University Press.

Mistri, Aisha Bint al-Shati. 1996. *Karbala ki Sher Dil Khatoon*, trans. Muhammad Abbas. Lahore: Maktaba-e Imamia Trust.

Moghissi, Haideh. 1994. *Populism and Feminism in Iran: Women's Struggle in a Male-Defined Revolutionary Movement*. New York: St. Martin's Press.

———. 1999. *Feminism and Islamic Fundamentalism: The Limits of Postmodern Analysis*. London: Zed Books.

Moinuddin, K. 1971. *A Monograph on Muharram in Hyderabad City*. Andra Pradesh, India: Indian Administrative Service.

Momen, Moojan. 1985. *An Introduction to Shi'i Islam*. New Haven, Conn.: Yale University Press.

Moore, Albert C. 1977. *Iconography of Religions*. London: SCM Press.

Morgan, David. 1998. *Visual Piety: A History and Theory of Popular Religious Images*. Berkeley and Los Angeles: University of California Press.

Mostowfi, Abdollah. 1997. *The Administrative and Social History of the Qajar Period*. Costa Mesa, Calif.: Mazda Publishers.

Motahhari, Morteza. 1985. *Hamaseh-e Hosayni*. Vols. 1–3. Tehran and Qom: Sadra Publishers.

Mottahedeh, Negar. 1997. "Scheduled for Judgement Day: The Taʿziyeh Performance in Qajar Persia and Walter Benjamin's Dramatic Vision of History." *Theatre Insight* 8(1), 12–20.

———. 1999a. "Bahram Bayzaʾi: Filmography." In *Life and Art: The New Iranian Cinema*, ed. R. Issa and S. Whitaker, 74–82. London: BFI.

———. 1999b. "Resurrection, Return, Reform: Taʿziya as Model for Early Babi Historiography." *Iranian Studies* 32(3): 387–399.

———. 2000. "Bahram Bayzaʾi's 'Maybe Some Other Time': The un-Present-able Iran." *Camera Obscura* 43(15.1): 163–191.

Mottahedeh, Roy. 1985. *The Mantle of the Prophet*. New York: Simon and Schuster.

Nadvi, A. A. 1991. *The Life of Caliph ʿAli*. Lucknow, India: Academy of Islamic Research and Publications.

Naficy, Hamid. 1994. "Veiled Vision/Powerful Presences: Women in Post-Revolutionary Iranian Cinema." In *In the Eye of the Storm: Women in Post-Revolutionary Iran*, ed. Mahnaz Afkhami and Erika Friedl, 131–150. Syracuse, N.Y.: Syracuse University Press.

Najmi, Naser. 1988. *Tehran-e ahd-e Naseri*. 2nd ed. Tehran: Entesharat-e Attar.

Nakash, Yitzhak. 1993. "An Attempt to Trace the Origins of the Rituals of Ashura." *Die Welt des Islams* 33: 161–181.

———. 1994. *The Shiʿis of Iraq*. Princeton, N.J.: Princeton University Press.

Naqvi, S. 1987. *Qutb Shahi ʿAshur Khanas of Hyderabad City*. Hyderabad, India: Bab-ul-Ilm Society.

Narang, Gopichand. 1986. *Sanahae Karbala baytaur sheoristeoara*. Delhi: Educational Publishing House.

Nashat, Guity, Ed. 1983. *Women and Revolution in Iran*. Boulder, Colo.: Westview Press.

Nasr, S. V. R. 1995. "Communalism and Fundamentalism: A Re-examination of the Origins of Islamic Fundamentalism." *Contention: Debates in Society, Culture, and Science* 4(2): 121–139.

Nayshaburi, Hasan Farahbakhsh (Zhu al-ʿedat). 1996. *Hamaseh saz-e Ashura*. Tehran: Entesharat-e Baqer al-Olum.

Nazmi, Mahdi. 1984. *Reg-i Surkh*. New Delhi: Abu Talib Academy.

Nelson, Cynthia. 1974. "Public and Private Politics: Women in the Middle Eastern World." *American Ethnologist* 1(3): 551–563.

Norton, Augustus Richard. 1987. *Amal and the Shiʿa: Struggle for the Soul of Lebanon*. Austin: University of Texas Press.

———. 2003. *Shiʿism and the Ashura Ritual in Lebanon.* New York: Al-Saqi.

Norton, Augustus Richard, and Ali Safa. 2000. "Ashura in Nabatiyye." *Middle East Insight* 15: 21–28.

Paidar, Parvin. 1995. *Women and the Political Process in Twentieth-Century Iran.* Cambridge: Cambridge University Press.

Pari, S. 1997. *The Fortune Catcher.* New York: Warner Books.

Pelly, Lewis. 1879. *The Miracle Play of Hasan and Husain, Collected from Oral Tradition.* Vol. 2. London: The India Office.

———. Pepper, Stephen. 1942. *World Hypotheses.* Los Angeles and Berkeley: University of California Press.

Peteet, Julie. 1996. *Gender in Crisis: Women and the Palestinian Resistance Movement.* New York: Columbia University Press.

Peters, Emrys. 1972. "Shifts in Power in a Lebanese Village." In *Rural Politics and Social Change in the Middle East,* ed. Richard Antoun and I. Harik, 165–197. Bloomington: Indiana University Press.

Peterson, Samuel R. 1979. "The Tazieh and Related Arts." In *Taʿziyeh: Ritual and Drama in Iran,* ed. Peter J. Chelkowski, 64–87. New York: New York University Press.

———. 1981. "Shiʿism and Late Iranian Arts." PhD diss., New York University.

———. 1988. *Taʿziyeh: Ritual and Popular Beliefs in Iran.* Hartford, Conn.: Trinity College, Hartford Seminary.

Pettys, Rebecca Ansary. 1982. "The Taʿziyeh Ritual of Renewal in Persia." PhD diss., Indiana University.

Pinault, David. 1992a. "Shiʿa Muslim Men's Associations and the Celebration of Muharram in Hyderabad, India." *Journal of South Asian and Middle Eastern Studies* 16: 38–62.

———. 1992b. *The Shiʿites, Ritual, and Popular Piety in a Muslim Community.* New York: St. Martin's Press.

———. 1998. "Zaynab Bint Ali and the Place of the Women of the Households of the First Imams in Shiʿite Devotional Literature." In *Women in the Medieval Islamic World,* ed. Gavin R. G. Hambly, 69–98. New York: St. Martin's Press.

———. 2001. *Horse of Karbala: Muslim Devotional Life in India.* New York: Palgrave.

Qaʾemi, A. n.d. *Naqsh-e Zanan dar Tarikh-e Ashura.* Qom, Iran: n.p.

Qajar, Nasir Din Shah. 1874. *Diary of the Shah of Persia during His Tour through Europe in 1873,* trans. J. W. Redhouse. London: John Murray.

Qommi, Ali Shaykh Abbas. 1964. *Kolliyat-e mafatih al-jenan.* Tehran: Chap-khaneh-e Mohammad Ali Elmi.

Qureshi, Regula Burckhardt. 1981. "Tarannum: The Chanting of Urdu Po-etry." *Ethnomusicology* 13(3): 425–468.

———. 1996. "Transcending Space: Recitation and Community among South Asian Muslims in Canada." In *Making Muslim Space in North America and Europe,* ed. Barbara Daly Metcalf, 46–64. Berkeley and Los Angeles: University of California Press.

Rachlin, N. 1978. *Foreigner: A Novel of an Iranian Woman Caught between Two Cultures.* New York: W. W. Norton.

———. 1983. *Married to a Stranger.* San Francisco: City Lights Books.

———. 1992. *Veils: Short Stories.* San Francisco: City Lights Books.

Ram, Haggay. 1994. *Myth and Mobilization in Revolutionary Iran: The Use of the Friday Congregational Sermon.* Washington, D.C.: American University Press.

Ramazani, N. 2001. *The Dance of the Rose and the Nightingale.* Syracuse, N.Y.: Syracuse University Press.

Rashid, Ahmed. 1995. "The Great Divide: Shias and Sunnis Battle It Out in Pakistan." *Far Eastern Economic Review* 158: 24.

Reeves, Minou. 1989. *Female Warriors of Allah: Women and the Islamic Revolution.* New York: E. P. Dutton.

Renard, John. 1996. *Seven Doors to Islam.* Berkeley and Los Angeles: University of California Press.

Reza'i, Ensiya Shaykh, and Shahla Azari, eds. 1998. *Gozaresh-ha-e nazmiy-yeh-e mahallat-e Tehran.* Tehran: Entesharat-e Sazman-e Asnad-e Melli-e Iran.

Richani, Nazih. 1998. *Dilemmas of Democracy and Political Parties in Sec-tarian Societies: The Case of the Progressive Socialist Party of Lebanon, 1949–1996.* New York: St. Martin's Press.

Richard, Y. 1995. *Shi'ite Islam.* Oxford: Blackwell.

Riggio, M., Ed. 1988. *Ta'ziyeh: Ritual and Popular Beliefs in Iran.* Hartford, Conn.: Trinity College, Hartford Seminary.

Rizvi, S. A. A. 1986. *A Socio-Intellectual History of the Isna 'Ashari Shi'is in India.* Canberra, Australia: Ma'refat Publishing House.

Robinson, Neal. 1996. *Discovering the Quran.* London: SCM Press.

Ryave, A. L. 1978. "On the Achievement of a Series of Stories." In *Studies in the Organization of Conversational Interaction,* ed. Jim Schenkein. New York: Academic Press.

Saad-Ghorayeb, Amal. 2002. *Hizbu'llah: Politics and Religion.* London: Pluto Press.

Sabagh, G., and Mehdi Bozorgmehr. 1987. "Are the Characteristics of Ex-
iles Different from Immigrants? The Case of Iranians in Los Angeles."
Sociology and Social Research 71: 77–84.

Sacks, Harvey. 1974. "An Analysis of the Course of a Joke's Telling." In *Ex-
plorations in the Ethnography of Speaking*, ed. R. Bauman and Joel Sherzer.
Cambridge: Cambridge University Press.

Sacks, Harvey, Emmanuel Schegloff, and Gail Jefferson. 1974. "A Simplest
Systemics for the Organization of Turn-Taking in Conversation." *Language* 50(4): 696–735.

Sadeghi. 1996. "Shahadat-e Zahra." In *Naghmeh-ha-e Karbala*, ed. Morteza
Dana'i. Tehran: Entesharat-e Sa'id Novin.

Sadeqi, Sayyed Rasul, ed. 1997. *Naghmeh-e Ashura*. Tehran: Entesharat-e
Yasin.

Sagaster, U. 1993. "Observations Made during the Month of Muharam,
1989, in Baltistan." *Proceedings of the International Seminar on the Anthropology of Tibet and the Himalaya*, ed. C. Ramble and M. Brauen,
308–317. Zurich: Ethnological Museum of the University of Zurich.

Salehirad, Hasan, ed. 1995. *Majales-e ta'ziyeh*. 2 vols. Tehran: Soroush
Press.

Sanasarian, E. 1982. *The Women's Rights Movement in Iran: Mutiny, Ap-
peasement, and Repression from 1900 to Khomeini*. New York: Praeger.

Scarce, Jennifer. 1976. *Isfahan in Camera: Nineteenth-Century Persia
through the Photographs of Ernst Hoeltzer*. London: AARP.

Schaefer, K. 1993. "Suffering with al-Husayn." *Bulletin of the Henry Martyn
Institute of Islamic Studies* (Hyderabad, India) 12(1–2): 74–84.

Schegloff, E., and Harvey Sacks. 1973. "Opening Up Closings." *Semiotica*
8(4): 289–327.

Schenkein, Jim. 1978. *Studies in the Organization of Conversational Interaction*. New York: Academic Press.

Schimmel, Annemarie. 1979. "The Marthiya in Sindhi Poetry." In *Ta'ziyeh:
Ritual and Drama in Iran*, ed. Peter J. Chelkowski, 210–221. New York:
New York University Press.

———. 1986. "Karbala and the Imam Husayn in Persian and Indo-Muslim
Literature." *al-Serat* 12, 29–39.

Schubel, Vernon James. 1991. "The Muharram Majlis: The Role of a Ritual
in the Preservation of Shi'a Identity." In *Muslim Families in North America*, ed. S. McIrvin Abu-Laban E. Waugh and Regula Burckhardt Qureshi, 118–131. Edmonton: University of Alberta Press.

———. 1993. *Religious Performance in Contemporary Islam: Shi'a Devo-*

tional Rituals in South Asia. Columbia: University of South Carolina Press.

———. 1996. "Karbala as Sacred Space among North American Shiʿa: 'Every Day Is Ashura, Everywhere Is Karbala.'" In *Making Muslim Space in North America and Europe,* ed. Barbara Daly Metcalf, 186–203. Berkeley and Los Angeles: University of California Press.

Shafeʿi, S. M. 1373 AH. *Payramun-e Hamaseh-e Ashura.* Tehran: Markaz-e Chap va Nashr-e Sazman-e Tablighat-e Eslami.

Shahidi, Enayatollah, and Bolukbashi Ali. 2001. *Pazhuheshi dar taʿziyeh va taʿziyeh khani az aghaz ta payan-e dowreh-ye Qajar dar Tehran.* Tehran: Daftar-e Pazhuhesh-ha-e Farhangi, Komisiyon-e Melli-e Yunesko dar Iran.

Shakir, Parvin. 1995. "Sadbarg." In *Mah-e tamam.* Delhi: Educational Publishing House.

Sharar, Abdul Halim. 1975. *Lucknow: The Last Phase of an Oriental Culture,* trans. E. S. Harcourt and Fakhir Husayn. Boulder, Colo.: Westview Press.

Shararah, Waddah. 1968. *Transformations d'une manifestation religieuse dans un village du Liban-Sud (Asura).* Beirut: al-Jamiʿah al-Lubnaniyyah, Ma'had al-ʿUlum al-Ijtimaʿiyah.

Sheil, Lady. 1856. *Glimpses of Life and Manners in Persia.* London: John Murray.

Sherzer, Joel. 1984a. *Language in Use: Readings in Sociolinguistics,* ed. John Baugh and Joel Sherzer. Englewood Cliffs, N.J.: Prentice-Hall.

———. 1984b. "Strategies in Text and Context: Kuna kaa kwento." In *Language in Use: Readings in Sociolinguistics,* ed. John Baugh and Joel Sherzer, 183–197. Englewood Cliffs, N.J.: Prentice-Hall.

Shirazi, Faegheh. 2001. *Unveiling the Veil: Hijab in Modern Culture.* Gainesville: University Press of Florida.

Shirazi, M. 1984. *Javady Alley.* London: The Women's Press.

———. 1991. *Siege of Azadi Square.* London: The Women's Press.

Sidiq-i-Akbar, M. H. 1976. *Hazrat Abu Bakr: Being a Biography of Abu Bakr the First Caliph and a History of Islam during the Caliphate of Abu Bakr.* Lahore: Ferozsons.

Singh, K. 1988. *Bloodstained Tombs: The Muharram Massacre, 1884.* London: Macmillan.

Stocchi, Sergio. 1988. *L'Islam nelle Stampe.* Milan: Be-Ma Editrice.

Sykes, Ella. 1910. *Persia and Its People.* London: Methuen.

Tabari, A., and Nahid Yeganeh, eds. 1982. *In the Shadow of Islam: The Women's Movement in Iran.* London: Zed Books.

Tabatabai, S. M. H. 1977. *Shi'ite Islam*. New York: University of New York Press.

Tancoigne, J. M. 1820. *A Narrative of a Journey into Persia and Residence at Tehran*. London: William Wright.

Taqiyan, Laleh, ed. 1995. *Ta'ziyeh va te'atr dar Iran*. Tehran: Nashr-e Markaz.

Ter Haar, Johan G. J. 1993. "Ta'ziye: Ritual Theatre from Shi'ite Iran." In *Theatre Intercontinental: Forms, Functions, Correspondences*, ed. C. C. Barfoot and Cobi Ordewijk, 155–174. Amsterdam: Rodopi.

Thaiss, Gustav. 1972a. "Religious Symbolism and Social Change: The Drama of Husain." In *Scholars, Saints, and Sufis: Muslim Religious Institutions since 1500*, ed. Nikki R. Keddie, 349–366. Berkeley and Los Angeles: University of California Press.

———. 1972b. "Unity and Discord: The Symbol of Husayn in Iran." In *Iranian Civilization and Culture*, ed. C. J. Adams. Montreal: McGill University, Institute of Islamic Studies.

———. 1994. "Contested Meanings and the Politics of Authenticity: The 'Hosay' in Trinidad." In *Islam, Globalization, and Postmodernity*, ed. Akbar S. Ahmed and H. Donnan. London: Routledge.

———. 1999. "Muharram Rituals or the Carnivalesque in Trinidad." *ISIM Newsletter*, 38.

Tohidi, N. 1993. "Iranian Women and Gender Relations in Los Angeles." In *Irangeles: Iranians in Los Angeles*, ed. Ron Kelley, and Jonathan Friedlander, and Anita Colby, 175–217. Berkeley and Los Angeles: University of California Press.

Torab, Azam. 1996. "Piety as Gendered Agency: A Study of Jalaseh Ritual Discourse in an Urban Neighborhood in Iran." *Journal of the Royal Anthropological Institute* 2: 235–252.

———. 1998. "Neighbourhoods of Piety: Gender and Ritual in South Tehran." PhD diss., University of London.

———. 2002. "The Politicization of Women's Religious Circles in Post-Revolutionary Iran." In *Women, Religion, and Culture in Iran*, ed. Sarah Ansari and Vanessa Martin, 143–168. London: Curzon.

Torabi, A. R. 1977. *Sham-e Ghariban Majles*. Tehran: n.p.

Torabi, Rashid. 1991. *Majales-e Torabi*, ed. Sayyed Zulfeqar Hosayn Hosni. 3 vols. Karachi: Mahfuz Book Agency.

Tsirkani, Sohrab Asadi. 1995. *Mas'eb-e a'emeh-e athar*. Tehran: Nashr-e Golfam.

Turner, Victor. 1969. *The Ritual Process: Structure and Anti-Structure*. Chicago: Aldine.

———. 1974. *Dramas, Fields, and Metaphors.* Ithaca, N.Y.: Cornell University Press.

Unvala, J. M. 1927. "The Moharram Festival in Persia." *Studie Materiale di Storia Delle Relegioni* 3: 82–96.

Van Der Veer, Peter. 1992. "Playing or Praying: A Sufi Saint's Day in Surat." *The Journal of Asian Studies* 51(3): 545–564.

Van Gennep, Arnold. 1960. *Rites de Passage,* trans. Monika B. Vizedom and Gabrielle L. Caffee. Chicago: University of Chicago Press.

Walbridge, L. 1996a. "Sex and the Single Shi'ite: Mut'a Marriage in an American Lebanese Shi'ite Community." In *Family and Gender among American Muslims: Issues Facing Middle Eastern Immigrants and Their Descendants,* ed. Barbara Bilge and Barbara C. Aswad, 143–154. Philadelphia: Temple University Press.

———. 1996b. *Without Forgetting the Imam: Lebanese Shi'ism in America.* Detroit: Wayne State University Press.

Waugh, Earle H. 1977. "Muharram Rites: Community Death and Rebirth." In *Religious Encounters with Death: Insights from the History and Anthropology of Religions,* ed. Earle H. Waugh, 200–213. University Park: Pennsylvania State University Press.

———. 1989. *The Munshidin of Egypt: Their World and Their Song.* Columbia: University of South Carolina Press.

Werbner, Prnina. 1988. "'Sealing' the Koran: Offering and Sacrifice among Pakistani Labour Migrants." *Cultural Dynamics* 1(1): 77–97.

Wills, C. J. 1883. *In the Land of the Lion and Sun, or Modern Persia.* London: Macmillan.

Wirth, Andrej. 1979. "Semiological Aspects of the Ta'ziyeh." In *Ta'ziyeh: Ritual and Drama in Iran,* ed. Peter J. Chelkowski. New York: New York University Press.

Wishard, John G. 1908. *Twenty Years in Persia: A Narrative of Life under the Last Three Shahs.* New York: Fleming H. Revell Company.

Workman, W. T. 1994. *The Social Origins of the Iran-Iraq War.* Boulder, Colo.: Lynne Rienner.

Yarshater, E. 1979. "Ta'ziyah and Pre-Islamic Mourning Rites in Iran." In *Ta'ziyeh: Ritual and Drama in Iran,* Peter J. Chelkowski. New York: New York University Press.

Zahedi, Ashraf. Forthcoming-a. *Challenging the Shah: Student Mobilization for Revolution.*

———. Forthcoming-b. *Women of the Confederation: From Triumph to Despair.*

Index

Page numbers in italic indicate illustrations.

211, 214–215, 222; Iraqi, 230–233, 248–255

women's participation. *See* private rituals; public rituals; women-only rituals

Yazdegerd the Third, 120

Yazid, 3, 10, 27, 31, 51, 53, 66, 77, 85, 94, 113, 114, 116, 121, 122–123, 128, 166, 167, 168, 174; camp of, 33; court of, 47, 50, 53, 113, 118n37, 148, 170, 252; in *ta'ziyeh*, 25, 29, 30; troops of, 40n14, 41n22, 53, 66, 68, 70, 83, 105, 164; uprising against, 3, 48, 148; *yazidiyyat,* 165, 248, 257

Yemen, 187, 189

zaban-e hal, 105–108, 112, 113

"*Zaban-e Hal:* Ali Mourning for Zahra," 105

"*Zaban-e Hal:* Roqayyeh (Peace Be Upon Her)," 113

"*Zaban-e Hal:* Sakineh (Peace Be Upon Her)," 113–115

"*Zaban-e Hal:* Zahra with Ali," 106

Zahra. *See* Fatemeh al-Zahra

zaker/zakereh, 76, 81, *144,* 148, 149, 151, 152, 156, 157, 159n22, 162, 166

Zaynab, 4, 10, 12, 16, 20n18, 47, 48, 49, 50, 51, 52, 80, 95, 96, 102, 109, 110, 113, 127, 134, 143, 164, 181n31, 193, 241, 248, 250; "authenticated," 242, 255–260; as critic, 10, 53, 128, 148, 165, 168, 174, 252, 257, 260; depictions of, 17, 18, 51, 82, 103, 107, 108, 110, 111, 112, 115, 116, 120, 121, 122, 126, 136, 163, 166, 169, 170–176, 242, 246, 255–258; in elegies, 108–110, 111–112, 174–176; identification with, 127–129, 256–260, 265n41; in *matam majales,* 65, 68, 85, 86, 143, 246, 252–253; in *nowheh,* 84, 85–86; as orator, 53, 116, 122, 127, 148–149, 164, 165–168, 176, 260; portrayed, *130, 132;* as role model, 54, 110, 112, 115–116, 120, 169, 172, 256–257, 259–260; shrine of, 161

zaynabiyyeh, 68, 72, 79, 145, 146, 150, 151, 154

ziyarat, 153, 156, 157, 160n47, 161, 189

Ziyarat Salman Pak, 230, 232–233, 236

Zu al-Jenah, 158n13, 204